A Christianity Today Reader

A
Christianity Today
Reader

Edited and with an introduction by Frank E. Gaebelein

MEREDITH PRESS   NEW YORK

By Way of Introduction

Anthologies are to be dipped into rather than read through systematically. In its field, a good anthology is a miniature library, and like a library it invites browsing. The reader who explores this volume will encounter discussions of theology and the Bible, the Church and its mission, Christian education and its problems, evangelism and world missions, national and foreign affairs, and science and the arts, interspersed with poetry and also with touches of humor, lest seriousness be equated with solemnity. But amidst this wide assortment of writings, the central point of reference is the historic evangelical faith, which is alien to no part of life.

Making an anthology demands a certain ruthlessness. Since its beginning in 1956, *Christianity Today* has printed a good many million words, of which some 100,000 have been selected for this anthology. Thus the problem of elimination has been acute. Here are essays, editorials, news reports, book reviews, and also some shorter pieces, chosen for their quality and for their reflection of what the magazine has stood for during its first ten years. In preparing these pages for publication in book form, there has been a minimum of editing, and this has been mostly confined to correction of typographical errors or essential updating. In the case of a few of the longer pieces, condensation has been necessary.

The past decade has been packed with stirring events; it has also witnessed a ferment in religious life probably unmatched since the Reformation. To include everything that *Christianity Today* has carried concerning even one major area of theological thought or social concern would take much of this book. Material is not arranged in chronological order; instead, the reader is offered samples of how this national journal of evangelical Christianity has dealt with a great many topics. What has given the magazine unity through the years—and what therefore unifies this book—is its dominant editorial commitment to the biblical revelation.

From sifting the more than 10,000 pages published during our first decade, one gains certain impressions. Fidelity to the purpose of *Chris-*

tianity Today has not hampered change. The use of special features began early in our history; among them have been a poll of doctrinal beliefs of Protestant ministers (1957–1958) and interviews with such world figures as Dr. Charles Malik (1960) and Bishop Otto Dibelius (1963). News events covered by staff members through extensive travel include Premier Khrushchev's American tour (1959), the World Council of Churches' meeting in New Delhi (1961), and Billy Graham's Latin American crusades (1960). The publication of Professor Cyrus Gordon's essay on the outmoded status of the documentary hypothesis of the Pentateuch (1959) opened our pages to distinguished Jewish scholarship. Sometimes there was sharp debate, as in several articles on capital punishment (1959–1960). More recently, Roman Catholic spokesmen have been heard and both the pros and cons of ecumenism discussed. But differing positions have always been set in the biblical perspective. The format has not remained static, the most extensive change having been the complete redesigning of the magazine in the fall of 1963. In other departures, cartoons were added (1965) and the cover design made more flexible (1966).

An editor's task, being largely anonymous, is a selfless one. He does some of his most significant writing in unsigned editorials, and much of the content of a journal reflects his planning. While this anthology contains only a small amount of material attributed to Dr. Carl F. H. Henry, the discerning reader will recognize that his editorial leadership has given *Christianity Today* much of its present place as a nationwide voice for evangelical Christianity, although—as Dr. Henry has often said—without a gifted staff this would not have been possible. Moreover, the magazine owes very much to the wise counsel and generous support of its Board of Directors in the fulfillment of its purpose.

May the reader enjoy this sampler of ten years of Christian journalism.

F. E. G.

Washington, D.C.
October, 1966

Contents

* This *Reader* follows the policy of *Christianity Today* in not naming writers of editorials.

A Christianity Today Reader

1 *Why* Christianity Today? *

Christianity Today has its origin in a deep-felt desire to express historical Christianity to the present generation. Neglected, slighted, misrepresented, evangelical Christianity needs a clear voice to speak with conviction and love, and to state its true position and its relevance to the world crisis. A generation has grown up unaware of the basic truths of the Christian faith taught in the Scriptures and expressed in the creeds of the historic evangelical churches.

Theological liberalism has failed to meet the moral and spiritual needs of the people. Neither the man on the street nor the intellectual is today much attracted by its preaching and theology. All too frequently, it finds itself adrift in speculation that neither solves the problem of the individual nor of the society of which he is a part.

For the preacher, an unending source of wisdom and power lies in a return to truly biblical preaching. For the layman, this same Book will prove to be light on the pathway of life, the record of the One who alone meets our needs for now and for eternity.

Christianity Today is confident that the answer to the theological confusion existing in the world is found in Christ and the Scriptures. There is evidence that more and more people are rediscovering the Word of God as their source of authority and power. Many of these searchers for the truth are unaware of the existence of an increasing group of evangelical scholars throughout the world. Through the pages of *Christianity Today* these men will expound and defend the basic truths of the Christian faith in terms of reverent scholarship and of practical application to the needs of the present generation.

Those who direct the editorial policy of *Christianity Today* unreservedly accept the complete reliability and authority of the written Word of God. It is their conviction that the Scriptures teach the doctrine of plenary inspiration. This doctrine has been misrepresented and misunderstood. To state the biblical concept of inspiration will be one of the aims of this magazine.

The doctrinal content of historic Christianity will be presented and defended. Among the distinctive doctrines to be stressed are those of God, Christ, man, salvation, and the last things. The best modern

* This *Reader* follows the policy of *Christianity Today* in not naming writers of editorials. Authors of all other selections are named.

scholarship recognizes the bearing of doctrine on moral and spiritual life. This emphasis will find encouragement in the pages of *Christianity Today*.

True ecumenicity will be fostered by setting forth the New Testament teaching of the unity of believers in Jesus Christ. External organic unity is not likely to succeed unless the unity engendered by the Holy Spirit prevails. A unity that endures must have as its spiritual basis a like faith, an authentic hope, and the renewing power of Christian love.

National stability and survival depend upon enduring spiritual and moral qualities. Revival as the answer to national problems may seem to be an oversimplified solution to a distressingly complex situation. Nevertheless, statesmen as well as theologians realize that the basic solution to the world crisis is theological. *Christianity Today* will stress the impact of evangelism on life and will encourage it.

Christianity Today will apply the biblical revelation to the contemporary social crisis by presenting the implications of the total gospel message for every area of life. This, fundamentalism has often failed to do. Christian laymen are becoming increasingly aware that the answer to the many problems of political, industrial, and social life is a theological one. They are looking to the Christian Church for guidance, and they are looking for a demonstration of the fact that the Gospel of Jesus Christ is a transforming and vital force. We have the conviction that consecrated and gifted evangelical scholarship can provide concrete proof and strategic answers.

Christianity Today takes cognizance of the dissolving effect of modern scientific theory upon religion. To counteract this tendency, it will set forth the unity of the divine revelation in nature and Scripture.

Three years in a theological seminary is not sufficient to prepare a student fully for the ministry. *Christianity Today* will seek to supplement seminary training with sermonic helps, pastoral advice, and book reviews by leading ministers and scholars.

The interpretation of the news becomes more and more important in the present world situation. Correspondents conversant with local conditions have been enlisted in the United States and abroad. Through their reports *Christianity Today* will seek to provide its readers with a comprehensive and relevant view of religious movements and life throughout the world.

While affirming the great emphases of the historic creeds, this magazine will seek to avoid controversial denominational differences. It does not intend to concern itself with personalities or with purely internal problems and conflicts of the various denominations. If significant enough, these will be objectively reported. Into an era of unparalleled problems and opportunities for the Church comes *Christianity Today* with the firm conviction that the historic evangelical faith is vital for the life of the Church and of the nations. We believe that the Gospel is still the power of God unto salvation for all who believe; that the basic needs of the social order must meet their solution first in the redemption of the individual; that the Church and the individual Christian do have a vital responsibility to be both salt and light in a decaying and darkening world.

Believing that a great host of true Christians, whose faith has been impaired, are today earnestly seeking for a faith to live by and a message to proclaim, *Christianity Today* dedicates itself to the presentation of the reasonableness and effectiveness of the Christian evangel. This we undertake with sincere Christian love for those who may differ with us, and with whom we may be compelled to differ, and with the assurance in our hearts that God's Holy Spirit alone can activate any vital witness for him.

Editorial   October 15, 1956

2 *Epistolics Anonymous*

EDMUND P. CLOWNEY

To the Editor:

Can you tell me, please, whether it is proper to launch an ICBM rocket with a bottle of champagne? Having flunked physics, I am somewhat unsure of myself in this atomic age. It would be great fun for an inveterate non-alcoholic to contribute some verbal pop and fizz to the launching of your new magazine.

I'm a little overawed. Your magazine, you say, is "designed for worldwide impact." Looking at your streamlined brochure and the impressive list of editors and contributors I can well believe it.

But sir, you need a Pseudonymous Letter Writer, for which position I herewith make application. I can hear you muttering, "The pseudonymous, while not synonymous with the anonymous, is equally pusillanimous . . ." I wish you wouldn't talk that way. Where would

American literature be without Mark Twain? Besides, as that great master of pseudonymity, Sören Kierkegaard, has explained, using a pseudonym may show too much courage rather than too little! My nom de plume suggests not a personality but a picture. Easy slumber under sound gospel preaching was fatal for Eutychus. The Christian Church of our generation has not been crowded to his precarious perch, but it has been no less perilously asleep in comfortable pews.

The resemblance to Eutychus does not end there. Eutychus prostrate on the pavement is more appropriate than we know as a symbol of Christendom today. To tap sleeping Eutychus on the shoulder, to embrace dead Eutychus in love, faith, and hope is your task.

Believe me, my heart is with you. "Evangelical Christianity." Never were those words more significant than in this time when many who falsely or foolishly claim the noun would assure us, in the name of unity, that the adjective is unnecessary.

But if we are to contend for the truth in love, humbling humor is good medicine. When men take a cause seriously enough, there is always great danger that they will take themselves too seriously. If we see ourselves as others see us, we may discover why everyone is laughing!

May your cause prosper, your letters-to-the-editor department flourish, and may I remain (this is a threat and a promise)

your humble scribe,

Eutychus   October 15, 1956

3 *A Civilization at Bay*

CHARLES H. MALIK AND CARL F. H. HENRY

Following is an abridged reproduction of a face-to-face interview with Dr. Charles H. Malik, former President of the United Nations General Assembly, conducted by the editor of *Christianity Today*.

Q. World history in our generation seems to be running on a Communist timetable. Do you see any outward signs, like those that once marked the decline of the Roman Empire, to suggest that the Communist thrust has passed its zenith?
A. I don't think so. I think we can expect it to register further gains. The question obviously takes one into the realm of sheer conjecture and prophecy, and I disclaim any prophetic powers. But I can only

say realistically that the Communists are still very vigorous, and the rest of the world is relatively rather weak.

Q. What are the symptoms of the Free World's deterioration? Do you think it is now too late to avert the final decline of the West?

A. Certainly it's not too late. It's never too late, given the freedom of man and given the grace of God. But symptoms of deterioration in the Western world are very evident. First and foremost is the lack of unity among the various components of the Western world. The statesmen congratulate themselves over that lack of unity, on the ground of their freedom and equal partnership. All this is fine—but what is the use if one keeps on losing? We keep saying we are good, we believe in civilization, we believe in freedom, we believe in equal partnership, and so on, yet we keep getting beaten. In the end it is not enough to be good; it is also necessary to believe that the good will win. And therefore one who really believes in the good must also believe that the cause of his losing is not the good in him but the bad in him. One aspect of Western lack of unity is the nationalism which is eating and corroding the life of the Western world. They have NATO, true, but they squabble; on many important issues they don't see eye to eye. I have seen it in the United Nations. To this squabbling I would add, as a weakness, materialism—sheer, crass materialism. I am not sure your Western materialism is better than the Soviet's. Another sign of weakness: Christians aren't speaking with conviction. Many Christians have become so worldly that one doubts whether their Christianity can resist the non-Christian and anti-Christian pressures. I could recite 20 or more signs of moral weakness in the Western world which are highly disturbing—weaknesses of people who ought to know better, people with a great tradition behind them, whose tradition alone can save them and the world ten times over if they understand it, and live it, and rise above their failures.

Q. How then do you define the decisive issues underlying the crisis of the twentieth century?

A. The issue, as I see it, is this. A rebellion within the Western world in the form of Marxism and Leninism has for its ultimate objective the destruction of the accumulated values that we have inherited from the Graeco-Roman-Christian civilization. Against this terrific rebellion our civilization is now engaged in a life or death battle. This rebellion gathers to itself all kinds of supporting forces in the world which have grievances against that civilization. Hence there is a mobilization of all forces in the world which hate freedom, man, God, objective truth, and the name of Jesus Christ. This to me is the greatest crisis that we face today. Marxism-Leninism is the vanguard of these forces running together against the inherited tradition, which stresses—or ought to stress, regardless of the unworthiness of some of its representatives—man, truth, God, and Jesus Christ.

Q. What has Christianity to say to both of the modern power blocs?

A. I don't completely understand what many Protestants mean by Christianity. There are 250 Protestant sects. One weakness of the West is its wide use of the word Christianity for a vague, "liberal," sentimental form of idealism. If you ask me what Christ's message is, I shall try to tell you. What he says to the two power blocs today is: Resolve your differences peacefully. If you must fight, be humane; and remember that history is completely in the palm of my hands and I am its Lord.

Q. Granted that Christian values are compromised on all the secular frontiers today, how would you assess the Free World and the Soviet sphere in terms of biblical ideals? How would you measure the extent of the revolt in the West and the East?

A. I don't agree with Karl Barth at all that it is, as it were, "six of one and a half dozen of the other." The governments of the Western nations have not become totalitarian. They have not turned against the Bible, against the Gospel. On the other hand, the totalitarian governments have taken a stand against the Gospel and Jesus Christ. The governments of the West are at least neutral with respect to the propagation of the Gospel. While we see very virulent movements of secularism and atheism in the West, yet organized society in the form of governments has taken no formal, official stand against religion, and against Christ, and many members of these governments are believers at least outwardly. When it comes to real faith in Christ, of course, the West has become very worldly, very soft. Still the Church is there, and the Bible is there, and Christians are living a free life, and it is their fault if they don't make good their claims.

Q. What bearing has the biblical view of God and man on the modern controversy over human rights and duties?

A. Every bearing in the world. Man is made in the image of God. Man has a dignity with which he is therefore endowed by his mere humanity; he has certain natural rights and duties which stem from his being the creature of God. It is interesting to note that this whole conception of rights and of the oneness of humanity and of the universal dignity of man has arisen only within the Christian tradition.

Q. Does Christianity bear also on property rights?

A. I believe that private property, including the ownership of the means of production, provided it be carefully and rationally regulated —and science and reason and moral responsibility are fully able to supply the necessary regulating norms—is of the essence of human nature, and is a Christian pattern. I believe therefore that the abolition of all private property, including the abolition of the private ownership of every means of production, is not just.

Q. What is the real hinge of history, Dr. Malik?

A. The real hinge of history to me is Jesus Christ.

Q. If that be so, how can the Christian remnant recover an apostolic initiative in witnessing to the world?

A. Not by magic; not by mechanical techniques which call for a special conference at six in the morning and another at eleven; not by many of the ways suggested in American theological literature, with their emphasis on methods and techniques of worship and of invoking the Holy Spirit; not by mass organization simply. But especially by ardent prayer for the Holy Spirit to come mightily into the hearts of men. That is the most important thing. Jesus did not concern himself mainly with "how to organize," although this is most important for the continuity of the Church.

Q. Where dare we as Christians hope for a breakthrough?

A. In the field of Christian unity there are great signs of hope, I believe. I am encouraged by the awakening of people as a result of suffering and the sense of danger, and by the way people are giving themselves once again to the discussion of fundamental questions. The greatest possibility for a breakthrough exists in prayer for the coming of the Holy Ghost. The Holy Ghost is, as it were, now knocking at the door, fluttering around about us on every occasion. We must open the door. To the extent that people ardently pray for his coming—well, that is the greatest victory we can hope for, the coming of the Holy Spirit.

Q. How effectively and properly, in your opinion, has organized Protestantism addressed the politico-economic crisis?

A. Economics and politics are certainly realities, but not the primary realities with which the Church has to deal. The Church can examine these things in the light of the Holy Ghost and with the mind of Christ. But primarily the Church ought to be above politics and economics, ought to feel that it can thrive even in hell. If it is going to wait until the economic and social order is perfect before it can tell you and me individually that right here and now we can be saved, no matter what this politico-economic order is, it will never accomplish its proper work. Think of Jesus Christ saying to us: "You've got first to perfect your government, to perfect your social system, to perfect your economic system, before you take your cross and follow me." He would never say that!

Q. *Do you feel then that there is too great a tendency for the Church to shape and approve particular programs of political and economic action, parties, and platforms, while principles are neglected?*

A. This happens at times and is very unfortunate. This does not at all mean that the Church does not have something to say about everything. But what it says about any situation should never so tie the Gospel down to that situation that the Cross and Christ and salvation and hope and faith and love become secondary and dependent upon such programs and pronouncements.

Q. *What is the main dynamism on which the Gospel of Christ relies for social transformation?*

A. The love of Christ. The indebtedness to Christ. The first commandment. I think that if Christians are infused with the mind of Christ and are socially conscious—believing in the reality of the social orders, and in their groundedness in man's nature as a social being— such Christians will be social and economic revolutionaries. They won't stand for injustice in the social order, and will do everything they can to transform it.

Q. *Today we often hear it said that the United Nations is "the world's best hope for peace." How do you feel about this?*

A. That formula is like all other clichés. While there is something to be said for it, it is more of a propagandistic cliché than a real statement of truth. The United Nations is a very interesting thing and has its own possibilities—possibilities that should never be minimized. But the United Nations isn't a cure for every problem. The United Nations is a great institution, it should be supported, it has done very well during the last 16 years. But it could have done much better. It isn't such that we can go home and rely on it alone.

Q. *Do you consider the Church more than the United Nations as the real bearer of peace on earth?*

A. Yes, sir! Certainly.

Q. *What do you personally think is the future of organized Christianity in our century?*

A. If you mean the Church, it has a good future. The Church will never die. The Church is absolutely assured by Christ that he will be with it until the end of time. Everything is going to vanish except the Church. It will go through trials, I assure you, and many so-called churches are going to find out that they are not as much the Church as they thought. The Church as God willed it, as God organized it, as it has existed throughout the centuries, as Christ has continued to build it up—that will not vanish from this earth until he comes. When he comes then everything will be transformed.

Q. How shall we regard the attitude one often hears in our current situation, namely, that Christians are pledged not to combat this or that particular ideology but to preach Christ?

A. I believe we must distinguish three things here. The first distinction is between the Church and those whom you call Christians: the two are not the same thing. The second distinction is with respect to the attitude of Christians or the Church vis-à-vis the final religious realities, the final revelation of God. And the third distinction concerns their attitude towards the various modes of organizing human life practically and politically, towards the present economic and social order. Under this third distinction it is most important to ascertain whether Christians or the Church believe that through the life of reason we may discover ultimate truth and falsehood in respect to social and economic orders. If you make these three orders of distinctions, I would briefly say concerning the first one that undoubtedly the Church as a body cannot rest its fate on the ups and downs of social orders. Its fate depends upon its fidelity, its faithfulness to that fund of truth and salvation and mediation between God and man that it has received from the Lord. On the other hand, Christians as individuals are duty bound to take a position concerning all kinds of social and economic situations, and have every right to make their own destiny rest on the position they take. But they cannot compromise the Church. The Church should not be compromised by taking stands on social and economic matters. About the second order of distinctions, it is part of my ecclesiology that the Church alone can speak authoritatively on matters of faith and morals. As to the third distinction, I would say that Christians can distinguish between right and wrong, justice and injustice; they can do this on the basis of rational observation, science, inquiry, the application of first principles, going deeply into things, and finally, expounding and showing to the world that one position more than another is in accordance with the truth.

Q. Where do you think that Christianity has failed in its day-to-day opposition to communism?

A. Christians have failed because they underestimated the nature of the Marxist-Leninist-Communist onslaught on the world. And its development during the last 40 years, I assure you, was anything but inevitable. It could have been arrested at a dozen different junctures; it was only the folly, stupidity, and complacence of the Christians that allowed it to reach its present dimensions.

Q. Would you spell that out just a bit more?

A. Yes. Our unfortunate minimizing and underestimating of the nature of Marxism-Leninism enabled that movement to attain the proportions it has. That is one cause of our failure to oppose communism. Another cause is the presence in Western society of economic and social and political injustices. If Christians had attended to these problems they could have spoken with far greater meaning, with clearer and less burdened consciences than they did, with all these problems existing in their own domain. And Christians did not work together. They were undermined by communism itself that entered their ranks and weakened them. There is so much sentimentalism, too, so much softheadedness, so much unauthentic interpretation of the Gospel, so much disconnection in the minds of many Christians with the real streams of history.

Q. What can Christians learn from the meteoric rise of world communism in little more than 40 years?

A. The most important thing to learn is that we are still living, as the Germans say, *zwischen den Zeiten,* "between the times," when demonic forces can quickly soar very high and can take possession of the world in very short order. If it isn't communism, it will be something else. This battle between Christ and the devil is an eternal thing until Christ comes again. Christians therefore should be alert. Christians cannot watch too closely. Christ told us to watch day and night; we don't know when he is coming again. The greatest lesson we can learn is that there is no security "between the times," no security whatever.

Q. Wherein lies our hope for defeat of the Communist ideology?

A. In our faith in Christ. In the unity of watching together. In never being soft. In being the first under any circumstances to step out and acquit ourselves honorably like men, not letting silly, soft propaganda weaken our determination. In being clear in our own minds about the ultimate issues in the world today. In praying day and night, day and night. If there is one thing I want to stress, even to the clergy, it is the absolute importance of prayer. This is the most important thing for all men who truly believe in God.

Q. Do you expect the Gospel of Christ again to become culturally and socially significant in our lifetime?

A. Yes, even in our lifetime. Undoubtedly. I hold Christ to be relevant to every situation. I hold him to be present even though we don't
see him.

*Q. In our quest for world peace what posture ought the Christian
Church to assume in the struggle against communism?*

A. The Communists say they want peace; the Christian Church wants
peace. But there is "peace" and peace! Some kinds of peace seem to
me to be unchristian, and the Church cannot condone them unquali-
fiedly. A peace that is based upon tyranny is not real peace. A peace
that is based upon fighting God and Christ is not the right kind of
peace. And a peace that is based upon international peace but is
simultaneously waging class war is not Christian. The Christian Church
ought to say, "We're all for peace; but we want a peace that respects
God and Christ and men; we want a peace that is not based on tyranny;
we want a peace that is 'all out' peace—peace between classes as much
as peace between nations."

Q. Is nuclear war inevitable?

A. No.

Q. If not, how can we avoid it?

A. Through greater unity in the Western ranks, through the development of new techniques for challenging the Communist threat, through
separating the people who are ruled by the Communist party from
their rulers. This is something that Western leaders have not dared
to do very much. They seem to think that the identification of ruler
and ruled behind the Iron Curtain is an ironclad and fixed identification. So there are many ways to avert nuclear war. One thing we must
never overlook, namely, the devastating cost of military weakness. We
ought to maintain and increase whatever strength we can have. I sincerely believe that the mobilized resources of the Free World—economic, political, moral, and spiritual—far outweigh any mobilized resources of the Communist world.

*Q. How firm should the Free World be in the face of Communist
aggression?*

A. Very firm, immovably firm.

Q. Who is winning the Cold War?

A. The Communists, if you compare their status in the world now
with their status 10 years ago, let alone 20.

*Q. What new ideology ought the Christian to look for as he peers
beyond communism into the future?*

A. A Christian ideology can only be one that is integrally grounded
in the mind of Christ. Such an ideology would place spiritual things

above material things; would affirm God the Creator, Christ the Redeemer, the Holy Ghost and Giver of life; would stress the Church; would stress man and his absolute dignity as the creature of God, created in his divine image and later redeemed by the blood of Christ. It would certainly have a social message, an international message of peace, equality, and mutual respect. The strong will come to the support of the weak, and the weak will be humble and not rebellious. The infinite potential of science and industry can be turned to the enrichment of human life in a completely unprecedented manner that would bring blessing and happiness to all mankind, insofar as these depend upon material things. Because of human sin and human corruption, government and order will be of the essence; the Christian ideology cannot be an anarchic ideology. Education will be stressed. But unless the intellectual, the political, and the economic are put in their proper place as instruments willed by God for the sake of man—who is created in God's image and has fallen away from that grace, and yet, thank God, has been redeemed by Christ—they always have a tendency to overwhelm the human spirit and to rebel against God. So this is my vision of what you termed "Christian ideology." While he hopes for these things, believes in these things, and works for these things, the Christian ought to be very humble; he should not expect miracles except as they are authentically wrought by the Holy Ghost.

Interview   November 24, 1961

4   *What Protestant Ministers Believe*

Professional pollsters conducted an important survey for *Christianity Today*. It provided key information on the convictions of clergymen.

Three out of every four Protestant ministers classify themselves as "conservative" or "fundamentalist," while the fourth says he is "liberal" or "neo-orthodox."

So indicates a representative nationwide survey of American ministers. The poll was conducted for *Christianity Today* by the Opinion Research Corporation of Princeton, New Jersey, using scientific random-sampling methods in October and November, 1957.

This question highlighted each survey interview:

Just how would you generally classify your theological position—

fundamentalist, conservative, neo-orthodox, liberal, or some other category?

This is a breakdown of replies:

Conservative	39%
Fundamentalist	35%
Liberal	14%
Neo-orthodox	12%

The classifications of theological position were left to the clergymen to define for themselves in their own understanding of the terms.

All were asked whether they felt it was essential to preach and teach the doctrines of: (1) God as creator of man, (2) the literal resurrection of Christ, (3) Christ as Saviour and Lord, (4) one sovereign God, (5) the Bible as the authoritative rule, (6) Christ as the Son of God, (7) the Bible as having been verbally inspired by God in original writings, (8) the virgin birth of Christ, (9) the vicarious substitutionary atonement of Christ, (10) the literal return or "second coming" of Christ, (11) the unity of all believers in Christ.

Virtually every minister said it is essential to preach and teach that God is creator of man, and that Christ is Saviour and Lord. An overwhelming majority said it is essential to preach and teach the Bible as the authoritative rule of life and death, the unique deity of Christ as the Son of God, and the unity of all believers in Christ.

However, 33 per cent said it is not essential to preach and teach that the Bible is verbally inspired by God in original writings. Other "is not essential" percentages included the literal return or "second coming" of Christ, 26 per cent; virgin birth of Christ, 18 per cent; vicarious substitutionary atonement of Christ, 17 per cent; historical, literal resurrection of Christ, 11 per cent.

Some 27 per cent feel that working for organic church unity is a "very important" task of the Church. Only 18 per cent of the ministers believe in church union through organic mergers. About 48 per cent believe in church unity only through doctrinal beliefs, while 24 per cent are against any form of merger.

The interviews indicated that most conservative ministers tend toward desire for church mergers on the basis of doctrinal beliefs only, while the liberal and neo-orthodox want mergers based on organic union.

In interpreting the survey, it should be noted that, generally speaking, theological liberalism exaggerates the immanence of God while virtually denying his transcendence. Hence, the doctrine of God's wrath, man's fall, miraculous revelation and redemption, a unique divine incarnation in Christ—all these are denied. The Bible is dismissed as nothing more than a record of "the highest religious and moral insights."

Neo-orthodoxy reacts against liberalism in exaggerating God's transcendence and emphasizing God's judgment, man's sin, and Christ as Lord and divine Saviour. But it carries forward the liberal rejection of revealed doctrines and precepts and asserts special divine revelation, formulating it as suprarational, non-intellectualistic confrontation of each individual as against a once-for-all revelation in Christ and the Bible.

Fundamentalism is at the extreme right of the theological scale. Conservative religious beliefs fall in between fundamentalism and neo-orthodoxy.

Of the ministers in the survey who call themselves "conservative," only 59 per cent said it is essential to preach and teach that the Bible was verbally inspired by God in original writings; 25 per cent in the neo-orthodoxy category and 23 per cent in the liberal classification felt the same way.

News   March 31, 1958

5 *The Book That Understands Me*

EMILE CAILLIET

Through my college days in France I was an agnostic. Strange as it may seem to the reader, I graduated without having ever seen a Bible. To say that the education I received proved of little help through front-line experiences as a lad of twenty in World War I would amount to quite an understatement. What use, the ill-kept ancient type of sophistry in the philosophic banter of the seminar, when your own buddy—at the time speaking to you of his mother—dies standing in front of you, a bullet in his chest? Was there a meaning to it all? The inadequacy of my views on the human situation overwhelmed me. One night a bullet got me, too. An American field ambulance saved my life and later restored the use of my left arm. After a nine-month stay at the hospital, I was discharged and resumed graduate work.

Needless to insist that the intellectual climate had changed as far as I was concerned. Reading in literature and philosophy, I found myself probing in depth for meaning. During long night watches a few yards from the German trenches, as I looked at swollen bodies dangling in the barbed wires, I had been strangely longing for . . . —I must say it, however queer it may sound—for a book that would understand me. But I knew of no such book. Now I would in secret prepare one for my own use. And so, as I went on reading for my courses, I would file passages that spoke to my condition, then carefully copy them in a leather-bound pocket book I would always carry with me. The quotations, which I numbered in red ink for easier reference, would lead me as it were from fear and anguish, through a variety of intervening stages, to supreme utterances of release and jubilation. The day came when I put the finishing touch to "the book that would understand me," speak to my condition, and help me through life's happenings. A beautiful, sunny day it was. I went out, sat under a tree, and opened my precious anthology. As I went on reading, however, a growing disappointment came over me. Instead of speaking to my condition, the various passages reminded me of their context, of the circumstances of my labor over their selection. Then I knew that the whole undertaking would not work, simply because it was of my own making. In a rather dejected mood, I put the little book back in my pocket.

At that very moment, my British-born wife—who, incidentally, knew nothing of the project I had been working on—appeared at the gate of the garden pushing the baby carriage. It had been a hot afternoon. She had followed the main boulevard only to find it too crowded. So she had turned to a side street which she could not name because we had only recently arrived in the town. The cobblestones had shaken the carriage so badly that she had wondered what to do. Whereupon, having spotted a patch of grass beyond a small archway, she had gone in with the baby for a period of rest. At this point in her story, she had a moment of hesitation. As she resumed her account, it turned out that the patch of grass led to an outside stone staircase which she had climbed without quite realizing what she was doing. At the top, she had seen a long room, door wide open. So she had entered. At the farther end, a white-haired gentleman worked at a desk. He had not become aware of her presence. Looking around, she noticed the carving of a cross. Thus she suddenly realized that this was a church—a Huguenot church, hidden away as they all are, even long after the danger of persecution has passed. The venerable-looking gentleman was the pastor. She walked to his desk and heard herself say, "Have you a Bible in French?" He smiled and handed over to her a copy which she eagerly took from his hand; then she walked out with a mixed feeling of both joy and guilt. (I should confess at this point that I had once for all made the subject of religion taboo in our home.) As she now stood in front of me, she meant to apologize. This was the way things had happened . . . She had no idea . . . But I was no longer listening:

"A Bible, you say? Where is it? Show me. I have never seen one before!"

She complied. I literally grabbed the book and rushed to my study with it. I opened it and "chanced" upon the Beatitudes! I read, and read, and read—now aloud with an indescribable warmth surging within . . . I could not find words to express my awe and wonder. And all of a sudden, the realization dawned upon me: This was "the book that would understand me." I needed it so much that I had attempted to write my own—in vain. I continued to read deep into the night, mostly from the Gospels. And lo and behold, as I looked through them, the One of whom they spoke, the One who spoke and acted in them, became alive to me. The providential circumstances amid which the Book had found me now made it clear that while it seemed absurd to speak of a book understanding a man, this could be said of the Bible because its pages were animated by the presence of the Living God and power of his mighty acts. To this God I prayed that night, and the God who answered was the same God of whom it was spoken in the Book. A decisive insight flashed through my whole being the following morning as I probed the first chapter of the Gospel of John.

I still proceed on the old theme of "the Book that understands me," the main difference being that I now capitalize the *B*. My devotional life springs from my conversations with Holy Writ. Whenever I am confronted with difficulties, with a puzzling situation, or with a call on which more light is needed, I turn to a set of similar circumstances as presented in Scripture. Or it may be that as I read the Bible as a normal, daily practice, a passage "jumps at me" and lights up the way I must go. Whatever the case may be, I pray over the page, waiting upon him who speaks through it in a joyful eagerness to do his will. I have learned to beware of putting too much trust in the immediate feelings that may thus be awakened in me, for I know that at such a time, first impressions may amount to mere wishful thinking. Rather, I allow life to take its course, in this way emulating the faith of the centurion. What is it that the Lord is trying to show me as actual situations develop? Thus I learn to "read" daily happenings in the light of Scripture. The margins of my Bible are marked with dates together with brief reminders of occasions when such a passage "spoke" to me and directed me.

An unexpected result of this approach has been its effect on whatever amount of scholarship I may be credited with. Thus is has sharpened my sensitiveness to the working of the Word in the achievements of such outstanding Christians as Pascal. Some of my students have caught the vision and proceeded upon it. It profoundly moves me to see how the faltering steps I have taken in the light of Scripture have become in their case a firm, steady walk. I think, for example, of some admirable young scholars who are interpreting patterns of Christian thought and life in great writers such as Milton, Bunyan, and Shakespeare. So true it is that any real achievement generally points to an enlightened insight of youth brought to fruition by maturity.

Theological hairsplitting may well suggest to some that a dividing line should be drawn between the scholarly and the devotional approaches to the Bible. All I can say is that things have not worked out this way in my case. My experience of the Bible, unsophisticated though it has continued to be, has actually inspired and directed the best of my efforts as a liberal-arts student.

Article   November 22, 1963

6 *My Father's Benediction*

RACHEL   CROWN

(Numbers 6:24-26)

Now he is gone, but he has left these words
Of benediction, inkwritten upon the flyleaf
Of the Book, which was his gift. I read

The Word he loved, gracious as dew of Hermon
Or the oil that covered Aaron: "The Lord
Bless thee and keep thee . . . make his face
To shine upon thee and be gracious unto thee:
The Lord lift up his countenance upon thee
And give thee peace." Almost unseeing I trace
The signature; then wordlessly his life
Shines as from an illuminated page:
Strangely he speaks who has no need of utterance.
Who, having blessed, is bathed eternally
In fuller light than shines upon the land.

January 5, 1959

7 Biblical Authority in Evangelism

BILLY GRAHAM

It is a sultry day with a hot breeze spinning little dust whirls down the winding road by the Sea of Galilee. There is an air of expectancy everywhere. We hear voices, raised to an excited pitch as friend calls a greeting to friend. Down every trail leading to Galilee little clusters of people make their way. Word has spread abroad that Jesus is returning to Galilee.

Suddenly he and his little band of followers come over the brow of a little hill on the Capernaum road. Following close behind swarms a vast multitude of people from Decapolis, Jerusalem, Judea, and beyond Jordan.

Quickly the word passes from mouth to mouth, "Jesus is coming." Crowds from Bethsaida and Capernaum soon appear and join the others. Together they follow the little band of thirteen men, simply dressed in flowing robes. As they reach the summit of the hill, where gentle winds afford relief from the heat, Jesus stops and motions for all to sit down and rest.

The air is tense. It is a moment to be captured and held for eternity. The crowd hushes as Jesus mounts a large rock and sits down. Quiet falls upon the multitude, their faces turned expectantly toward Jesus. Then he moves his lips and begins to speak.

What he was saying there, on that Mount of Beatitudes in faraway Palestine, was to illuminate the pages of history. The most profound, the most sublime words ever uttered were spoken there that day. In simple words, Jesus revealed to his dumbfounded hearers the inner depth of God's commandments and a new way of life.

No one who once heard Jesus could ever again be the same. What was the secret of this Master Teacher? How did he hold those crowds spellbound?

"And it came to pass, when Jesus had ended these sayings, the people were astonished at his doctrine: for he taught them as one having authority" (Matt. 7:28, 29). Is not this authoritative note part of the secret of the earthly ministry of Christ?

The great prophets of the past had also spoken with authority. The impact of their preaching cannot be traced simply to an authoritative technique. Nor was their authoritative note based on confidence merely in the rightness of their own intentions and speculations. Their secret is traceable to nothing less than the confidence that they were the mediators of divine revelation. Throughout the Old Testament we find Isaiah, Jeremiah, Hosea, and the other prophets continually using such expressions as "The word of the Lord came unto me" or "Thus saith the Lord." The flaming prophets of old gained their authority from this: they were not simply speaking their own words; they were mouthpieces for God.

The authority of Jesus is more than a prophetic authority. The Christian Church rightly acknowledges that in him alone the incarnate God entered history; the very words he spoke are the words of the one and only God-man. Yet the remarkable fact is that in his teachings Jesus continually referred to passages in the Old Testament as fully authoritative. His Messianic self-consciousness, his very authority as the Son of God, are combined with the highest regard for the Old Testament as the authoritative record of the will of God.

Even a casual study of Church history will reveal that the great giants of pulpit and pen, from Augustine to Wesley, relied heavily on Scripture for their authority. In this, they followed a sacred precedent hallowed by Christ and the apostles.

In 1949 I had been having a great many doubts concerning the Bible. I thought I saw apparent contradictions in Scripture. Some things I could not reconcile with my restricted concept of God. When I stood up to preach, the authoritative note so characteristic of all great preachers of the past was lacking. Like hundreds of other young seminary students, I was waging the intellectual battle of my life. The outcome could certainly affect my future ministry.

In August of that year I had been invited to Forest Home, Presbyterian conference center high in the mountains outside Los Angeles. I remember walking down a trail, tramping into the woods, and almost wrestling with God. I dueled with my doubts, and my soul seemed to be caught in the crossfire. Finally, in desperation, I surrendered my will to the living God revealed in Scripture. I knelt before the open Bible and said: "Lord, many things in this Book I do not understand. But thou hast said, 'The just shall live by faith.' All I have received from thee, I have taken by faith. Here and now, by faith, I accept the Bible as thy Word. I take it all. I take it without reservations. Where there are things I cannot understand, I will reserve judgment until I receive more light. If this pleases thee, give me authority as I proclaim thy Word, and through that authority convict me of sin and turn sinners to the Saviour."

Within six weeks we started our Los Angeles crusade, which is now history. During that crusade I discovered the secret that changed my ministry. I stopped trying to prove that the Bible was true. I had settled in my own mind that it was, and this faith was conveyed to the audience. Over and over again I found myself saying, "The Bible says." I felt as though I were merely a voice through which the Holy Spirit was speaking.

Authority created faith. Faith generated response, and hundreds of people were impelled to come to Christ. A crusade scheduled for three weeks lengthened into eight weeks, with hundreds of thousands of people in attendance. The people were not coming to hear great oratory, nor were they interested merely in my ideas. I found they were desperately hungry to hear what God had to say through his Holy Word.

I felt as though I had a rapier in my hand and, through the power of the Bible, was slashing deeply into men's consciences, leading them to surrender to God. Does not the Bible say of itself, "For the word of God is quick, and powerful, and sharper than any two edged sword, piercing even to the dividing asunder of soul and spirit, and of the joints and marrow, and is a discerner of the thoughts and intents of the heart"? (Heb. 4:12.)

I found that the Bible became a flame in my hands. That flame melted away unbelief in the hearts of the people and moved them to decide for Christ. The Word became a hammer breaking up stony hearts and shaping them into the likeness of God. Did not God say, "I will make my words in thy mouth fire" (Jer. 5:14) and "Is not my word like as a fire? . . . and like a hammer that breaketh the rock in pieces?" (Jer. 23:29)

I found that I could take a simple outline and put a number of pertinent Scripture quotations under each point, and God would use this mightily to cause men to make full commitment to Christ. I found that I did not have to rely upon cleverness, oratory, psychological manipulation of crowds, or apt illustrations or striking quotations from famous men. I began to rely more and more upon Scripture itself, and God blessed.

I am convinced, through my travels and experiences, that people all over the world are hungry to hear the Word of God. As the people came to a desert place to hear John the Baptist proclaim, "Thus saith the Lord," so modern man in his confusions, frustrations, and bewilderments will come to hear the minister who preaches with authority.

I remember how in London many secular and religious journalists remarked on this very point as being perhaps the greatest secret of the meetings there in 1954. One of the thousands who came to commit their lives to Christ in that crusade was a brilliant young Communist. She was a student at the Royal Academy of Drama and Arts, and was already a successful young actress. She had joined the Young Communist League because the members were zealous and seemed to have the answers to the problems of life. Out of curiosity she and some of her fellow students came to our meetings at the Harringay Arena "to see the show." She later testified how startled she was to hear not a lecture on sociology, politics, psychology, or philosophy, but the simple Word of God quoted. This fascinated her and her companions. They came back several nights until the Word of God did its work of breaking open their hearts. They surrendered their lives to Christ.

I am not advocating bibliolatry. I am not suggesting that we should worship the Bible, any more than a soldier worships his sword or a surgeon worships his scalpel. I am, however, fervently urging a return to Bible-centered preaching, a gospel presentation that says without apology and without ambiguity, "Thus saith the Lord."

The world longs for authority, finality, and conclusiveness. It is weary of theological floundering and uncertainty. Belief exhilarates the human spirit; doubt depresses. Nothing is gained psychologically or spiritually by casting aspersions on the Bible. A generation that occupied itself with criticism of the Scriptures all too soon found itself questioning divine revelation.

It is my conviction that if the preaching of the Gospel is to be authoritative, if it is to produce conviction of sin, if it is to challenge men and women to walk in newness of life, if it is to be attended by the Spirit's power, then the Bible with its discerning, piercing, burning message must become the basis of our preaching.

From my experience in preaching across America, I am convinced that the average American is vulnerable to the Christian message, if it is seasoned with authority and proclaimed as verily from God through his Word.

Do we not have authority in other realms of life? Mathematics has its inviolable rules, formulas, and equations; if these are ignored, no provable answers can be found.

Music has its rules of harmony, progression, and time. The greatest music of the ages has been composed in accordance with these rules. To break the rules is to produce discord and "audio-bedlam." The composer uses imagination and creative genius, to be sure, but his work must be done within the framework of the accepted forms of time, melody, and harmony. He must go by the book. To ignore the laws of music would be to make no music.

Every intelligent action takes place in a climate of authority.

I use the phrase "The Bible says," because the Word of God is the authoritative basis of our faith. I do not continually distinguish between the authority of God and the authority of the Bible because I am confident that he has made his will known authoritatively in the Scriptures.

The world is not a little weary of our doubts and our conflicting opinions and views. But I have discovered that there is much common ground in the Bible—broad acres of it—upon which most churches can agree. Could anything be more basic than the acknowledgment of sin, the Atonement, man's need of repentance and forgiveness, the prospect of immortality, and the dangers of spiritual neglect?

There need be no adulteration of truth nor compromise on the great biblical doctrines. I think it was Goethe who said, after hearing a young minister, "When I go to hear a preacher preach, I may not agree with what he says, but I want him to believe it." Even a vacillating unbeliever has no respect for the man who lacks the courage to preach what he believes.

Very little originality is permitted a Western Union messenger boy. His sole obligation is to carry the message he receives from the office to the person to whom it is addressed. He may not like to carry that message—it may contain bad news or distressing news for some person to whom he delivers it. But he dare not stop on the way, open the envelope and change the wording of the telegram. His duty is to take the message.

We Christian ministers have the Word of God. Our Commander said, "Go, take this message to a dying world!" Some messengers today neglect it, some tear up the message and substitute one of their own. Some delete part of it. Some tell the people that the Lord does not mean what he says. Others say that he really did not give the message, but that it was written by ordinary men who were all too prone to make mistakes.

Let us remember that we are sowing God's seed. Some indeed may fall on beaten paths and some among thorns, but it is our business to keep on sowing. We are not to stop sowing because some of the soil looks unpromising.

We are holding a light, and we are to let it shine. Though it may seem but a twinkling candle in a world of blackness, it is our business to let it shine.

We are blowing a trumpet. In the din and noise of battle the sound of our little trumpet may seem to be lost, but we must keep sounding the alarm to those in danger.

We are kindling a fire in this cold world full af hatred and selfishness. Our little blaze may seem to have no effect, but we must keep our fire burning.

We are striking with a hammer. The blows may seem only to jar our hands as we strike, but we are to keep on hammering.

We are using a sword. The first or second thrust of our sword may be parried, and all our efforts to strike deep into the enemy flank may seem hopeless. But we are to keep on wielding our sword.

We have bread for a hungry world. The people may seem to be feeding busily on other things, ignoring the Bread of Life, but we must keep on offering it to the souls of men.

We have water for parched souls. We must keep standing and crying out, "Ho, every one that thirsteth, come ye to the waters."

Give a new centrality to the Bible in your own preaching. Jesus promised that much seed will find good soil and spring up and bear fruit. The fire in your heart and on your lips can kindle a sacred flame in some cold hearts and win them to Christ. The hammer will break some hard hearts and make them yield to God in contrition. The sword will pierce the armor of sin and cut away self-satisfaction and pride, and open man's heart to the Spirit of God. Some hungry men and women will take the Bread of Life and some thirsting souls will find the Water of Life.

Preach the Scriptures with authority! You will witness a climactic change in your ministry!

Article   October 15, 1956

8 *The Stadium Story*

GEORGE BURNHAM

The first news editor of *Christianity Today* describes one of the highlights of the New York Crusade.

The center field sign at Yankee Stadium read, "Say Seagram and be sure."

Directly behind home plate was a banner, "Jesus said, I am the Way, the Truth and the Life."

Jammed between the two viewpoints were 100,000 people—the largest crowd ever to attend any event in "The House that (Babe) Ruth built" in 1923. An estimated 20,000 were turned away after standees filled the outfield area.

The wide-open spaces, usually covered by the likes of Joe DiMaggio and Mickey Mantle, were covered by the Smiths and Joneses from Manhattan, the Bronx, Brooklyn, and Jersey City.

It was the hottest night of the year, with reporters in the dugouts perspiring more than Casey Stengel during a ninth-inning rally. Seventy persons were treated for heat exhaustion. Over 2,500 ushers did a magnificent job of keeping confusion to a minimum.

Shortly before 7 P.M. a wave of applause began rippling across the stands and grew into a mighty sound. Walking side by side toward the platform at second base were Billy Graham and Vice President Richard M. Nixon. They were trailed by guards, friends, and a few who sneaked in under the blanket of applause.

In the opening moments of the program the 100,000 voices joined in praying the Lord's Prayer. Later another mighty sound rolled across the surrounding blocks as the huge crowd sang "All Hail the Power of Jesus' Name."

It seemed impossible that complete quietness could come to such a throng, but it did as George Beverly Shea and the 4,000-voice choir, superbly led by Cliff Barrows, sang "How Great Thou Art."

Roger Hull, chairman of the executive committee, announced that the Crusade, scheduled to end July 20 at Yankee Stadium, was continuing at Madison Square Garden for three weeks. A great burst of applause warmed the words.

After moving his eyes slowly around the vast expanses, Graham said in his opening remarks:

"They said Yankee Stadium wouldn't be filled. But it is. God has done this and all the honor, credit, and glory must go to him. You can destroy my ministry by praising me for this. The Bible says God will not share his glory with another."

Mr. Nixon, who was given a standing ovation, said:

"I bring you a message from one who is a very good friend of Billy Graham and one who would have been here if his duties had allowed him—the greetings and best wishes of President Eisenhower."

Noises from planes taking off from LaGuardia Field drowned out some of the early parts of the program. A telephone call to the airport brought quick results. The tower instructed all pilots to turn away from Yankee Stadium.

Graham, citing the perils of communism from without and moral deterioration from within, said, "I believe there is a glorious hope. There is only one solution for our collective problems that can guarantee the survival of America and its continued prosperity. Jesus Christ is the only answer."

Clutching his familiar Bible, he gave the listeners a choice between heaven and hell. "You make the choice by accepting or rejecting the Son of God, Jesus Christ. There is no middle ground."

With no room for people to walk to the platform, he asked all who would accept Christ to stand. An estimated 2,500 did so.

One man had made his decision before the address began. Posing as an usher, he collected about $500 in the bleachers when the offering was given. He was caught and arrested. (Graham attended the official hearing a few days later and, in love, offered him the riches of Christ. The man rebuffed Graham and refused Christ. Then the evangelist went another mile. He gave the man a job.)

News   August 19, 1957

9   *Where Is Evangelical Initiative?*

The other day brought a letter from a student in one of our leading Christian colleges. "I 'explode' because I don't feel I want to identify myself with it," he wrote of the way our evangelical cause is addressing —or rather, failing to address—the world crisis. "Perhaps that is my biggest reason for not going into the ministry," he added. "As I look at the world situation I wonder if it is even worth giving one's life to the Church anymore. In terms of long-range prospects, I am sure the answer is yes. But I now find that those who think make the mission field or ministry the last thing on their agenda of possible vocations. . . . I don't think Christian education is going to succeed. . . . My heart is really in politics. . . . If one has a real passion for the world and for lost souls, he must pick a medium which interacts with society and people."

That letter didn't come from a young radical. It came rather from the son of a seminary professor and Christian editor. It came, in fact, from the writer's own son. He is a symbol of a generation of evangelical youth who feel that organized evangelical structures today are so unconcerned for the world dying around us that legislative and political dynamisms now seem more potent channels of social change than our sacred evangelical and spiritual dynamisms. He writes: "I realize that politics is not the ultimate factor in changing society" (and I am thankful that he well realizes that regeneration is the decisive factor), but, he adds—and this mood is to be found among quite a few of our young evangelicals—"the organized Church as we know it today has had it."

It is not only our children who wonder where we as evangelical Protestants are in the world conflict today. Who has not himself awakened at three in the morning, restless with a conviction that, if we are really going to get a fresh hearing for the Gospel, we must address the trial and trouble of the needy masses in a way that links the emptiness of their lives to the suffering agony of Christ's cross? What threatens our evangelical witness today is not lack of enduring doctrine and principle, for we have held fast what has been delivered once for all. What threatens our witness is lack of spiritual power, reliance on past achievement that stifles creative concern, and lethargy and inertia in applying our sacred convictions.

The big debate over American goals carries sobering lessons for evangelical Protestants. The Protestant vision once supplied the sense of ultimate purpose and the reservoir of regeneration that held off and healed the social disorders in this privileged land. That vision has long since faded: the dominant climate is no longer Protestant, and it is less evangelical than ever.

A sense of dissatisfaction among evangelicals themselves over organized evangelical structures now runs deeper than before. There is dissatisfaction over our evangelical churches, over evangelical education, and over the evangelical image. This dissatisfaction calls for new power to face our terrible era, not merely a holding operation in a time of unusual disorder. Not a few of the young evangelicals of the oncoming generation shock us by swift and sure judgments on much of what our own generation has taken for granted.

When we answer back only with the old clichés, as if this atomic age were no different from any other, as if a century with communism on the march calls for nothing new, as if a generation with Romanism threatening to reverse most of the gains of the Protestant Reformation is just like any other, as if a decade in which the direction of Protestant theology (in its movement from Barth to Bultmann) may be sealed for our lifetime makes no special demands upon us—then our sons and daughters are prone to prize existentialism above evangelical theology and to share the mood (if not the intention) of the Communist verdict that "the Church has had it! . . . It's time for another day!" A religious commitment without flaming significance for a world whose walls are daily pushed out by rockets and missiles and whose inhabitants are daily threatened with extinction, or for a world in which communism is daily on the loose, or in which Romanism reaches daily for power, or in which the daily theological engagement has to do only with reaction to the initiative of others, holds little appeal for the next generation of Christian youth, and may God bless them for that!

We stand at one of the most important crossroads in modern times for the evangelical witness. Evangelical patriarchs are prone to exaggerate our gains, while evangelical youth are prone to exaggerate our losses. Both mistakes are costly. While the younger generation grows pessimistic over the broken dynamic displayed by organized evangelical structures, the older generation becomes optimistic because larger doors are now opening to evangelical leaders on the American scene. It is easy to forget how much of this development represents the mere semblance of progress, how much of it represents actually a freer expression of a proportionate voice once denied evangelicals by liberal ecclesiastical strategists when Protestantism was still the majority mood in America and when in fact evangelicals were the Protestant majority. There is no need for evangelical self-congratulation, if the larger "acceptance" of the evangelical voice takes place in a society which year by year becomes more pluralistic and less evangelical, and which welcomes evangelicals simply because their god is one of the many curiosities in the gallery of American faith. What is really at stake, in this decade of the twentieth century, is whether the "Golden Sixties" will mark an end-time in which the period from the Protestant Reformation to the Russian Revolution is closed off as an historical parenthesis, after which paganism once more becomes the controlling subject of Western thought and life.

We hear so much about "trends facing evangelicals today." Everything is facing us today—theological trends, social trends, politico-economic trends; the world has the initiative, and we seem resigned forever merely to react to that initiative. When the evangelical movement begins instead to face the trends, searching them to their depths, laying bare their weaknesses, taking them by storm, flashing the Gospel's power with the Apostle Paul's courage in the mighty pagan Roman Empire of his day—fashioned for a Nero or a Khrushchev ("there is none righteous, no not one"), a rejoinder to Stoics and Epicureans and no less to Marxists ("God . . . hath determined the times before appointed . . . and now commandeth all men everywhere to repent")—then our young people will lose their semi-paralysis in the face of competing theologies and philosophies; they will glory in a mightier than Khrushchev; and they will detect in history the sure hand of the eternal God no less than the grasping fingers of modern tyrants.

One of the Communists has said, "The Christian Church is dead; it just does not know how to lie down and be buried." There is profound wisdom in our ignorance of how to conduct a funeral for Christ's Church, and it springs from the glory of the Resurrection. Christ's resurrection took place in a graveyard. As long as we live in fallen history the Empty Tomb is the promise of a new day. We are thrust into the world as light and life, not to grovel about like moles in a subversive underground.

Editorial   May 22, 1961

10 *The Service of Worship*

CALVIN D. LINTON

Great truths are often weakened because the words by which we identify them become so familiar. How rich a theme, for example, is signified by the words which appear somewhere in almost every church bulletin: "worship service." Let us glance briefly at these words as if we were defining them for the first time. But first, a prefatory comment.

The original harmony of the spheres and the perfection of joy which caused the sons of God to shout have been shattered by discord and rebellion, begining with Satan's first "I will not serve" and lasting to the present moment. No longer is it "natural" to conduct oneself in accordance with the divine orderliness which emanates from the being and nature of God, and which unites all creation (save man, the rebel) in a vast and exquisite artifice permeated by the driving force of love, all manifesting itself in total beauty. The Satanic temptation is always aimed at the disciplined orderliness of right hierarchy. If creation may be likened to an orchestra (a popular simile in the seventeenth century), Satan may be likened to a tempter who whispers to the bassoon played: "You are not properly appreciated. You are not being permitted to play loud enough or often enough, and you can't even make up your own melodies! Play your own way, make up your own tunes— and for heaven's sake (if you will pardon the expression) play louder!" Such a violation of discipline, of order, of "acceptable service" the Renaissance writers often refer to as violation of "degree," the divine ladder of hierarchy. And so Shakespeare has Ulysses in *Troilus and Cressida* say: "O, when degree is shak'd, which is the ladder of all high designs, then enterprise is sick!"

Now all this may seem a "long preamble to a tale" when our only purpose is to engage in a little semantic exercise; yet it is all to the point, for the service of worship implies no less than a completely restored inward and outward harmony for man as he takes his place once more in the perfect order of the kingdom of heaven. From God, the motionless center of the turning wheel, emanate all values, all relationships, all concepts of decorum. And the ultimate decorum which man must relearn shows forth his relationship to the infinite majesty of God and to his creation.

As the final comment in our preface we must note an often ignored fact; fallen man is completely unable to worship God in any way whatever. "The sacrifice of the wicked is an abomination unto the Lord." The problem of worship simply does not exist for him, any more than the problem of how to honor and serve his betrayed king existed for the medieval outlaw. The right to serve was an honor deprived the outlaw as a penalty for his rebellion against his monarch's rule and law. Indeed, the analogy may be pushed a bit further, for just as clearly as the outlaw was able to return to his king's favor and thus to resume his service only as the king permitted, so clearly can fallen man be restored to citizenship and divine favor only on God's terms. The pagan, therefore, deceives himself when he thinks he is worshipping God in his humble adoration of the night sky, or in his outpoured libations; and so does the modern, more sophisticated pagan in his self-appointed ritual of culture, or aesthetic response, or even good works. Further, all men do not worship the same God "by whatever sign or name he may be known"—Allah, or Dagon, or the Life Force. (Whatever were the shortcomings of the Crusaders, this is one error they did not make, as they battled the "paymin," worshippers of Allah!) To all who worship on their own, as it were, come the tragic words: "Ye worship ye know not what." Worship is not a sort of general spraying in all directions of reverence and awe, to be soaked up by whatever deity exists. It must, rather, be based on communion between two self-conscious beings who know each other.

Turning at last to our basic definitions, we note that "worship" comes from the Old English "weorthscipe" (Middle English "worschippe") and that it denotes in its first syllable inherent value, ultimate merit. In short, it is a word primarily relating to a value judgment, and we know that value must be determined within a frame of reference, according to a hierarchy. Most of our value judgments day by day are comparative; that is, we compare the valued object with others of its class or group. Thus in feudal terms, for example, a count is of more "worth" than a baron; a duke is "worthier" than a count—all in "priority, and place, insisture, course, proportion, season, form, office, custom, in all line of order," as Shakespeare explains.

So when worth is ascribed, one must know within what system of evaluation the term is used. Man's systems vary with each age, each society, almost each individual, and that which is worthy to one group at any given time is offensive to another. Indeed, there is no more poignant evidence of man's spiritual confusion, of his "fragmentation," than his total inability to agree on any single system of establishing that which is good, worthy. Even in evaluating himself, he varies wildly, either shouting with Swinburne, "Glory to man in the highest!" or agreeing with Stevenson that man is a mere "disease of agglutinated dust." Paul warns us not to think of ourselves more highly than we ought, but rather to think of ourselves in terms of the only absolute measure, the only changeless standard, the only infallible system of evaluation—the standards of God. By the terms of righteousness within that divine standard, man's natural condition is simply and bluntly given in Scripture: "Thou art worthy to die." But there is another dimension to be included, the infinite measure of God's love, and by that measure man, though bereft of self-pride, stands immeasurably high, for while we were yet sinners God loved us.

For the Christian, then, the word "worth" has only one absolute application: the infinite worth of God. To acknowledge the absolute worth of God is the first step of worship; indeed, it is the first requirement. "Give unto the Lord the glory due unto his name." "I am the Lord, and there is none else, there is no God besides me." When the Church acknowledges "worth-ship" as it exists totally and uniquely in God, it simply joins in with the "voice of many angels round about the throne, and the beasts, and the elders: and the number of them was ten thousand times ten thousand, and thousands of thousands; saying with a loud voice, Worthy is the Lamb that was slain to receive power, and riches, and wisdom, and strength, and honor, and glory, and blessing."

Although such an acknowledgment can be made only after man has obeyed God's command to "turn" to him, it is still simply the first step. The perfect communion with God which each creature seeks must be based on harmony of will and desire, not on intellectual assent alone. So we turn to the original meaning of the two words most often translated "worship" in English; and we find that both "shachah" in the Old Testament and "proskuneo" in the New carry the force of submission, obedience, "to kiss the hand toward someone in token of submission, to bow down in submission."

This concept takes us into the heart of the mystery of worship. Intellectual truths may be forced on us; the facts may simply overwhelm the mind until we cry out, "Enough! I am convinced." But at the same time, in the secret place of our heart, we may whisper, "But I will not obey." Hypocrisy, says Milton, is the only evil whose operation is so entirely inward that only God can know surely when it is present. It is an interesting question whether true submission can be willed. We can force our bodies to make those gestures which indicate submission; but can we by willing so alter our nature as to make it harmonious with, submissive to, a pattern of values foreign to it? To the Christian, of course, the answer is easy: such a change is not alteration; it is re-creation, a new birth, and only God can accomplish it. For the human-ist, however, man need obey nothing unless he chooses. He is born with an unextended allegiance which he can, if he wishes, cherish throughout life as a king might his crown. Scripture teaches otherwise. Man is born in the kingdom of Satan and is under his domination. Sub-mission to the will of God, central to worship, is a transferred alle-giance, not a pristine bestowal of it. Writes Isaiah: "O Lord our God, other lords besides thee have had dominion over us: but by thee only will we make mention of thy name. They are dead, they shall not live; they are deceased, they shall not rise: therefore hast thou visited and destroyed them, and made all their memory to perish" (26:13-14).

So here again is emphasized the fact that the high privilege of wor-ship is all of grace. God must of his grace reveal himself sufficiently to man for man to acknowledge his being and his worth; but even more of grace is his victorious battle over the power of Satan and of his dark subordinates in our hearts. Man cannot serve two masters, and the evil king we are born under must be driven from his throne by a power mightier than the combined might of man.

The paragraph above has led us to the term "service." It is impos-sible to speak long about "worship" without using the word, for wor-ship exhibits itself outwardly in service. It comes second, but it is not secondary. Man is not a static awareness, a mere abstract state of knowing and submitting; he is a dynamic creature whose very purpose of creation was that he might "serve" God. When he fell, he forgot every act and gesture appropriate to true service, for he was com-pletely turned about, completely disoriented. So the detailed ritual of the Mosaic code of worship began to retrain him, to acclimate him once more to heaven.

From all of Scripture we know one thing that "service" does not mean, and that is "performance of labor for the benefit of another." God did not create man simply because he needed anything done for him. And yet the thought that when we serve God in worship we do something for which he should be grateful is widespread. It is even supported, innocently, by certain hymns—"God has no hands but mine his work to do," for example. This attitude is an example of imperfect reorientation. We are still too steeped in the world's system of values, even its understanding of love. As T. S. Eliot is fond of pointing out, earthly love is inseparably linked with the idea of exchange, or bartering something we have for something we want. Apart from revelation, indeed, it is unlikely that man could ever imagine motiveless love.

No, the service of worship is not something rendered to God in order that he may generously remunerate us. So we look further down the list of definitions, until we come to one emerging from the philosophy and the social structure of the Middle Ages. (And the feudal system, whatever were its human perversions and injustices in practice, shows forth in its ideal concept the nature of divine orderliness better than any other system.) There, we note, "service" had the sense of being permitted to do that which fulfilled and enriched the person so serving. When the knight was permitted to serve his lady, or the liegeman his lord, he was (under the ideal if not the reality) given freedom to be his best self, to exercise his capacities as they were meant to be exercised, to become a living, working part of the whole beautiful, divinely ordained structure. Service was a privilege, an honor, a release from unworthy servitude. It was motivated by reference, gratitude, and love.

And so first and foremost, our service to God consists of living as we were originally intended to live, in obedience and perfect love. Such service is freedom because such living for the re-created creature is natural. God created us for his glory, and our purpose is to glorify him and enjoy him forever. This is our "acceptable service." We can never live it fully in this life—the process of perfection is not completed —but we can practice.

Then we look at one more pertinent definition: "service" as "an office of devotion" performed by a priest. It was the priest, we know, who under the Mosaic law was "ordained to offer gifts and sacrifices," "to serve" before the Lord. Under grace, every Christian is entered into the priesthood of all believers and is thus similarly "ordained." In a very significant way, this fact most clearly exemplifies the whole wonderful meaning of worship, for it shows a rebellion overthrown, a breach healed, an evil covered, a communion restored.

Since, then, service emanates from a living relationship, our service of worship is continuous, as continuous as those who serve before the thunderous throne itself in heaven. The condition of the believer is not one of normal, everyday separation from God occasionally interrupted by periods when he is admitted to the Divine Presence. Rather it is one of permanent restoration to a vital relationship. In this life, however, this truth is never fully realized; so it is proper, and sanctioned by Scripture, that man should from time to time celebrate in a particular way his restored relationship to his Creator. And it is right, too, that these worship services should be made so decorous and comely that the spiritual reality is shown forth in pleasing outward signs. What in detail constitutes appropriate ritual is a matter of endless discussion among the various denominations, and it is no part of this writing to touch on the problem. But one thing is clear: any detail of the ritual which ignores, weakens, or contradicts any spiritual reality underlying the outward form is improper at best, offensive to God at worst.

Really, everything is summed up in a command and a promise. The command: "Whatsoever ye do in word or deed, do all in the name of the Lord Jesus, giving thanks to God and the Father by him." And the promise: "If a man love me, he will keep my words: and my Father will love him, and we will come unto him, and make our abode with him."

Article   July 20, 1959

11   *"Of Man's First Disobedience and the Fruit . . ."*

ELVA McALLASTER

Firm-winged, the gulls, this shining afternoon
Glide past my window. Glide alone, in threes.
Glide without effort. Curve and turn and rise.
Enthralled, I watch. No strain, no struggle in
Firm-sinewed wings; no crashes in mid-air.
No suicidal anguish pulls apart
The rhythm of their wing-beats. For such flight
Gull wings were made. Gull wing-bones.
    Feathers, too.

So ought the soul to be; it, too, was made
To soar in upper regions undismayed,
Yet hobbles, hobbles, hobbles over stones,
Wing-broken, feathers draggled. Thing of
    groans.

February 4, 1966

12 *The Spirit's Certainty*

G. C. BERKOUWER

No one was better than Luther at uttering quotable phrases. Many of his pointed verbal crystals have been swept into the public domain and become familiar to people who know little else of Luther's theology. But, of course, all great phrasemakers have suffered this. Besides, Luther's little remarks often contain a good bulk of theology in themselves.

Take, for instance, the famous words: *simul peccator et justus,* sinner and just at the same time. This phrase became the focal point of any number of theological controversies. Roman Catholics saw it as a betrayal that Luther meant to teach that grace remained wholly external to the Christian. There was a word of forgiveness, a word of pardon, but no grace that entered a sinner to make him a new and better man. The phrase revealed, Luther's opponents said, that Luther was content to let the sinner remain a total sinner while enjoying the free grace of God.

But there are other phrases that Luther made immortal. I am thinking just now of this: *Spiritus Sanctus non est scepticus.* He said this in a context that included the remark that no more miserable state of mind existed than that of uncertainty. Luther told us that we must remember that the Spirit writes no doubts and no mere opinions in our hearts. The Spirit breathes certainty.

In a time of uncertainty like our own, these words need capital letters. The truth of what Luther said is reflected in the Gospel. For if one thing is true of the New Testament, it is that the Spirit is set out in it as the faithful witness of Christ in the world. Anyone with a notion of studying this facet of the New Testament further would do well to look into two books: *Der Paraklet,* by O. Betz, published in 1963, and *Zeuge und Märtyrer: Untersuchungen zur frühchristlichen Zeugnisterminologie,* by N. Brose, published in 1961.

But in the event that the reader does not get to these books, he can do even better by comparing Luther's words to the witness of Scripture itself. Perhaps Karl Barth had Luther in mind when he said that the word No is never a final piece of wisdom, and that he himself came increasingly to realize that the positive and the certain were the decisive things men had to live and die by. (See the foreword to his *Kirchliche Dogmatik,* IV/3.)

We live in a time when even theology is exploding with new and revolutionary problems. There is a danger that the serious student will be so impressed by all the problems in theology that he will circle all certainties by a ring of questions. When this happens, an inverse Pharisaism sets in. The doubting student says: I thank thee, Lord, that I am not as certain as those naïve people. Let Luther say it again: *Spiritus Sanctus non est scepticus.* Indeed, the Spirit is not a skeptic.

Well, of course, these words must not be allowed to cover up a simplistic certainty that is achieved by solving problems even before they have really been stated. The Spirit is no wavering doubter. But this does not mean that we know everything or can solve every problem. Paul, hardly a skeptic, did admit that he saw through smoky lenses. And even Luther often warned against false security.

That much must be said. But we have to watch out for people, including ourselves, who enjoy playing games with problems and glorifying uncertainty. Let Luther's words be a living warning against such vicious sport. When problems pop up like bubbles in boiling water, doubt threatens to win the day from certainty. The impression is sometimes given that anyone having certainty has plucked a cheap triumph out of the air. I recall someone's saying once that all certainty has something demonic in it.

The Reformation gave us a different outlook. Perhaps Reformed Christians more than anyone else have to be on guard against being know-it-alls. We know only in part, said St. Paul in connection with the riddles and the dark mirror we look through. But remember that he wrote this about not knowing it all in the chapter on love. He points a way through the riddles, a way that transcends the partial knowledge, a way we can walk in with blessing (I Cor. 13).

Discriminating between evangelical certainty and false security may not be easy. We have to recognize the caricatures that even the friends of certainty make of it. But we want to brush aside caricatures only to get at the genuine article. If we really want to follow the right way into certainty, without falling into cheap security, we are going to have to remember that the Gospel is, after all, not *yes* and *no,* but only *yes.* We are going to have to keep in mind that the Gospel calls us into knowledge and not doubt, to certainty and not skepticism. Forgetting this, a man can stand in our day as an impressive poser of problems, but withal not as a witness.

We are not apostles, needless to say. But the message is here, and we are called to be witnesses. If the Spirit is in fact not a skeptic, then there are human witnesses to the truth. The witness must be faithful. We are not allowed to pass out opinions and guesses as if they were divine revelation. But we must stick to the message that points a way to certainty for doubting and problematic people. There is a right way to say, "We know." It must be said without pride if it is to be said in a way that will serve as a blessing to others and ourselves. But it can be and must be said—always humbly, but said nonetheless. To change Luther's words just a bit: *Christianus non est scepticus*—The Christian is not a skeptic. *Veni, Creator, Spiritus!*

Current Religious Thought   October 22, 1965

13 *"What If . . ."*

JOHN LAWING

LAWING

Here I stand . . . at present . . . I think . . . but then again, I could be wrong.

December 4, 1964

14 *The Continental Divide in Contemporary Theology*

BERNARD RAMM

From Canada to Mexico runs the continental divide, along which two raindrops falling just a few inches apart can end up in two different oceans. There is also a continental divide in contemporary theology. Certain truths and doctrines characterize historic Christianity and, if rejected, necessarily involve its repudiation.

The present state of contemporary theology is certainly one of confusion. Whom are we to believe? Weimann with his natural theism? Bultmann with his demythologized New Testament but existentially impassioned kerygma? Barth with his massive tomes quarried from a dozen different pits? Berkouwer with his scintillating restatement of Calvinism? Bishop Robinson with his theological first-aid kit? Ebeling with his vast historical learning used to buttress the new hermeneutic? What makes the situation really confusing for the layman, the seminary student, and the average minister is that all these theologians use the same Bible and the same or similar terminology, tackle the same or similar problems, teach in historic Christian schools, work in historic denominations, and practice the same sacramental life.

In a preliminary way we can find three different strands in contemporary theology. (1) There is the orthodox strand, which includes the Roman Catholic and the Eastern Orthodox theologian, the traditional Calvinist, and the Methodist. It is characterized by the belief, common to all versions of orthodoxy, that Christianity is essentially a religion of supernatural salvation wrought by the death and resurrection of Christ and appropriated through faith (and the sacraments). (2) There is the modernist strand, which believes centrally that Jesus revealed perfect spirituality; this may be interpreted according to Schleiermacher as perfect God-consciousness, or according to Ritschl as perfect filial trust, or according to Tillich as the norm of new being. In modernism there is no supernatural salvation to be appropriated by a definitive act of saving faith. (3) There is also liberalism, religious faith which is built on some form of philosophical idealism or existentialism but which denies that there is anything crucial in the person of Christ or the Holy Scriptures. The liberal may include Jesus and the Bible in his system, but only because he shares in Western culture—not from principle or necessity.

It is obvious that, though modernists differ from liberals in that they insist on the centrality of Jesus to their theology and with it some normative status for the Bible, nevertheless modernism and liberalism are one in rejecting orthodoxy as the only valid version of Christianity. In a sense the modernist believes that all versions of Christianity are true. Insofar as every version of Christian theology attempts to preserve the Jesus mystique (using the term for something very real but yet so elusive that it defies precise definition), it is true Christianity. It may be surrounded with the heavy timber of antiquated theology, as in Roman Catholicism, or by experiential phenomena, as in Pentecostalism. But it is still there. And it is this pervasive Jesus mystique in all Christian bodies that is the rationale for the modernist's participation in the ecumenical movement. We are all Christian brothers, because each in his own way embodies the Jesus mystique. But of course the modernist believes that his version is the best to date, as it is supposedly freest from those elements that offend educated and cultured people.

According to modernism, all men really or potentially have this mystique. In the "unchurched" it lies dormant, but the Christian is the person who has positively responded to the Jesus mystique and conducts his life accordingly. God is every man's Father, and each man is brother to every other man. The human race is thus one great household of God divided into the obedient sons and the ignorant or even disobedient sons. The historic notion of men as lost sinners is rejected. The world is not divided into saved and lost, regenerate and unregenerate. The "new look" in evangelism is not reaching the lost or rescuing the heathen by Christian missions. Evangelism and missions are now creative sharing! Thus, according to Tillich, all men share to some degree in new being. Therefore, all men (in the older terminology) are saved; evangelism is the attempt to stir up a little more new being in the Christian West, and the missionary enterprise is creative sharing with non-Christian religions our mutual experience of new being.

On one side of the continental divide in contemporary theology stand the orthodox; on the other stand the modernists and liberals in their common rejection of supernatural salvation. But theologies do not come neatly labeled. Criteria must be used to evaluate them. The following criteria are meant to be representative rather than exhaustive as guides for finding this divide in theology.

1. Revelation. Theologians have tried to show that revelation is dynamic, not static; event, not information; existential, not intellectual; God's personal presence, not a piece of writing; holy history, not holy writings. Certainly no orthodox theologian wants a dry, flat rationalistic, intellectualistic view of revelation. If the orthodox doctrine of revelation was becoming arid because doctrinaire, it can profit from recent writings on revelation and correct its deficiencies. But what is the critical issue in any theology of revelation? It is this: Revelation may be many things but it must at least be truth. There must be a conceptual or a propositional element in revelation or otherwise revelation is no more the Word of God as truth.

Orthodox theology in all its versions believes that theology can originate only in truth, be the explication of truth, and be controlled by truth. If revelation is not at least truth, then Christian theology is impossible, for no reliable and authentic theology can be built from non-truth materials. There can be no logos of that which is by principle non-logos. The frequent attack in contemporary theology on "propositional revelation" never gets around to explaining how theology can be written from "non-propositional" revelation. Thielicke in *Between Heaven and Earth* sees the fundamentalists' drive for verbal inspiration and inerrancy as a fanatic bid for religious certainty, but he fails to see that pulsing beneath this doctrine of Scripture is a tremendous passion for truth.

Whenever revelation is defined exclusively as insight, or religious experience, or existential communication, or a felt Presence, then that view is unorthodox. It is not true that the orthodox theologian is an unreconstructed rationalist and therefore fears the existential, the symbolic, the mythological, the divine as a mysterious Presence. The orthodox theologian believes that religion may have many such overtones, and he would not wish to rob Christian faith of depth by being an unreconstructed rationalist. His point is that theology is *logia* and that a *logia* is possible only when there are *logia* materials. No *logia* is possible from the *non-logia* of intuition, religious experience, existential leap, or encounter. Therefore, he insists that revelation must at least be the Word as truth.

Certainly Tillich with his notion of revelation as ecstatic and Bultmann with his notion of revelation as a new self-understanding have broken with the historic doctrine of revelation. Barth and Brunner have a theology of the cracks! In that Barth stresses revelation as the personal presence of God, God as subject, as encounter and not as knowledge, his view is in the Ritschlian tradition and therefore is modernist. In that he stresses the objectivity of revelation in the Incarnation and the authoritative witness to revelation in Holy Scripture, he assents to revelation as truth. Thus his view of revelation is in the crack between modernism and orthodoxy.

In that Brunner emphasizes God as mystery, God as subject, revelation as address and encounter, he continues the modernists' view that revelation is not truth. In that he insists on the Incarnation as the supreme event of revelation and sound doctrines as the necessary presupposition for Christian faith, he assents to revelation as truth. So his theory of revelation also is in the cracks.

2. The Incarnation. The Incarnation is the unpredicted and unpredictable, sovereign, gracious, and absolute entrance of God into this world and our humanity in the person of Jesus Christ. It is God the Son freely, sovereignly, graciously uniting himself with a specific human nature. The verb "taking" (Phil. 2:7—*labōn*) affirms that he who was in the form of God and equal with God did of his own sovereign decree determine to enter the human race as Jesus of Nazareth. This has been the orthodox stance in Christology in all the various communions.

This doctrine of the Incarnation was spelled out at Chalcedon. Charges that Chalcedon is the product of the corruption of Christian theology by Greek metaphysics do not weigh seriously with the orthodox. The orthodox believe that Chalcedon can be reconstructed from the exegesis of the New Testament. Tillich and a host of modern theologians with him believe that the term "two nature" Christology is almost a dirty expression.

The real issue is not whether Chalcedon represents a timeless statement of Christology but whether contemporary theologians have remained true to the New Testament in shooting down Chalcedon. We can illustrate this briefly at one point: "the Word became flesh" (John 1:14). Here we have the divine expressed by "the Word," the human expressed by "flesh," and a union expressed by "became." It would seem that shooting down the "two nature" Christology of Chalcedon also manages to shoot down John 1:14.

Orthodox theologians believe that contemporary theology is riddled through and through with adoptionism, the belief that Jesus was a Palestinian Jew who existed in his own right, with his own parents, in his own family, and in his own vocation, and that God elected him and adopted him and called him to be the Christ. Thus the ordinary Jesus becomes the special Christ by God's gracious adoptive act. Orthodox theology resists this with all its power, because this Christology negates the entire scheme of supernatural salvation obtained by the incarnation, crucifixion, and resurrection of Jesus Christ.

Schleiermacher's Jesus as the model example of God-consciousness is adoptionism; the Ritschlian version of Jesus as the model example of filial piety is adoptianism; the Hegelian Christology which sees in Jesus the principle of divine-human continuity is adoptianism; Tillich's Christology of the man Jesus surrendering himself to the Christ of new being is adoptionism; Bultmann's Christ-event as the perfect existential example of dying to the world and rising to openness to the future is adoptionism; the new hermeneutic with Jesus as the perfect example of "the word" of existential communication is adoptionism; and all the recent expressions of young theological Turks who destroy traditional Christology but still find some kind of mystique in Jesus are adoptionism.

3. Sin. In orthodox theology, sin is primarily an offense against the holiness of God. It therefore excites the wrath of God. Few concepts of the older theology have been so belittled or so categorically rejected as the wrath of God. In the caricature God is pictured as a peeved deity, or a blood-thirsty deity, or a terrible-tempered Mr. Bang. To the modernists the wrath of God is an unfortunate imputation to God of a human weakness—namely, uncontrolled and ugly temper.

To the orthodox theologian the wrath of God is the proper response of the holy God to the human infraction of the good, acceptable, and perfect will of God. To the orthodox theologian the denial of wrath in God is a denial of all moral fiber in God. The wrath of God stands for the moral integrity of God, and thus, for the orthodox, to deny the wrath of God is to render ambiguous the moral integrity of God.

No orthodox theologian would deny the personal and social evil of sin. The liar damages himself. The racially prejudiced person creates great social evil. The international evils of Stalin and Hitler beggar description. But the essence of sin is not its destructive effect on the self nor its cancerous influence in society but its defiance of the good, acceptable, and perfect will of God. David committed adultery with Bathsheba and caused the death of Uriah, yet in his anguish cried out, "Against thee, thee only, have I sinned" (Ps. 51:4). He furthermore recognized the rightness of God's wrath toward him for his sin, for he said that God's sentence was justified and his judgment blameless.

In the modernist, liberal, and existentialist view, sin appears as an expected human foible. It is like making an error in mathematics, or a mistake in an experiment, or a blunder in social conduct. The game of life is complicated; no man can pick his way through it without some mishap. Man is really more a victim of sin than an agent of sin. It is hardly fair to blame a teen-ager for being unruly, if he comes from a broken home; the professional thief is a product of inner-city decay; the drunkard is the hapless victim of destructive psychodynamics; and the homosexual is the pitiful product of a pathological home.

This is to say nothing new. Chapters 4-11 of Genesis have been called the greatest theological tract on sin in the Old Testament. They reveal that, once sin is let loose in the race, man as a matter of fact is as much victim of sin as he is agent. This does not lessen our view of sin but reveals its tragic character.

Because man is both victim and agent of sin, the final assessment of a man's life can be made only by God. God alone can sort out a man's life and determine that which is victim and that which is agent. An inhuman and graceless moralism or legalism in regard to sin is not part of the orthodox view of sin. No orthodox theologian wishes to minimize the destructive effects of sin in personal and social life. No orthodox theologian wants to judge heartlessly the poor victims of the destructive forces of sin. But the orthodox theologian insists that those theologians who see in sin only human foible, only human error, only human miscalculation, only existential unauthenticity, who do not see sin as defiance of the good and perfect and holy will of God nor the wrath of God as that which corresponds to this defiance, do not measure up to historic orthodoxy or to the biblical revelation. Thus as long as Barth and almost all neo-orthodox and existentialist theologians along with him teach that the wrath of God is merely the inverse side of his love, or, with C. H. Dodd, teach that the wrath of God is merely the personal, social, and historical consequences of sin, they fail the biblical revelation of the wrath of God.

4. Salvation. In all versions of orthodoxy, salvation is the person and work of Christ, particularly his vicarious death and his resurrection. Personal salvation is the faith response to the supernatural salvation in Christ. The entire process from incarnation to regeneration is through and through supernatural.

In liberalism it is meaningless to talk of salvation, for there is nothing to be saved from except an attitude of irreligion, and that cannot be very serious if there is no such thing as lostness or damnation. In modernism, salvation is not really being saved but is merely the arousing of a religious potential that lies dormant. Preaching the perfect spirituality of Jesus sparks to life the religious element in men who previously were irreligious. Thus the difference between Christian and non-Christian becomes relative rather than absolute.

Representative of much current thought is the theology of Paul Tillich. All men have ultimate concern and therefore "new being," or, in more conventional existential language, "authentic existence." If they did not have some ultimate concern, some new being, they would cease to be men. Buddhists, Communists, and atheists have ultimate concern in their lives and hence new being. Christians differ from them only in that they believe that in Jesus as the Christ we have the norm for judging all instances of new being. In short, modernism in all its forms is universalism. Nobody is really counted out. As one modernist phrased it, the difference between Hitler and Gandhi was purely relative; Hitler was way down on the scale of spirituality (but not lost!) and Gandhi was way up (but not because he was justified or regenerated).

The continental divide in modern theology is revealed in the varying answers to the Philippian jailer's question: "What must I do to be saved?" One would say, "Make the existential leap and thou shalt be saved." Another would say, "You are saved, you fool. Just start living that way." Another would say, "Clean up the conditions in the jail and go to work on the social injustices in Philippi, and you are being saved." Still another would say, "My dear man, in view of our present knowledge of the Bible and the modern mentality you have asked a meaningless question. This selfish business of personal salvation was a bit of primitive nineteenth-century evangelism. Christianity is not being saved—perish the thought; it is identifying oneself with the forces of love and justice in the reconstruction of society." According to such answers, Paul never could have been more wrong than when he replied, "Believe on the Lord Jesus Christ, and thou shalt be saved."

5. Sacramental theology. Orthodox theology in all its versions believes that the sacraments either convey supernatural grace or witness to supernatural grace imparted by the Holy Spirit. Sacramentalism and non-sacramentalism in orthodoxy are both grounded in the supernatural grace of God founded in the death and resurrection of Jesus Christ.

The consistent liberal must deny the sacraments. His "naturalistic theism" takes the ground from under them. The modernist believes that Christian fellowship must include the liturgical, and so he retains the sacraments as a form of Christian fellowship. But only the most naïve person would ever believe that a modernist intends by baptism and communion what an orthodox person does. When a Lutheran or a Presbyterian in the orthodox tradition baptizes an infant, it is within the schema of the supernatural salvation obtained by Jesus Christ or the covenant relation of God's supernatural grace. But a modernist Lutheran or modernist Presbyterian cannot baptize the infant on these grounds. To him infant baptism represents the Christian estimation of children, or the responsibility of parents in Christian nurture, or the place of the whole family in the Christian Church. But it is not a witness to the supernatural salvation of Christ realized in the infant by the supernatural power of the Holy Spirit.

One has to ask what a sacrament can possibly mean to Bultmann or to Tillich or to Ebeling, because all these men deny a supernatural act of God either in the deed of Christ or in the sacrament.

6. The Church. In historic orthodox theology of all versions, the Church is based upon the supernatural salvation wrought by Christ in his death and resurrection and communicated in a supernatural act by faith in regeneration and justification, and the supernatural binding of believers together by the mystical but real bond of the Holy Spirit. When modernists deny a supernatural salvation in Christ, deny a supernatural act of salvation by the Holy Spirit, and deny the supernatural connectedness of all believers by the mystical union of the Holy Spirit, they destroy the historic, orthodox Christian understanding of the Church.

What takes its place? The Church becomes a society, a natural, human, non-supernatural religious community. It is bound together by purely natural ties, such as a common heritage in the Bible, a common belief in some sort of uniqueness in Jesus, a common belief in the historical continuity of Christians, and a common ethic of love. Now the Church is a society. But this is secondary to its being the supernatural body of Christ. Modernism in all its forms, the older Fosdickian version or the new hermeneutic, reduces the Church to a religious society, nothing more, nothing less; for it denies the entire supernatural foundation upon which the historic doctrine of the Church was built.

The conclusion is that there is a continental divide in contemporary theology. Despite all the confusion that exists, this divide can be located in "Jesus Christ the same yesterday, and today, and forever." Those who really know the cardinal doctrines of the Christian faith can differentiate the kind of theology which falls on the right side of this continental divide from that which falls on the wrong side.

Article   October 8, 1965

15 *Rebels and Causes*

J. D. DOUGLAS

A story about Speakers' Corner in London purports to quote the words of a stolid bobby directing people at the gate of Hyde Park: "Those in favor of burning down Buckingham Palace, on the right; those plotting to blow up the Houses of Parliament, on the left." The story is doubtless apocryphal, but it truly reflects a cosmopolitan institution that could flourish only under English skies.

Here on a Sunday afternoon converges a motley collection of individualists to hold forth in an atmosphere of high good humor, putting the world right, setting brother against brother, and exchanging frightful insults with fellow speakers and with hecklers. All, that is, but the Man with the Silent Message, who just stands aloofly on his platform. A smiling young man with a peculiar swaying motion is selling Onkism to a fascinated audience who don't understand a word of it, yet feel they are on the verge of hearing something for their soul's good. "I am sick of all the isms," he yells at them, "because isms bring schisms, and there are as many divisions in the schisms as there are schisms in the isms." An impatient hearer in a cloth cap gets a word in at last: "Hey, Mac, what are you talking about?" The Onkist fixes him with a compassionate eye, then in lofty tones refers the questioner to the Book of Onk, chapter 1980, verse one-million-and-something: "All is Onk, and Onk is all."

The Man with the Tattooed Face is boasting as usual that he'd been deported from America, while the Irish Anti-Partitionist nearby is settling the age-old problem of the six counties. "What are you doing in our country?" an African speaker on immigration challenges an interrupter. "Why don't you go back to Australia?" The Singing Woman, who is in particularly good voice, is making some extremely personal remarks about a fat little speaker before she bursts into more Victorian ballads. The fat man ignores her, but finally gives up and hands over his platform to a West Indian, to whom he gives a muttered word of encouragement: "Carry on with the old rubbish." The West Indian immediately becomes the target for a heckler who has a low view of the new man's mental capacity. The latter proves himself no slouch. "My friend," he retorts, "if I am stupid, then that's an accepted fact. But you are even stupider, because you stand there and listen to me."

Notably absent on this showery Sunday in mid-April is any sort of orthodox Christian message. A little group of elderly people stand singing evangelical choruses of poor quality, one after another, under a banner inscribed on one side "Flee from the Wrath to Come," and on the other "The End Is at Hand," but none of them deigns to interpret these somewhat unhelpful warnings.

A few yards off, a large crowd gathers around an elderly man in a clerical collar who is defending the government's new budget and belaboring the opposition. To a heckler in the crowd he replies: "That's just what I've been saying, if you'd only listen." Then (taking the crowd into his confidence), "I know it must be very embarrassing for our friend here to have people agree with him, but I must insist on doing it. . . ." On this speaker's platform are the words: "West London Methodist Church." He is Dr. Donald O. Soper. Attracted by the man, some listen a while, then depart, perhaps wishing he had spoken a good word for Jesus Christ. Maybe he was leading up to it.

News   May 7, 1965

16 *Do We Need a Christian University?*

Christian colleges dot our land. Most of them are affiliated with and partly supported by particular denominations. Most of them are in financial trouble, and a large number of them could immediately take more students without straining their facilities. Many offer an educational experience acceptable by secular educational standards; a few— a very few—offer work of exceptional quality in one field or another.

Why, then, is there talk of establishing a "Christian university"?

Why not put the money into the hard-pressed Christian colleges already in existence?

Among the several answers that might be made, this writing considers only the one which emerges from this statement: it is not proposed to set up just another Christian college (or university, in the larger view) but a university of the highest academic excellence. This need is not filled by existing institutions. With full credit to those very few Christian colleges which enjoy the full and well-deserved respect of the world of secular higher education, the fact remains that such academic distinction is definitely the exception. What is looked for, then, is a university dedicated not only to the Faith but also to the highest and most rigorous academic standards, a university demanding the respect of the secular world of scholarship in the arts and sciences, and in the professions. At the core, solid, dynamic Christian unity; in the branches, solid and creative scholarship.

One need not profess Christianity to see the desperate need in American higher education for unity of purpose, for an agreed-to set of values. To teach facts without teaching values is worse than useless; it is dangerous. The power of knowledge put to evil use plagues our planet, and may plague it to death; it troubles the very footstool of God's throne (Job 1:6). Few convictions are so deadly as that one which equates knowledge with virtue as well as with power.

And yet secular colleges and universities make little pretence that they still teach the ends to which the power of knowledge should be directed. Science, the keystone of our education, not only confesses, it asserts, that it has nothing whatever to do with value judgment. Long since lost is the implied unity of purpose implied by such phrases as "community of scholars" and "men and women joined in the fearless pursuit of truth." In the now-standard jest, we have not so much universities as multi-versities sharing the same plumbing system— often suffering from edifice complexes. The wholeness and oneness once provided, at least in some measure, by common acceptance of Christian theology, philosophy, and ethics has exploded into fragments. A typical college student, taking five courses from five different instructors will, in any given week of attendance, hear either openly avowed or subtly implied five different value systems. (Among them, however, there may well be a clear, scholarly Christian point of view, for the situation is not so entirely black as some believe.)

But, it may be asked, is it possible to create a truly distinguished Christian university? Distinguished, that is, in the view of the world?

Is there not something incompatible between true Christian education on the one hand and high standing in the secular world of scholarship on the other? Can one seek the approval of God and that of the secular world of scholarship at the same time?

Any full answer would be long, complex, and controversial. But one important facet of the answer is clear: every educator will be able to list offhand, in his own field of specialization, the names of many men who are eminent scholars and who are at the same time dedicated Christians. Gather enough of them together and the Christian university has its faculty. Typically, however, the most eminent of these men are now mostly to be found on the faculties of secular institutions. The existing avowedly Christian colleges have not attracted all the top Christian scholars.

Why not? Again, the answer would be long and controversial, but we may at least suggest a part of it by speaking of that sometimes bewildering thing, the "scholarly mentality." (Remember, now, we are speaking of Christian education, not Christian evangelism.) That mentality demands a very specific kind of environment. Among the lesser things it demands are scholarly facilities (such as libraries and laboratories), the companionship of other dedicated scholars, encouragement by the administration of independent research, challenging and intellectually competent students, graduate-level teaching. But above all else it demands intellectual freedom.

Now, granted that "freedom to pursue the truth and to teach it without let or hindrance" may become merely a pious phrase, and granted that it even may be made a cloak to cover subversive intent, it yet suggests something absolutely essential to academic excellence. It is too often lacking at denominational colleges. When, in its recruitment of teachers, the Christian college demands subscription to a detailed code of conduct as well as to a basic statement of Christian faith and commitment, many Christian scholars decide that they can do their work better in the freer atmosphere of a secular institution. This is, of course, a problem which sets ganglions quivering, and has done so for some centuries. In its larger implications it plagued the apostolic Church. When all the talk is done, it adds up to this: No Christian university can hope to gather to it distinguished Christian scholars if it forgets the force of Peter's question to the legalists at Jerusalem: "Now therefore why tempt ye God, to put a yoke upon the neck of the disciples, which neither our fathers nor we were able to bear?" (Acts 15:10) Nor can it succeed if it forgets James's ruling: "For it seemed good to the Holy Ghost, and to us, to lay upon you no greater burden than these necessary things . . ." (Acts 15:28).

Are we then to argue that a Christian university should require no more of its faculty members than they be excellent scholars and vaguely devoted to "good things"? Not unless we attribute the same nonsense to Paul when he stood up against Peter (before Peter was, rather laboriously and at some trouble to God, enlightened on legalism) and when he stood up against the legalists at Jerusalem. It is beyond dispute that there are "necessary things," the unalterable bases of our faith revealed in God's inerrant Word, but we must not confuse these things with details of conduct. Indeed, it probably would be difficult to do better than to require assent to the articles of the Apostles' Creed (taken for what they clearly say, without mental reservation and without "interpreting" them away) as the chief basis of Christian unity.

None of this line of thought is intended to deny that an individual's conduct is part of his testimony, nor to deny the legitimacy and importance of supporting denominational colleges which, in details of conduct as well as in creedal statements, require conformity with what is most sincerely believed by members of the denomination. Rather, it is intended to distinguish between the denominational colleges which we now have and the kind of institution which is being proposed. Not all Christian scholars receive the missionary calling which leads them to serve in the more cloistered religious college. All honor—very great honor—to those who are so called. They often sacrifice distinguished careers on the altar of missionary service. But honor, too, to those who achieve eminence in the world of scholarship in secular institutions without for a moment compromising the "things necessary" to our Christian faith. It is these who must be attracted to a Christian university which seeks the highest academic reputation.

But there are students as well as teachers in the classrooms of our colleges, and the students, in their own academic excellence, must challenge and stimulate the teachers. This means that admissions standards must be set high. There must be no thought of substituting a "high degree of Christian commitment" for solid academic attainment, as demonstrated by scores made on such tests as are put out by the College Entrance Examination Board. Presumably, indeed, there should be no requirement that incoming students sign a statement certifying their Christian faith. The usual evidence bearing on good moral qualities will be sufficient, for surely one of the greatest services to be performed by the proposed Christian university will be to introduce uncommitted students to the intellectual validity, ethical grandeur, practical applicability, and unifying comprehensiveness of Christian philosophy. They thus may be led to the ultimate value, the discovery of the saving power of the Lord Jesus Christ, who alone is the Way, the Truth, and the Life. But this last is evangelism. The proposed Christian university must first and foremost be an educational institution.

The world has long sought to exhibit Protestant Christianity as essentially anti-intellectual, and all too often there has seemed to be evidence to show it. The proposed Christian university will confront many problems, but the chief one will be to hold high and clear the two basic characteristics sought: deep Christian faith and unity, and academic excellence. Fortunately, they are not incompatible.

Editorial   October 10, 1960

17 *Why Did I Ever Leave Cardiff?*

In the autumn of 1923 I arrived from Wales, my native land, with the party of David Lloyd George, famed British Prime Minister. I soon found myself the guest of the African Inland Missionary Home in Brooklyn, a guest who was a very lonely and homesick young man. A large group of retired lady missionaries, sensing my loneliness, arranged an afternoon tea to help dispel my gloom. At the close I was asked to say a word to the assembled ladies, and looking them squarely in the face I exclaimed, "What language is there to describe my gratitude to you dear women for all this kindness? What word can describe my feelings?" Then in a burst of enthusiasm I thundered, "I know just the word, you are without doubt the most homely women I have ever met." Brother, I learned the hard way that there are words used in the old country that are never used here, even if homely in Wales does mean wholesome, gracious, kind, loving, and motherly.

DR. PETER R. JOSHUA, Presbyterian Evangelist, Geneva, Illinois.

Preacher in the Red   June 8, 1962

18   *The Plight of the Church College*

CARL F. H. HENRY

Perhaps nothing in American education is more important than the role of Christian institutions in our present secular culture. Of the national population, 85 million persons are presently twenty-four years of age or under; by 1980 more than 35 per cent of the population will be between sixteen and twenty-five. Sunday-school enrollment is not keeping pace with population growth, and youth evangelism faces growing odds if church colleges do not counterbalance the secular trend of public education and, in fact, sacrifice one biblical truth after another to modern alternatives.

The Danforth Foundation, which has made many notable contributions to American education, has undertaken an appraisal of the 817 religiously oriented colleges and universities throughout the United States. Statisticians agree that public education will in the future even more overwhelmingly overshadow church colleges and universities in size, facilities, and total financial support than it does now. If, despite this service to a declining percentage of college students, church colleges are to fulfill a highly important leavening role, far-reaching changes are demanded.

So much new knowledge has emerged, along with a growing thirst for its assimilation within a reasoned outlook on life, that Christian colleges face a remarkable opportunity to confront the academic world in a fresh spirit of intellectual adventure. But without constructiveness of purpose, clarity of objective, and authentic spiritual vision, they are doomed first to irrelevance and then to extinction.

What distinctive role has the Christian college? To emphasize the humanistic values in Western culture? The better secular campuses now do this in their humanities courses. To add a religion department to a secular curriculum? Already eighteen state universities have established full-time religion departments; learning about religion is no distinctive of church-related education but an integral element in a complete liberal arts education. To stress "Hebrew-Christian values" or "the basic truths of life"? An academic institution that seeks to perpetuate these values in a metaphysical vacuum has learned little from the drift of Western thought and life, and its cherished "vital truths" usually become so broad that little depth remains. Sometimes church-related colleges differ little from others except in preserving corporate worship or a moral code that erases biblical patterns less swiftly than that of secular campuses.

Since the questioning of religious beliefs is a widespread characteristic of American secular education, what special obligation have the church-related campuses? They are accused by some of neglecting the development of a philosophy of life and assuming unjustifiably that a reasoned outlook emerges automatically from a college education. At a time when many forces are inimical to historic Christianity, a steady stream of graduates sensitive to modern ideas and equipped for intellectual leadership could exert significant influence both in the churches and in secular society. The Christian campus might thus supply the guiding principles of the future as a by-product of its illumination of the liberal arts by the Christian faith.

No mere addition of "a religious tone" to the liberal arts will dispel the present spiritual vacuum, to which paradoxically many of the churches are contributing. The theological and ethical uncertainty in the seminaries and in the churches is surely one of the chief causes of uncertainty in the church-related colleges. The major universities have, in fact, sloughed off their church-relatedness except when crusading for funds or recalling their origins. Some secular educators cherish the strange notion that the academic excellence of colleges is proportionate to their lack of church-relatedness. And not a few surviving church colleges tend to look upon their church affiliation as a liability. They perpetuate no fixed Christian beliefs, consider chapel attendance optional, pay no serious attention to religion, and emphasize their non-sectarian character.

Despite the ecumenical tendency to speak of "church colleges," this term now covers a spectrum of institutions of such divergent commitments that it serves only a statistical purpose. For obvious reasons, Roman Catholic educators would rather speak of their institutions as Catholic colleges, while evangelical educators speak of Christian colleges. One Presbyterian college president, asked what religious beliefs he requires of faculty, replied: "Only that they be church members; we assume that this establishes their evangelical commitment." The term "church-relatedness" implies nothing definitive in the way of theological commitment; what it assures is little more than favored tax treatment for ordained members of the teaching staff.

The weakest link in the effort to revive the importance of the church colleges is their unsure sense of the role of truth in Christianity. This uncertainty is doubly distressing at the present moment, when public education is groping to understand the role of religion in the curriculum and when the main vacuum in many church colleges is their lack of an integrating world-life view.

At a time when the winds of modernity have swept over many religious campuses, administrators speak of the need for faculty diversity —for "ventilation"—as a guarantee of intellectual ferment, despite the fact that the fundamental problem in church-related institutions is their neglect of Christian perspective. When the Christian faith has been all but blown away by modernity, sensitive educators ought to think about closing some doors rather than opening more windows. The times being what they are, the need is not for more "ventilation"— the thing that already accounts for the secularizing of many church colleges—but for greater consistency in the relevant exposition of Christian truth and the relating of all subjects to the Judaeo-Christian revelation.

The plea for vitality in learning is, of course, well taken. It has been rightly said that students ought to "field the question" before teachers suggest the answers. No Christian faculty is worthy of its academic responsibilities if it can sustain intellectual excitement on campus only through the presence of unbelieving colleagues. This device may be dramatic, but it tends to neglect the best resources for academic vitality—such things as the full use of library holdings, the conflict in the minds of students, the spirit of the classroom, panel discussions including outside participants, and visiting lecturers.

The Christian campus does not need a devil on its faculty; a devil's advocate will do. The devil will be active enough on his own account. Even an ideologically united faculty usually includes a considerable amount of diversity, simply because sanctification is not glorification. Those who make room for a Unitarian on a seminary or college faculty may have a church-related institution, but its Christian integrity is compromised. The advocates of "ventilation" offer no objective gauge of when such contrary winds become objectionable. But faculty members who contend that unbelievers ought to be able to teach in a Christian college classroom should apply to a secular institution, since the main distinction between a church college of diverse religious outlooks and a secular college is usually the latter's academic superiority.

Behind the advocacy of "ventilation" is not so much a desire for intellectual excitement, which can be achieved in other ways, as a surrender of the traditional view of the Christian college as a propagatory institution or medium of indoctrination. The campus cannot be the Church, requiring an affirmation of the historic faith from its students. Its role cannot be defined as pastoral and protective. Nor is the classroom the place to press for conversion. Its main traffic is in ideas; intellectual content is its commodity. But liberal arts education presumably is interested in the whole truth. Just as physicians are bound by the Hippocratic oath to preserve life, so teachers ought to consider themselves academically responsible to purvey truth in its entirety. And a company of scholars who agree about a corpus of spiritual truth that they are willing to expose to the same searching scrutiny they give other ideologies has every academic right, and in fact an obligation, to pass this truth on.

Non-evangelicals who disbelieve biblical truths will hesitate to inculcate these truths, but it should be clear that it is the truths and not the indoctrination that they oppose. Whoever thinks that only evangelical or fundamentalist campuses practice indoctrination is due for some higher education. Every campus, and, in fact, almost every teacher, does this; the difference between liberal and conservative teachers and colleges in this regard is not *whether* but *what*. If conservative colleges are characterized as defenders of the faith, the plain fact is that the liberal college not only has lost the historic faith and is confused about what to substitute but also serves an intellectual smorgasbord, with ardent promotion of one specialty or another by the various classroom chefs.

The notion that academic freedom is inconsistent with the presentation of a body of truth to which a college faculty subscribes is unconvincing. The difference in this matter among the religiously oriented campuses is one of degree, not of kind. Few if any church-related colleges will tolerate an atheist as a professor, and probably none would tolerate a known Communist. All religious institutions have specific faculty requirements. If academic freedom is thwarted by an intellectual requirement, then all church-related campuses are in the same predicament. What is really objectionable about evangelical institutions from the liberal standpoint is the requirement of faculty adherence to articles of the historic faith that the non-evangelical has surrendered, and that are a barrier to faculty eligibility unless religious symbols are rationalized to mean what they once did not mean. Every educational institution gathers a company of scholars subscribing to its purposes, and no institution grants its faculty members freedom to destroy those purposes. If an institution allows academic license to erode its objectives in the classroom, the dissident faculty will in time preside over the death of these objectives.

Let no one consider this a brief for run-of-the-mill fundamentalist education. It is the academic shortcomings of these institutions that lend artificial credence to liberal contentions. Their ingrown faculties, their worship of Ph.D's more than good teachers, their contentment with graduates who have not really won the faith for themselves but "parrot" it, their elevation of the campus code to an authority paralleling that of divine articles of faith, their inclusion in required faculty statements details on which even evangelicals disagree widely, their failure to produce a comprehensive literature articulating the Christian faith in the context of contemporary thought, their smug withdrawal from the secular academic scene—all these elements and more call for a new day in conservative education.

But non-evangelicals are in no position to gloat over this list of shortcomings, since some of their own campuses reflect certain of these tendencies also. And the so-called "liberal" campus that boasts about its academic freedom often has bolted the doors against first-hand reflection of evangelical convictions, and, even more often, presents them second-hand in the spirit of effigy-burning. As a matter of fact, some "liberal" liberal arts colleges wholly bypass evangelical faculty prospects. Nor are theological seminaries an exception; at one period or another campuses of the stature of the University of Chicago Divinity School have displayed this same exclusive temper. As many graduates complain of the academic illiberality of liberal institutions as protest the closed mindedness of conservative campuses. One would be hard put to it to draw up a list of evangelical professors teaching philosophy in non-evangelical church colleges. The libraries of non-evangelical institutions are often woefully lacking in evangelical reading resources, and course requirements and reserve reading shelves frequently bypass conservative literature entirely.

The liberal complaint that conservative institutions necessarily transgress academic freedom by their doctrinal requirements really springs from a quite different motivation—in a word, from skepticism about basic evangelical tenets. Often, in fact, this skepticism runs much deeper; there is doubt of the reality of any divinely revealed truths whatever, or of the existence of a fixed body of truth of any kind. This attitude implies not so much a concern for freedom, of which Christ is the font, as an uncertainty that Christ is the font of truth and that the Christian campus can know absolute truth about the spiritual world.

Precisely this mood has led the church colleges to their present predicament, in which the relation between religion and truth is highly ambiguous. In fact, religion and intellect are sometimes viewed antithetically. This is all the more apparent when liberal educators, troubled about the decline of Christian conviction on church-related campuses, speak of their institutions as stronger academically than religiously. The contrast of truth and religion is one that neither Augustine nor Aquinas, Luther nor Calvin, would have tolerated. But the liberal tradition from Kant through Ritschl, Schleiermacher, and Kierkegaard refuses to acknowledge the competency of reason in the metaphysical realm. Evangelical scholars insist that this competency has been impaired by sin; but this is quite different from the emphasis that man cannot have objective knowledge of ultimate reality on any basis whatever, divine creation and redemption included.

What underlies the liberal outlook pervading many denominational colleges today is the arbitrary denial of the ontological significance of reason—that is, of the biblical fact that the Logos is structurally constitutive of all reality. That a rational God is Creator of all things, that in Jesus Christ the divine Logos has become incarnate, that the rational nature of man and the laws of logic belong to the *imago Dei*—all this has been surrendered to the waves of modernity. The instrumental philosophy of John Dewey, the anti-metaphysical theology of influential European modernist, dialectical, or existential scholars, have squandered all this—and more. What more? The historic Christian assurance that divine revelation has communicated trustworthy knowledge of God and his purposes. In a word, the whole biblical and traditional confidence in divinely revealed truths is gone.

This situational fact, much more than genuine theological renewal, explains the success of ecumenism in our time. And its implications for the church-related colleges are plain. If evangelical confidence in revealed truths is misplaced, if no genuine metaphysical knowledge is possible, if there is, in fact, no body of fixed truth, and if religion thrives in the absence of any universally valid truth-content, then it is perfectly clear why many insist that Christian colleges need "ventilation," why the "ideal" Christian campus will not defend a "faith which was once for all delivered," and why the insistence on creedal subscription conflicts with academic freedom. Surely no scholar wants to be chained to what he considers error.

Much of this kind of thinking motivates the emphasis that students best acquire a unified view of life from the encouragement of professorial example. This emphasis is popular among liberals who are disillusioned about the ability of a structure of courses (particularly "the religion department") to achieve the integration of learning. Surely no one will doubt the importance of professorial example, particularly in the matter of a unified view of life. The teacher should teach by example outside the classroom what he teaches by precept in the classroom. But it should be crystal clear that, at this level, we are speaking of something considerably less than an integrated Christian world-life view, something, shall we say, answering to the Communist *Weltanschauung.*

The evangelical, the modernist, and the humanist have strikingly different convictions about what delivers man from inner personality discord and unifies his personality and outlook on life. And it is the evangelical today who insists on the role of reason in religious experience. The others insist, no doubt, that the purpose of education is not simply to amass a great quantity of facts but "to make the students' eyes shine." But all the "posies, punch, and platitudes" cannot conceal the fact that most church college campuses are evasive at the point that needs most clearly to be articulated—namely, whether the Christian religion is true. That Christianity is the highest religion, that it is unique, that it is redemptive—all this may be asserted. But no college campus that professes to be Christian can evade an academic duty to deal with the truth-claim of historic Christianity in relation to the truth of philosophy, science, and history. Is the truth of the Christian religion universally valid? If a church-related campus cannot give a reasoned affirmative answer to that question, it deserves to go out of business. In fact, it really has gone out of business so far as its religious claim is concerned.

Article   May 21, 1965

19   *A Scientist's Beliefs*

I believe:
That the power of God is complete,
That the authority of God is absolute and final,
That God is both Creator and Redeemer,

That in his providence, God is in control of his creation, and that
he rules in the affairs of men, and that for this, Christ is his
instrument and our contact,
That God is just (yet I do not always understand),
That God is loving, for he has provided a way through Jesus Christ
so that by commitment to him we may meet God's requirements
and be acceptable to him,
That the Bible, as the revealed Word of God, is the supreme authority for my faith and life.

DR. ELMER W. ENGSTROM
President, Radio Corporation of America
August 27, 1965

20   *Youth in Search of a Mission*
DAVID E. KUCHARSKY

*In a day of general apathy and delinquency, collegians demonstrate their
interest in sacrificial missionary service. IVCF convention shows evangelical vitality, broadening social interest.*

Gathered in the mammoth University of Illinois Assembly Hall, 7,000
youthful delegates lifted hearts and voices in climactic lines approaching the pitch of a battle cry:

We are on the Lord's side,
Saviour, we are Thine!

Perhaps it was their way of repudiating student escapades at Hampton
Beach, New Hampshire, and Seaside, Oregon. Or perhaps the Congo
martyrdoms had stirred a new measure of spiritual vitality. Whatever
the reasons, the Seventh Inter-Varsity Missionary Convention held
during the last five days of 1964 could show the world an army of
Christian collegians in a sincere quest for purposeful living and service.

At the same time, 3,500 Methodist college students and campus
ministers met at Lincoln, Nebraska, for the Eighth Quadrennial Conference of the Methodist Student Movement. At Richmond, Virginia,
the Eighth Quadrennial Youth Convention of the Presbyterian Church
in the United States drew 540 students.

The Urbana-Champaign, Illinois, convention, sponsored by Inter-
Varsity Christian Fellowship in the United States and Canada, drew

its record turnout from nearly a thousand campuses. Almost too restrained at the outset, the students proved to be earnest seekers and intent listeners. Only on the last night did an unruly element protrude. Announcement of a ban on picture-taking by Dr. John W. Alexander, IVCF's newly appointed general director, was greeted by a defiant succession of camera flashes. When Alexander was left speechless, the crowd roared in good humor. That episode aside, delegates behaved in a way becoming their collective destiny: tomorrow's missionary task force.

The Urbana convention has become the world's leading trade fair of the foreign missions enterprise and the most productive medium of missionary recruitment.

"It's a candidate secretary's dream," said Dr. Horace L. Fenton, associate general director of the Latin America Mission. "These delegates badger us from early morning until late at night. What's more, they voice important concerns, not things like 'What's there to eat on the field?' "

One missionary representing a major denominational board reports that more than 50 per cent of its candidates for overseas service have had IVCF contacts. To buy up opportunities, that board sent four staff members to man its displays. Another missionary board executive said that fifteen of its 1964 recruits had attended Inter-Varsity's last convention.

A total of ninety denominational and independent missionary boards were represented by convention displays. The exhibits stretched across nearly a half mile of concourse corridors in the circular, ultra-modern hall. Walkways were remarkably clean, indicating a minimum of waste among the 1,000,000 or more pieces of literature that changed hands during the convention.

The cresting interest of denominational boards in Inter-Varsity candidates provides a widening wave of evangelical missionary commitment within mainstream churches. It also works to diminish the embarrassing number of conservative missionaries abroad who avoid an ecumenical identification or association.

Among the delegates were the editor-in-chief of the student daily at Yale, a nephew of Kenya's Tom Mboya, a drama student from Korea, and the son of a missionary martyred in Bolivia. In all, some seventy-five denominations were represented, including Roman Catholicism: at least eight trainees for the priesthood were on hand. In the absence of a category of "observers," under which they had proposed to attend, they registered as delegates.

The breadth of concern among delegates carved out new avenues of involvement for Inter-Varsity. Questions sent to panel discussions by the students dealt largely with racial justice and Roman Catholicism. Student sensitivity to these issues obviously will encourage Inter-Varsity to regard them as focal points for future campus discussion and planning.

As new general director, the 46-year-old Alexander assumes responsibility for the movement's strategy. His credentials include a distinguished academic career at the University of Wisconsin and visiting professorships at Harvard and U.C.L.A. He comes to an organization which has been plagued by internal strife despite a realization of unparalleled opportunities for Christian outreach on secular campuses throughout North America. The academic world ignores Christianity before exploring it, he says, and thus rejects an unknown.

IVCF's response to the temper of the times was stamped indelibly on the convention program. Easily the most electrifying suggestion to come out of the panels on social issues was one which challenged missionary boards to reject financial aid from churches which deliberately encourage segregation. Further underscoring the intensity of the racial problem was panel member Ruth Lewis, who was one of the first Negroes ever to enroll at the University of Alabama and who is now studying for a doctorate there. Arthur Glasser, home director of China Inland Mission–Overseas Missionary Fellowship, predicted that missionaries' concern for racial justice would be "determinative."

Students also will remember the quietly persuasive appeal for Christian unity voiced by Executive Secretary I. Ben Wati of the Evangelical Fellowship of India, the plea for "a lifetime of Bible study" uttered by Rev. John R. W. Stott of the Church of England, and the articulate delineation of the convention theme—"Change Unparalleled, Witness Unashamed, Triumph Unquestioned"—by Dr. Eugene Nida, translations secretary of the American Bible Society.

Evangelist Billy Graham told a crowd of 13,500 that the academic world is losing its influence among students because it avoids the issues of sin, suffering, death, and the purpose of history. Only the Bible, he said, speaks to the ultimate situations.

Other highlights of the convention program included a memorial service for martyred missionaries and a New Year's Eve communion service.

News   January 15, 1965

21 *"Look on the Fields"*

RUTHE SPINNANGER

I never knew
    Thy way would lead
        across these fields
untouched by ocean's hue.
I thought
        there would be far-off scenes
        the challenge of "lost souls"
Till Thou did'st show
        in seas of sameness
            ordinary folk
                I passed
        in blind familiarity—
        more lost than those
            whom distance still enhances.

April 23, 1965

22 *Criteria of Biblical Inerrancy*

EVERETT F. HARRISON

Inerrancy is not a formally stated claim made by the Scriptures on their own behalf. It is rather an inference that devout students of the Word have made from the teaching of the Bible about is own inspiration.

If the Spirit of God has really wrought in the production of this Book from start to finish, it is hard to conceive of error save such as may have crept into the text in the course of its transmission.

The appeal to the original texts of the Old and New Testaments has indeed often been ridiculed as an unworthy refuge. Who has seen the so-called infallible originals? So the query goes. No one in our time, certainly. No one in possession of the facts would argue that the text of Scripture has come down to us unchanged from the beginning. The Scriptures contain no promise of the supernatural overshadowing of the transmitters of the Word such as is claimed for the writers. The variations are numerous, though mostly unimportant in relation to the message of Scripture. But we have no reason to conclude from the data of textual criticism that the writers of Scripture were so left to their own devices that error should be expected in the autographs.

If the Bible were of such a nature that it was composed by men and only subsequently was adopted by God and breathed into by the Holy Spirit, then it might conceivably be allowed that God was so concerned with the spiritual message that he tolerated a measure of error in the factual material. But this is not the scriptural doctrine of its own origin. Rather, it is insisted that the Spirit was active and controlling in the very production of the Word in its entirety.

Granted that the spiritual message is intrinsically more important than the historical minutiae of the narrative framework, yet the Scripture gives no hint of distinction as far as trustworthiness is concerned. This is understandable since the historical element is itself the unfolding of God's providential and saving activity. Herein lies the fallacy of the kernel-husk solution to the problem we are considering. The history of biblical interpretation shows that the abandonment of the inerrancy of Scripture in non-doctrinal items has a tendency to make criticism of the doctrinal data much easier.

Consequently, it is not wholly satisfactory to rest in the solution that the Bible is "the only infallible rule of faith and practice" and be indifferent to the question of its infallibility in areas that do not directly relate to faith and practice. Evidence is lacking in the statements of Scripture for the notion that the Word is the product of a division of labor, God working with the writers on doctrinal matters and leaving them to their own wisdom on historical matters.

Approaching inerrancy then as a corollary of the biblical exposition of its own origin, there seems to be every reason to insist upon it. But when the data of Scripture are examined, many problems present themselves, problems that seem to make the retention of inerrancy difficult if not impossible. Parallel accounts appear to contradict one another, and quotations from the Old Testament do not always agree with the Old Testament text we have or even with the text of the Septuagint as we have it. So if the fact of inerrancy is to be derived from Scripture deductively, the form that our view of inerrancy ought to take is to be derived inductively from the data of the text.

It may be helpful to start with the negative approach. Certain criteria of inerrancy ought not to be applied. One is the insistence that there should be verbal agreement in multiple accounts of the same event. Such agreement would involve mechanical control over the writers of Scripture such as is not suggested by the liberty given to them to utilize their own vocabulary and style of writing. Or, on the supposition that they consulted one another's work, it would make them echoes and rubber stamps of one another. Identity of language in such instances could even suggest the distinct possibility of collusion, which would tend to destroy confidence in the record. It is widely recognized, especially in courts of law, that witnesses may diverge from one another in details and even in perspective without being chargeable with untruth.

This should be kept in mind when one is wrestling with the problems of the Resurrection narratives in the Gospels. Again, in the account of Jesus' baptism, Mark reports the voice from heaven as saying, "Thou art my beloved Son." Matthew puts it in the third person, "This is my beloved Son." It is disingenuous to insist that the voice can only have spoken in one way, so that one of the reports must be erroneous. Mark gives the words in the form of direct address as they are found in Psalm 2. Matthew puts the words in the third person, possibly to emphasize that the baptism was properly witnessed, and by no less a witness than God himself. Testimony to the divine sonship is equally clear in both accounts.

Another criterion to be avoided is that there should be the same degree of completeness and finality in the statements of Scripture at all periods. There is such a thing as progress in the Word of God, and that progress is discernible both in the area of revelation and in the area of reception and response. The early chapters of Genesis have a primitive, almost naïve, character about them that befits the record of events in the distant past. Only when the Son of God was revealed could the knowledge of God be at all fully communicated or a fully adequate response by men be expected.

The claim of inerrancy should not be made dependent upon verbal exactness in quotation. It is anachronistic to apply the standards of our own time to the Scripture. With our wealth of printed books and other materials, all so easy of access, we can justly demand that quotations be verbally accurate. But such was not the standard of antiquity when written materials could be consulted only under great difficulties. Quotation from memory was common.

We ought not to expect scientifically precise statements of natural phenomena. The very thought that the biblical writers should be required to anticipate the discoveries and the terminology of modern times is altogether incongruous. As we might expect, their descriptions of nature are popular and not technical. What is more, we can still use the language of Scripture touching scientific matters without being counted antiquarian or incorrect. Even the scientists do it in ordinary conversation.

Finally, difficulties ought not to be prejudged as errors. The folly of this has been demonstrated many times over. One of the best-known examples is the case of Sargon, mentioned in Isaiah 20:1 but unknown otherwise. Hostile criticism did not hesitate to pronounce the Scripture inaccurate. But now Sargon's palace has been excavated and his royal records uncovered. Some items in the Word of God remain to be confirmed, such as the enrollment under Cyrenius (Luke 2:2). Some may never be confirmed. But lack of confirmation is no basis for repudiation.

Having cleared the ground somewhat, it is well to ask ourselves, What then are the proper criteria of inerrancy? Three, at least, are worthy of special consideration.

First, the Bible must be evaluated in terms of its cultural milieu. If the soul of Scripture is universal and eternal, its body remains Oriental. It was written by men who had patterns of thought that differ from ours at many points. The more one can steep himself in these, the better will be his position as translator or interpreter. With us, for example, the word "son" has one commonly accepted meaning. But in Scripture it sometimes means descendant. It may also connote the possession of certain characteristics, as in the phrase "sons of darkness" or "sons of disobedience." Still other nuances of thought are conveyed by this word. The symbolic use of numbers, to take another example, is more congenial to the ancients than to our mental climate. Only occasionally does one get the impression that numbers in Scripture are given with great precision. Those who know most about the East tell us that the Bible is eminently true to the life and setting of the Orient as it persists today.

Second, diversity in Scripture statements is not incompatible with the unity of truth they represent. It was recognized in the early Church that differences existed in the Gospel accounts, but the prevailing attitude was that this did not disturb the unity of presentation, which was guaranteed by the operation of the sovereign Spirit upon the writers.

This is the testimony of the canon of Muratori (*ca.* A.D. 170) and of Irenaeus a few years later. Doubtless these men were therefore not sympathetic to the idea of presenting the Gospel narrative in one continuous account so as to relieve the story of apparent contradictions, the very thing which was done by Tatian in his *Diatessaron* at about the same period. The Apostle Paul had advanced the thought, in dealing with spiritual gifts, that there are diversities of operation but it is the one Spirit who works through them all. Our Western way of thinking, patterned closely after the Greek, inclines to demand uniformity. We tend to associate diversity with deviation and so with error. Apart from the question as to which outlook is correct, we ought not to sit in judgment on Scripture as untrustworthy because of a variety of presentation of the same basic material. It is a well-known fact that our Lord accepted the Old Testament of his day as the Word of God which could not be broken. In that Old Testament are many duplicate narratives, such as the accounts in Kings and Chronicles of the reigns of the kings of Judah. Evidently the compiler of Chronicles made use of Kings as source material, having also the records of certain prophets to draw upon. Even where the same event is being described, it is not always told in the same way, certainly not in the same words. All we are concerned to point out here is the fact that our Lord, familiar as he was with both portions, apparently accepted both as equally the Word of God. The bearing of this on the Synoptic problem is quite obvious.

Third, Scripture must be judged in terms of faithfulness to the purpose in view. A change in readers often necessitates a change of statement in order to achieve communication. In the account of the Triumphal Entry, Matthew and Mark have the words "Hosanna in the highest." Luke has instead, "Glory in the highest." "Hosanna," being a Semitic word, would be unintelligible to Luke's Gentile readers. One of our greatest authorities on the language of the Gospels, Gustaf Dalman, says, "It cannot be doubted that *hosanna* was understood to be a cry of homage in the sense of *glory* or *hail to the Son of David.*" The change was imperative, but it was made without falsification.

One of the knottiest problems in the New Testament is the evaluation to be put upon the discourses in John's Gospel. They are quite different from anything to be found in the Synoptics. Did the Lord actually speak them? Are they authentic reproductions of what he said? It is no doubt an oversimplification to quote Jesus' prediction about the Spirit bringing to the remembrance of his disciples whatever he had said to them. The Saviour also predicted that the Spirit would lead his followers into all truth. We need a combination of these two sayings to explain the discourses in John. That they rest upon Jesus' utterances we have no doubt. That they constitute in part an interpretation of those utterances under the tutelage of the Spirit we have no doubt also.

Our conception of inerrancy ought not to require us to adopt an a priori position about verbatim reporting. Our concern ought to be to learn with all humility as much as we can of the methodology that God the Spirit has chosen to use in giving us the Word of God. Those who are hostile to the claim of the veracity of Scripture commonly expect too little of the Bible. Its friends, on the other hand, may err in expecting too much.

Article   January 20, 1958

23   *Higher Critics and Forbidden Fruit*

CYRUS H. GORDON

Though Bible scholars live in an age of unprecedented discovery, they stand in the shadow of nineteenth-century higher criticism. There was a time when the label "conservative" meant the rejection of that higher criticism, but now the conservative mind often latches onto higher criticism even though archaeology has rendered it untenable. My conservative critics, some of whom are on the faculties of Protestant, Catholic, and Jewish seminaries, find fault not because my writings run counter to any particular religious tenet, but because I am not devoted to JEDP: the badge of interconfessional academic respectability.

All of my Bible professors were conservative higher critics with a positive appreciation—and in some instances, with a profound knowledge—of the archaeological discoveries bearing on the Bible. I was trained simultaneously in higher criticism and biblical archaeology without at first realizing that the two points of view were mutually exclusive. By this I mean that a commitment to any hypothetical source-structure like JEDP is out of keeping with what I consider the only tenable position for a critical scholar: to go wherever the evidence leads him.

When I speak of a "commitment" to JEDP, I mean it in the deepest sense of the word. I have heard professors of Old Testament refer to the integrity of JEDP as their "conviction." They are willing to countenance modifications in detail. They permit you to subdivide (D_1, D_2, D_3, and so forth) or combine (JE) or add a new document designated by another capital letter; but they will not tolerate any questioning of the basic JEDP structure. I am at a loss to explain this kind of "conviction" on any grounds other than intellectual laziness or inability to reappraise.

The turning point in my own thinking came after (and in large measure because of) a four-year hiatus in my academic career during World War II. Coming out of the army and back into teaching, I offered a course on the Gilgamesh Epic. In the eleventh tablet I could not help noting that the Babylonian account of the construction of the Ark contains the specifications in detail much like the Hebrew account of Noah's Ark. At the same time, I recalled that the Genesis description is ascribed to P of Second Temple date, because facts and figures such as those pertaining to the Ark are characteristic of the hypothetical Priestly author. What occurred to me was that if the Genesis account of the Ark belonged to P on such grounds, the Gilgamesh Epic account of the Ark belonged to P on the same grounds— which is absurd. The pre-Abrahamic Genesis traditions (such as the Deluge) are not late P products; they are essentially pre-Mosaic and it is not easy to single out even details that are late. This has been indicated by Sumero-Akkadian tablets for a long time; it is now crystal-clear from the Ugaritic texts, where whole literary themes as well as specific phrases are now in our possession on pre-Mosaic tablets, as well as in our canonical Bible. Ezekiel (14:13-19) thus refers to an ancient Daniel, a model of virtue who emerged together with his progeny from a major disaster. We now have the Ugaritic Epic of this Daniel on tablets copied in the fourteenth century B.C., when the story was already old. Like many another psalm ascribed to David, Psalm 68, far from being late, is full of pre-Davidic expressions some of which were not even understood before the discovery of the Ugaritic poems. In verse 7, for example, *kosharot* means "songstresses" as in Ugaritic, so that we are to translate "He brings out prisoners with the songstresses," meaning that when God rescues us from trouble, he brings us joy as well as relief. He frees the prisoner not into a cold world but into one of joyous song. The Kosharot were just as much a part of the classical Canaanite heritage of the Hebrews as the Muses are a part of our classical Greek heritage.

The question the biblical scholar now asks is not "How much post-Mosaic (or post-Exilic) is this or that?" but rather "How much pre-Mosaic (or pre-Abrahamic)?"

The urge to chop the Bible (and other ancient writings) up into sources is often due to the false assumption that a different style must mean a different author.

When the subject matter is the same, different styles do ordinarily indicate different authorship. But any one author will employ different styles for different types of subject matter. A lawyer uses different styles depending on whether he is preparing a brief, or writing a letter to his mother. A clergyman does not use the same style in making a benediction and in talking to his children at the breakfast table. No physician writes in prescription style except on prescription blanks. Accordingly the technical style of Genesis in describing the Ark is no more an indication of different authorship from the surrounding narrative than a naval architect's style in describing the specifications of a ship makes him a different author from the same architect writing a love letter to his fiancée.

Minds that are incapable of grasping whole entities are tempted to fractionalize the whole into smaller units. The Book of Job, for all its difficulties, is infinitely greater than the sum of its parts after the critics have hacked it to bits. Ancient Near East literature makes it abundantly clear that Job as it stands is a consciously constructed single composition. The kind of criticism that detaches the prose prologue and epilogue from the poetic dialogues on stylistic grounds (that is, that "prose and poetry don't mix") runs counter to ancient Near Eastern rules of composition. From many available illustrations, let us single out Hammurapi's Code in which the prose laws are framed within a poetic prologue and epilogue, giving the composition what may be called the ABA form. This means that the main body of the composition is enclosed within language of a contrasting style. The structure of Job ("prose-poetry-prose") exemplifies this ABA scheme. Moreover, the structure of Daniel ("Hebrew-Aramaic-Hebrew") also reflects the ABA pattern, and the book should be understood as a whole, consciously composed unit.

No one in his right mind would want to outlaw the study of the component parts of biblical (or any other) books, but a sane approach to scriptural (or any other) literature requires that we take it on its own terms, and not force it into an alien system.

One of the commonest grounds for positing differences of authorship are the repetitions, with variants, in the Bible. But such repetitions are typical of ancient Near East literature: Babylonian, Ugaritic, and even Greek. Moreover, the tastes of the Bible world called for duplication. Joseph and later Pharaoh, each had prophetic dreams in duplicate. In Jonah 4, the prophet's chagrin is described at two stages, each accompanied by God's asking "Are you good and angry?" (vv. 4, 9). Would anyone insist that such duplicates stem from different pens?

One particular type of duplicate is especially interesting because of the extrabiblical collateral material at our disposal. Judges 4 gives the prose and Judges 5 the poetic account of Deborah's victory. The two accounts confront us with variants. The usual critical position is that the poetic version is old; the prose version later. The assumption of disparity in age or provenance between the two accounts on stylistic grounds is specious. Historic events were sometimes recorded in Egypt simultaneously in prose and poetic versions, with the major differences appropriate to the two literary media. (Sometimes the Egyptians added a third version—in pictures.) In approaching matters such as the date and authorship of Judges 4 and 5, it is more germane to bear in mind the usages of the Bible world than it is to follow in the footsteps of modern analytic scholars who build logical but unrealistic systems.

One of the fragile cornerstones of the JEDP hypothesis is the notion that the mention of "Jehovah" (actually "Yahweh") typifies a J document, while "Elohim" typifies an E document. A conflation of J and E sources into JE is supposed to account for the compound name Yahweh-Elohim. All this is admirably logical and for years I never questioned it. But my Ugaritic studies destroyed this kind of logic with relevant facts. At Ugarit, deities often have compound names. One deity is called Qadish-Amrar; another, Ibb-Nikkal. Usually "and" is put between the two parts (Qadish-and-Amrar, Nikkal-and-Ibb, Koshar-and-Hasis, and so forth), but the conjunction can be omitted. Not only biblical but also classical scholars will have to recognize this phenomenon. In *Prometheus Bound, Kratos Bia-te* "Force-and-Violence" is such a combination. If any further proof were necessary, Herodotus provides it in his history (8:111), where he relates that Themistocles tried to extort money from the Andrians by telling them that he came with two great gods "Persuasion-and-Necessity." The Andrians refused to pay, and their way of telling him "You can't squeeze blood from a turnip" was that their gods were unfortunately "Poverty-and-Impotence." Thus it was a widespread usage to fuse two names into one for designating a god. The most famous is perhaps Amon-Re who became the great universal deity as a result of Egyptian conquest under the eighteenth dynasty. Amon was the ram-headed god of the capital city, Thebes. Re was the old universal sun god. The fusion of Re's religious universalism with the political leadership in Amon's Thebes underlies the double name "Amon-Re." But Amon-Re is one entity. Scholars can do much to explain the combination of elements in Yahweh-Elohim. Yahweh was a specific divine name, whereas Elohim designated "Deity" in a more general, universal way. The combination Yahweh-Elohim is probably to be explained as "Yahweh = Elohim," which we may paraphrase as "Yahweh is God." But when we are told that "Yahweh-Elohim is the result of documentary conflation, we cannot accept it any more than we can understand Amon-Re to be the result of combining an "A" document with an "R" document.

Older documents do underlie much of the Old Testament. Our Book of Proverbs is compiled from collections indicated as "The proverbs of Solomon, son of David" (1:1), "The proverbs of Solomon" (10:1), "These also are sayings of the wise" (24:23), "These also are proverbs of Solomon which the men of Hezekiah king of Judah copied" (25:1), "The words of Agur" (30:1), and "The words of Lemuel, king of Massa, which his mother taught him" (31:1). The individual psalms must have existed before our canonical book of 150 Psalms was compiled. Many of the psalms bear titles ascribing them to specific authors. But other biblical books do not have titles heading the text. The scroll of Ruth begins, "Now it came to pass in the days when the judges ruled"; Leviticus opens, "And Jehovah called unto Moses"; and so on. Since some biblical books are compilations (like Proverbs and Psalms) and since titles were often omitted (as in Ruth or Leviticus), it follows that certain biblical books can be compilations of earlier sources unidentified by titles.

If JEDP are artificial sources of the Pentateuch, are there any real ones? Yes, and one of them happens to be the book of the Wars of Jehovah cited in Numbers 21:14. Another ancient source used by the authors of both Joshua and Samuel is the book of Jashar, excerpted in Joshua 10:13 and II Samuel 1:18 ff. The second of these excerpts is the beautiful dirge of David for Saul and Jonathan, which was used for teaching the troops of Judah heroism and skill in the art of war (note, for teaching the sons of Judah bowmanship—in v. 18). There can be little doubt that the book of Jashar was a national epic, commemorating the heroic course of Hebrew history from at least the conquest under Joshua to the foundation of the Davidic dynasty. Like other national epics, including the *Iliad* and *Shah-nameh*, the book of Jashar was used for inspiring warriors to live, and if necessary to die, like their illustrious forerunners. If the entire book of Jashar was characterized by the high quality reflected in David's dirge, we can only hope that future discoveries will restore it to us. It might successfully compete with the Homeric epic as a masterpiece of world literature.

The books of Kings draw on earlier documents, such as, "the book of the acts of Solomon" (I Kings 11:41); and "the chronicles of the kings of Judah" and "the chronicles of the kings of Israel." The canonical books of Chronicles cite a host of sources by name. The time is ripe for a fresh investigation of such genuine sources of Scripture, particularly against the background of the Dead Sea Scrolls.

No two higher critics seem to agree on where J, E, D, or P begins or ends. The attempt to state such matters precisely in the Polychrome Bible discredited the use of colors but not the continuance of less precise verbal formulations. The "history" of Israel is still being written on the premise that we can only do so scientifically according to hypothetical documents to which exact dates are blandly assigned. While most critics place P last chronologically, some of the most erudite now insist that P is early, antedating D in any case. Any system (whether P is earlier or later than D in such a system makes no difference) that prevents us from going where the facts may lead is not for me. I prefer to deal with the large array of authentic materials from the Bible world and be unimpeded by any hypothetical system.

There may well be quite a few sources designated but not generally recognized as such in the Bible. Just as an older Deluge story is incorporated in the Gilgamesh Epic, another older variant Flood account has been, I think, excerpted in Genesis. The Hebrew word *toledot* (literally "generations") can designate a "narrative" or "story." In Genesis 6:9 "This is the Narrative of Noah" (literally, "generations of Noah") may well have conveyed to an ancient Hebrew what a title does to us. The account of nature in Genesis 2:4 ff. is introduced by "This is the Account of the Cosmos" (literally, "the generations of the heavens and the earth") and might possibly have been intended as a title indicating a biblical source.

Let us keep our eyes open and our minds sharp. Let us make observations and check them against the available facts. But let us not erect vast edifices on shifting sands.

The excavations at Ugarit have revealed a high material and literary culture in Canaan prior to the emergence of the Hebrews. Prose and poetry were already fully developed. The educational system was so advanced that dictionaries in four languages were compiled for the use of scribes, and the individual words were listed in their Ugaritic, Babylonian, Sumerian, and Hurrian equivalents. The beginnings of Israel are rooted in a highly cultural Canaan where the contributions of several talented peoples (including the Mesopotamians, Egyptians, and branches of the Indo-Europeans) had converged and blended. The notion that early Israelite religion and society were primitive is completely false. Canaan in the days of the Patriarchs was the hub of a great international culture. The Bible, hailing from such a time and place, cannot be devoid of sources. But let us study them by taking the Bible on its own terms and against its own authentic background.

If there is any expression in the Hebrew language that is charged with meaning for the intellectual person devoted to his biblical heritage, it is *simhat torah,* "the delight in studying Scripture." I am familiar with this delight and I like to see others have the opportunity of experiencing it. I am distressed to meet ever so many intelligent and serious university students who tell me that their teachers of Bible have killed the subject by harping on the notion that biblical study consists of analyzing the text into JEDP. The unedifying conclusion of all such study is that nothing is authentic. That this type of teaching should go on in our age of discovery when biblical scholarship is so exciting is, so to speak, a perverse miracle.

A professor of Bible in a leading university once asked me to give him the facts on JEDP. I told him essentially what I have written above. He replied: "I am convinced by what you say but I shall go on teaching the old system." When I asked him why, he answered: "Because what you have told me means I should have to unlearn as well as study afresh and rethink. It is easier to go on with the accepted system of higher criticism for which we have standard textbooks."

What a happy professor! He refuses to forfeit his place in Eden by tasting the fruit of the tree of knowledge.

Article   November 23, 1959

24 *Humpty Dumpty*

EDMUND P. CLOWNEY

Here is a lesson for your readers in what critical exegesis can do for them in dealing with a familiar text. The original source material which follows shows the value of such scholarly interpretation:

> *Humpty Dumpty sat on a wall:*
> *Humpty Dumpty had a great fall.*

We need not stop to discuss the critical questions which surround this classical text. It is generally understood by modern scholars to be a conflation of H and D. The Humptyist (H) may well have written, "Humpty sat on a wall." The original Deutero-Dumptyist (D²) probably had the reading, "Dumpty had a fall." A later redactor, acquainted with both traditions, and struck by the rhyming possibilities (Humpty/Dumpty; wall/fall) joined the conflicting accounts in a couplet. The adjective "great" is almost certainly a later gloss, which may be traced to lapsarian circles in Great Falls, Minnesota. The *formgeschichtlich* school traces the term to a *sitz-im-kindergarten* which favored exaggeration and legendary embellishment, but this has now been decisively rejected by I. E. Hohlkopfig (Z.A.G. XCMIII: 4, p. 116).

Our primary interest, however, is not in the vicissitudes of history which led to the challenging statement of the text. The fascinating speculations of Glowinkel linking our couplet with the festival of the Easter egg roll cannot be commented on here. We pass over the moralizing and allegorizing that many have found in C. Dodgson, *Through the Looking-Glass* (Ch. VI, "Humpty Dumpty").

Instead we turn to the simple declaration of the text. To be sure, the literal picture of an animate egg in a sitting posture on a stone wall is absurd from the scientific standpoint, for it escapes scientific categories. This fall did not occur in calendar time, but in the egg's act time, primal history. It gives mythological expression to the human predicament. As the Monarchist observes in those existential lines which he has had added in conclusion:

All the king's horses
and all the king's men
Couldn't put Humpty
together again.

Eutychus   November 25, 1957

25 A Theology That Walks the Earth

GEOFFREY W. BROMILEY

A review of *Evangelical Theology: An Introduction*, by Karl Barth, translated by Grover Foley (Holt, Rinehart and Winston, 1963).

For his final lectures as professor of dogmatics at Basel, Karl Barth gave a special series of 17 addresses as an introduction to theology. (Subsequently he delivered the first five of these at Chicago and Princeton on his American tour.)

In these lectures Barth has deliberately avoided giving yet another synopsis of the *Church Dogmatics*. Instead, he has gathered together in more compendious form his thinking concerning the nature, theme, and practice of theology itself. Students familiar with the *Dogmatics* will recognize many things that they have read before. Indeed, it is an astonishing fact that in this fundamental field Barth has changed little during the past 30 years. On the other hand, what has previously been scattered is here brought into a single volume and presented as the mature thinking of one who has devoted the last four decades, and more than half of his own life, to active dogmatic work.

Of the 17 addresses, the first is an introductory "Commentary" in which Barth explains why he is undertaking to introduce evangelical theology. In the first main section he then discusses the place of theology, with successive lectures on the Word, the witnesses, the community, and the Spirit. He then moves on to a second section on theological existence, which he considers from the successive standpoints of wonder, concern, commitment, and faith. The third section deals with the threat to theology in the three forms of solitude, doubt, and temptation, with a final lecture on hope. The last section is devoted to theological work, which is discussed in terms of prayer, study, service, and love.

For the purposes of a critical assessment of Barth's theology nothing very new is to be gleaned from these lectures. The main dogmatic elements are to be found in the first section. Here Barth insists again on the objectivity which will be sought by evangelical theology (i.e., as distinct from Roman Catholic and liberal) in relation to God as its theme. Theology is a true science not when it imitates the sciences which deal with creation, but when it is content to be good theological science, with a logic which derives from the Logos. This leads us at once to the familiar threefold structure of authority as Barth understands it. The primary authority is the Word itself, i.e., the divine self-revelation. This is the Word which God has spoken, speaks, and will speak in the history of Jesus Christ as the fulfillment of the history of Israel. The secondary authority is the immediate and normative witness to this Word in the Old and New Testaments, which are the work of prophets and apostles whom God specifically "ordained, appointed and elected" for this purpose. The subsidiary authority is the dependent testimony of the Church, and especially of its theology, in the canon, the creeds and confessions, and the fathers. In relation to all these fields strong emphasis is laid on the work of the Holy Spirit as the divine "spiration." Theology in particular needs this moving of the Holy Spirit if it is truly to be the logic of the divine Logos attested in the written word. In face of constant attempts either to resist the Spirit or to control him, Barth believes that theology must always pray: *Veni, Creator Spiritus.*

The valuable points in this presentation are evident. In contrast to earlier trends in his work, he rejects the concept of the Wholly Other and insists on the high and necessary place of logic in theology. He also sets his face firmly against any form of subjectivism as an ultimate theological principle, while recognizing that theology must accept its distinction from other sciences by virtue of the distinctive nature of its "object," i.e., God. The Christological concentration and the regard for the active nature of revelation are healthy in themselves, as is also the judicious attitude to indirect and relative authorities in the Church. No one can reasonably quarrel with the emphasis on the ministry of the Holy Spirit, especially in relation to theological endeavor, and Barth's mention of the special divine appointment of the biblical witnesses will be noted with satisfaction.

Nevertheless, the place of Scripture remains the area of greatest difficulty. Barth does not touch on inerrancy or inspiration in this series, nor do we meet with his concept of saga except in an incidental reference to the creation stories. To this degree, the work is less controversial than earlier writings, though it also does nothing to meet earlier objections. In terms of the material before us, we may ask whether the concept of witnesses is really adequate in itself to describe all that the Scriptures are. Do they not have a far more direct role in the divine act of revelation? While their words are witness, are they not witness in forms other than that of mere testimony? Does not the divine work itself come in and through them even in their original setting? Furthermore, if we rightly stress the ministry of the Spirit, should we not plainly recognize that the Spirit who rested on Christ, and who now illumines Scripture and guides theology and preaching, was no less active in the biblical authors and in their specific work of composition? Is there really such rivalry between the incarnate and the written word, between the Spirit and the letter, that we can exalt Christ and the Holy Ghost only by relative depreciation of the Bible? To be sure, the primacy of Christ and the sovereignty of the Spirit are to be maintained. Even on Barth's view, however, Scripture is a decisive link in the chain of divine self-revelation. God ordained that there should be this witness, and the Holy Spirit uses it as the absolute norm of faith and practice. Is it not essential, then, that there should be a strong statement here, not in opposition to Christ, or the Spirit, or even human proclamation, but in honor of Christ, in responsibility to the Spirit, and for the sake of pure proclamation?

When we turn to the wider themes of the attitudes, problems, and actions of the theologian, we enter a less debatable sphere in which one need not agree with all Barth's dicta to catch the wise and reverent spirit of the whole. Here is a high understanding indeed of theology, the theologian, and the theological task. Humility, devotion, and wholehearted commitment are required. There must be a readiness to withstand isolation from without, doubt from within, and the possibility of divine withdrawal from above. None may dare to undertake this task, nor may he continue in it, unless he is prepared to engage unceasingly in prayer, not merely in the sense of an attitude, but in definite acts of Sabbath refreshment. The study demanded is not to be for pragmatic reasons such as earning degrees, nor can it be regarded as a purely temporary engagement. Theology is a ministry: it is service to God, for in theology, too, God is to be praised in the beauty of holiness; it is also service to fellow Christians for upbuilding in knowledge and greater effectiveness in proclamation; and finally it is service to the world. Above all, theology also is a walk in the Spirit, so that the theologian must be a man of faith, hope, and love.

In face of a presentation and confession of this kind, it would be impertinent to praise and churlish to condemn. In objective evangel-

ical theology, pursued in loyalty to the biblical testimony and to orthodox tradition, we shall come to many conclusions different from
Barth's. But it is to be wished that we may do so with the same high
conception of our task, with the same spirit of reverence, humility, and
prayer, and with the same ultimate desire that the Gospel may be
prospered, that the brethren may be edified, and that God may be
glorified.

Book Review   January 4, 1963

26   *The Centrality of the Cross*

According to an old legend, the Cross on which Jesus Christ was crucified was set at the center of the world. And so it was—historically and
spiritually. The Cross is the center of the divine continuum of redemption. For it, God caused the Incarnation; as a result of it, the Resurrection occurred, the Ascension took place, and the Second Advent will
usher in the consummation of the Kingdom.

Good Friday, or in earlier usage "God's Friday," is a day of deepest
meaning. It reveals the enormity of sin and the greatness of God's love.
It was a brutal business done at Golgotha, the place of a skull, that
April day early in the first century. The shame of public execution, the
pounding of nails through hands that had healed the afflicted, the cruel
mockery of him "who did no sin" and "who when he was reviled, reviled not again," the bitter sponge pressed to the parched lips and
swollen tongue that had spoken words of life, and, most profoundly
of all, the dereliction of soul during the three dark hours—these show
the awful actuality of sin. Yet out of such suffering endured in love for
the lost, the Sin-bearer spoke seven words—words of forgiveness, assurance, filial concern, agony of soul, bodily thirst, triumphant victory,
and committal of spirit.

The Crucifixion is unique. And its uniqueness derives from the Person who was crucified rather than from the Cross itself. In the words of
Cecil Alexander's hymn,

> *There was no other good enough*
> *To pay the price of sin,*
> *He only could unlock the gate*
> *Of heav'n, and let us in.*

Yet unique though it is, the Crucifixion does not stand in isolation. Not only is it the center of God's redemptive plan; it is also related to the Resurrection as cause to effect.

According to the writer of Hebrews, "The God of peace . . . brought again from the dead our Lord Jesus, that great shepherd of the sheep, through the blood of the everlasting covenant." Here in words of surpassing beauty is the inevitable connection between the Cross and the empty tomb. Good Friday had to be vindicated by Easter. "The blood of the everlasting covenant" which was "shed for many for the remission of sins" had to be ratified by the mighty power of God in raising up him who could not be held by "the pains of death." Had there been no Good Friday, there never would have been an Easter; and had there been no Easter, the death of Christ would have had no saving efficacy. Therefore to deny the Resurrection is to deny the Gospel itself.

Like a priceless jewel with its facets, the Atonement has its different aspects. Down through the ages theologians have variously seen the work of Christ on the Cross as a ransom paid to Satan, as moral influence, as an expression of God's moral government, as mystical, or as victory over sin and the devil. Despite some real elements of truth, these theories, even taken together, are not a complete explanation of the Atonement. Although theology must continue to search the meaning of the Cross, Christ's saving work is never exhaustively defined by any human theological statement.

The substitutionary understanding of the Cross is not just one of a number of alternate views of what took place at Calvary, an optional interpretation to be accepted or rejected as one wishes; according to Scripture, it is the very heart of the Atonement. The "great shepherd of the sheep" actually took the place of the sheep. As Isaiah wrote, "All we like sheep have gone astray . . . he is brought as a lamb to the slaughter . . . he bare the sin of many." When Paul said, "The Son of God loved me and gave himself for me," he put the fact of what Christ did at Calvary in personal terms that are as true today as in the first century. Granted that in depth of meaning the fact is inexhaustible, it is not irrational nor beyond all comprehension. One need not be a theologian to apprehend its personal meaning. The individual who looks to the crucified Saviour and says in faith, "He died for me," affirms the Good Friday fact that God vindicated at Easter.

The death of Christ in the place of sinful men, the suffering of the just for the unjust, is a once-and-for-all event. Yet its proclamation continues "till he come." It is good for the Church to take time on "God's Friday" to recall the Lord's suffering and death. But it is also dangerous. To see the Crucifixion as a moving religious spectacle and nothing more is to join the Roman soldiers of whom Matthew said, "And sitting down they watched him there." No man has the right just to look at Golgotha; through his sin he is a participant in what happened there. And only by faith does he have life through Christ's death. The power of the Cross is not confined to the solemn festival of a single day but is ever available to all who believe.

For the preacher, the truth he proclaims on Good Friday is truth for every day. There is not the slightest indication that Paul came to Corinth on a Good Friday. But we have his passionate avowal to the Corinthian church, "I determined not to know anything among you, save Jesus Christ, and him crucified." For Paul the Cross was always at the center. For us too it can occupy no other place.

Significant also is the Apostle's statement of the manner of his proclamation of the Cross: "And I, brethren, when I came to you, came not with excellency of speech or of wisdom . . . my speech and my preaching was not with enticing words of man's wisdom, but in demonstration of the Spirit and of power." Today when philosophy is invading the pulpit and when there is a tendency to substitute existential jargon for basic Christian concepts, these words of Paul need pondering. If the message of Christ crucified is for all, young and old, it must be presented so that those who hear may lay hold upon its truth. Today as in Paul's day the preacher is obligated to reach both the Greeks and the barbarians, both the wise and the unwise. Aside from the power of the Spirit, the greatest gift a preacher may have is the gift of plain speech. To proclaim the Cross with a clarity that reaches the common man actually takes more of concentrated study and disciplined use of language than to speak to an audience of scholars.

A searching test of any minister's preaching is for him to ask about his every sermon, "Have I in some way preached Christ crucified in this message?" Not that every sermon must follow an evangelistic stereotype nor that it must refer at length to the Cross; preaching must be as various as human life and its needs. But always, whether the sermon deals with social justice, moral problems, life situations, history, or prophecy, Christ crucified must be in it. He must be there if for no other reason than that no minister can know whether his is the last voice to reach some listener whose heart is open to receive new life in Christ. Preaching devoid of the Good Friday truth may be eloquent, learned, fascinating, and even spiritually helpful; but if it contains no reference at all to the central fact of Christ crucified, it is open to the charge of inadequacy and unfaithfulness.

Editorial   March 13, 1964

27 *Remorse*

SUE FIFE

To have been the cup
His lips touched and blessed,
To have been the bread
Which He broke;
To have been the cloth
He held as He served,
Or water He poured
As He spoke;

To have been the road
He walked on the Way,
To have been His print
In the sand;
To have been the door
That opened the tomb,
But I was a nail
In His hand.

April 1, 1966

28 *The Easter Event*

F. F. BRUCE

What is it that the Christian Church celebrates year by year on Easter Day? Or what is it that the Christian Church celebrates week by week on Sunday? One might go even further to the root of the matter and ask what it was that brought the Christian Church into being as a force to be reckoned with in history, for the answer would still be the same. The resurrection of Christ, which is commemorated every week on Sunday and every year on Easter Day, brought the Christian Church into being; apart from his resurrection, we may be sure, nothing would ever have been heard of the Church.

What do Christians mean when they speak of the resurrection of Christ? For some it is sufficient to hold that although he was put to death, his spirit and power revived and lived on in the life and activity of his followers, as in measure they still do. When, for example, we contemplate the life-work of such a man as Albert Schweitzer, we may say, quite truly, that the spirit of Jesus is not yet dead. From this point of view, the event that the Church celebrates Sunday by Sunday and Easter by Easter is the moment when the dejected followers of Jesus suddenly became aware that their crucified Master was not really dead, because his power had invaded their lives as it had never done before, giving them courage and strength to go out and begin to win the world for him.

All that is true as far as it goes, but it is not the whole truth. Our earliest witnesses to the Easter event tell a story that goes far beyond this.

One of our earliest pieces of documentary evidence can be dated less than twenty-five years after the Easter event, at a time when many people were alive who had had first-hand experience of that event. This document is one of the letters sent by Paul, apostle to the Gentiles, to the community of Christians in the city of Corinth. As he wrote to them he had occasion to remind them of the message that he had brought when first he had visited their city. What adds weight to this message is Paul's assurance that he himself had first "received" it before he "delivered" it to others, and that it differed not at all from the message proclaimed by those who were apostles before him. Here, then, is Paul's summary of those features of the message that he reckoned to be of first importance: "that Christ died for our sins in accordance with the scriptures, that he was buried, that he was raised on the third day in accordance with the scriptures, and that he appeared to Cephas, then to the twelve. Then he appeared to more than five hundred brethren at one time, most of whom are still alive, though some have fallen asleep. Then he appeared to James, then to all the apostles. Last of all, as to one untimely born, he appeared also to me. . . .

Whether then it was I or they, so we preach and so you believed" (I Cor. 15:3-11, RSV). This is not the earliest New Testament document absolutely to mention the resurrection of Christ, but it is the earliest one to assemble so much evidence for it. And the evidence here assembled, apart from the clause "last of all . . . he appeared also to me," was common ground to all Christian preachers in the first twenty-five years of their preaching, however great and many might be the other differences among them.

There is, indeed, good reason to believe that this body of evidence is very primitive. Apart from Paul's reference to his own experience, it falls into two series of resurrection appearances—one headed "he appeared to Cephas" and the other headed "he appeared to James." Cephas is an alternative name for Peter, the first of the apostles, and James was the brother of Jesus. Now, when Paul visited Jerusalem in the third year after his conversion, he stayed with Peter for two weeks but saw none of the other apostles except James. So he tells us himself in Galatians 1:18, 19. This was almost certainly the occasion when he "received" the account of appearances of the risen Christ that he subsequently "delivered" to others. This, in other words, was the established account of the matter some five years after the death of Christ.

The Gospels and the Acts of the Apostles, which were written at various times in the later decades of the first century, reproduce this primitive apostolic witness in considerably greater detail. The incidents which they narrate are difficult to fit neatly together, partly because they represent only a selection from an abundance of stories of how Jesus appeared alive again after his death and burial; but this is the essence of their testimony:

Jesus died on the cross and was buried on the Friday of Passover Week (probably April 6, A.D. 30). On the following Sunday morning some of his friends went to place in his tomb the funeral spices that they had been unable to bring earlier, since the intervening day was the Jewish Sabbath. But when they arrived at the tomb, they found it empty. Not long afterwards, one and another of his followers saw him alive. Some of them were alone when they saw him, but for the most part he appeared to smaller or larger groups of them, both in Jerusalem and in Galilee. This went on for six weeks or so, and then the appearances ceased. But seven weeks after the first of those appearances a crowd of pilgrims who had come to Jerusalem for the festival of Pentecost were surprised to see a small group of men stand up and publicly declare that Jesus of Nazareth, who had been crucified just outside that city less than two months previously, had been raised from the dead and had been seen alive by them. They argued that therefore his claim to be the long-expected Messiah of Israel—a claim that had been rejected by the Sanhedrin, the supreme court of the nation—was vindicated by God. And so powerfully did they present their case that many of their hearers were convinced of its truth and joined their ranks. That day, the first Christian Pentecost, is accordingly reckoned to be the birthday of the Christian Church; but there would have been no such birthday but for the resurrection experience.

The most surprising feature of this last incident lies in the character of the men who made this bold claim. They were the followers of Jesus who, in spite of their protestations of loyalty to him, took to their heels when he was arrested. Their leader, whose affirmations of loyalty had been most emphatic, swore repeatedly that he had never set eyes on Jesus. They hid themselves for safety behind locked doors in the upper room of an obscure house in Jerusalem—and now they appear in public, proclaiming themselves to be Jesus' followers and charging the supreme court of the nation with having put their Messiah to death. What brought this change about?

Jesus' death had been, to all outward appearance, the tragic defeat of a noble ideal. The high hopes that had been placed in him collapsed; he had not lifted a finger to save himself. It looked as if he would follow into obscurity other leaders of popular movements in Israel who had come to grief. His followers were disillusioned and dejected. And then, beyond all expectation, everything was changed; their sun rose again and shone more brightly than ever. What was the cause?

Their own account was that they saw him alive again. It was not an empty tomb that brought them new faith and hope; it was a living Christ. Yet the empty tomb must not be dismissed as irrelevant to the Resurrection. If his tomb had not been empty, neither they nor anyone else would have believed that he had risen from the dead. To them resurrection did not mean the survival or revival of a man's spirit and power in the lives of others; those who regard the resurrection of Jesus as meaning that and nothing more are giving the word "resurrection" a meaning different from its New Testament usage.

Nor will it suffice to say, with one writer, that "once the disciples were convinced by the visions they had had that Jesus was alive and active despite his death on the cross, their belief that his tomb must therefore be empty would follow inevitably as the night the day, whether there was any actual evidence for it or not." We should try to use a little realistic imagination. Had his tomb not been empty, or had his body been moved somewhere else, then as soon as his followers began claiming that they had seen him alive again, the authorities would have taken steps to disprove their claim by producing the body. And had they been able to do so, no one would have believed that Jesus had risen from the dead. To the disciples themselves, and to all other Jews of that time, resurrection meant bodily resurrection.

Such arguments can be countered, no doubt, by the assertion that the body of Jesus was not placed in Joseph's tomb, as the gospel narrative states; that it was thrown into the common criminals' pit in the Valley of Hinnom or elsewhere. But when this assertion is made, one may ask on what grounds it is made. It is difficult to avoid the suspicion that sometimes it is made on no other grounds than a desire to dismiss the first-century evidence for Jesus' burial as irrelevant and useless as testimony in the case for his resurrection. In the Pauline passage quoted above, the clause "that he was buried" is inserted between those clauses that affirm his death and resurrection in such a way as to imply that the body in which Jesus rose was the body that had been taken down from the cross and laid in the tomb—transformed, indeed, into what Paul elsewhere calls a "spiritual body" or a "body of glory," but nevertheless maintaining some continuity and identity with his "body of humiliation."

We have no description of the actual resurrection of Jesus. All the "resurrection narratives" that we have in the New Testament, whether their location is near the tomb or elsewhere, are narratives about what happened after Jesus rose from the dead. But no one saw him rise. Whether or not there is any probability in such a suggestion as that made by Dorothy Sayers in *The Man Born to Be King* about the dissolution of the physical elements of Jesus' body in the tomb and their reassembly outside is something on which a physicist is better qualified to pronounce judgment than the present writer.

The disciples' claim did indeed receive powerful support from the evidence that was soon produced that the mighty works performed by Jesus were still being performed by his followers in his name. And that the claim was made in utter sincerity is clear from the readiness with which they staked their lives on its truth. That the "resurrection faith" is a firm historical datum is generally conceded even by those who find it difficult to accept the "resurrection fact."

But what gave rise to the resurrection faith if it was not the resurrection fact? If the resurrection appearances were wholly subjective, they cannot be said to conform to the conditions that normally govern such experiences. Usually in such experiences people see something else and mistake it for what they expect to see. But the disciples did not expect to see Jesus alive again. And repeatedly when they did see him alive again, they mistook him for someone or something else— the gardener, or an unknown fellow traveler, or an apparition—and needed some convincing that it was really he.

The obvious suggestion that he had not really died on the cross but regained consciousness in the cool of the tomb will not account for the events that followed his appearances. One who had luckily survived several hours of crucifixion would have been a broken and pitiable object of a man, quite unable to fill those who saw him with new life and new confidence that he was the Conqueror of death and the Lord of life. The sequel to that kind of survival would have been the sort of thing that George Moore brilliantly relates in *The Brook Kerith;* but that masterpiece of imaginative fiction has nothing to do with the history of apostolic Christianity. It is not very profitable to set up one alternative explanation after another, only to knock them down like so many Aunt Sallies; but the history of apostolic Christianity, and the history of post-apostolic Christianity as well, demands an adequate cause. The New Testament offers us one: "Christ has been raised from the dead." Need we look for another?

Most of the witnesses of the risen Jesus were his former disciples. But some were not. His brother James, for example, had not been a follower of his before the Cross. The family of Jesus had grave misgivings about his ministry, and when at last he was arrested and crucified, they probably felt with sorrow that their fears and warnings had been only too well founded. Yet James appears in later years as the trusted leader of the Jerusalem church, a man whose piety won him the esteem, moreover, of the non-Christian Jews of Jerusalem. What caused the change in James's attitude to Jesus and his cause, at this precise juncture when his worst fears had been realized? Paul gives us the explanation he had probably received from James himself: "He appeared to James."

"Last of all," says Paul, "as to one untimely born, he appeared also to me." Paul's antecedents are well enough known; he, at any rate, was not psychologically predisposed to believe that Jesus had conquered death. Those who went about claiming that they had seen Jesus alive again had no more relentless opponent than Paul; and we have no reason to believe that during his persecuting activity he had any qualms of conscience, any inward doubts, about the rightness of his course. What was it that convinced such a man of the wrongness of his course, and led him so decisively to abandon his most passionately cherished convictions for the cause which he had so vigorously assailed, but for which he was henceforth prepared to sacrifice everything? Paul's own account of the matter, that the risen Christ appeared to him personally, is an adequate explanation; it would be difficult to find another.

When we are dealing with a unique situation, generalizations and analogies are inapplicable. And the situation is indeed unique when we are confronted by the incarnate Son of God, divinest when he most was man. That the incarnate Son of God should die is wonder enough. But as the disciples looked back, they recognized more and more how impossible it was that their Master should stay dead, such was the impact he had made on them. It was not this impact that gave rise to the resurrection experiences. But when these experiences took place, the disciples realized their utter fittingness and inevitability. "God raised him up, having loosed the pangs of death, because it was not possible for him to be held by it" (Acts 2:24).

Article   March 27, 1964

29   *Exile*

EVANGELINE PATERSON

Yes, it is beautiful country,
The stream in the winding valley, the knowes
   and the birches,
And beautiful the mountain's bare shoulder
And the calm brows of the hills;
But it is not my country,
And in my heart there is a hollow place always.

And there is no way to go back.
Maybe indeed the miles, but the years never.

Winding are the roads that we choose,
And inexorable is life, driving us like cattle

Farther and farther away from what we
remember.

But when we shall come at last
To God, who is our Home and our Country,
There will be no more road stretching before us
And no more need to go back.

April 29, 1966

30 *The Mission of the Church*

J. HOWARD PEW

A vital question before the United Presbyterian Church is whether or
not the church, as a corporate body, should involve herself in economic, social, and political affairs. Many of its leaders, by precept and
example, have already given an affirmative answer to this question,
and much of their activity is concerned with civil affairs. The church
has become involved through pronouncements, through appeals to
political pressures, and through lobbies in Washington. Other denominations could be cited as examples, but this article discusses only the
situation within the United Presbyterian Church. So far as Presbyterians are concerned, the elders are responsible for the spiritual welfare of the church. The very term "ruling elder" indicates an active role
in governing the church.

In the United Presbyterian Church, a manual entitled *Consider
Your Ministry* has been produced to help in governing the church.
The second chapter defines the mission of the Church; its trust is
that the Church should be planted "in the middle of life with its everyday decisions." No one would seriously deny that the individual Christian must relate his Christian convictions to the society of which he
is a part in the economic, social, and political life about him. He must
live out his Christianity in every phase of life, showing that he is salt
and light in an unbelieving world. Nor is the right of the pulpit to speak
out according to moral, ethical, and Christian principles in question.
But Chapter II declares these things are also the responsibility of the
corporate congregation. If the thesis of this chapter is true, then a ses-

sion should involve the congregation "in the jobs men do to earn a living, in the power structures of the social order, in the decisions of politics, in the relationships of persons with one another as neighbors and members of various groups and clubs" (pp. 18, 19).

A paragraph on page 21 indicates the type of guidance a session should provide for the congregation:

> But there are also things that the congregation as a corporate body can do; there are ways for the congregation itself to accept its being sent out into the world. A congregation may provide forums for the exploring of crucial issues, or it may conduct a survey of housing or job opportunities for minority groups, or it may establish an agency to meet the recreational needs of youth. It may deal forthrightly with some corruption of justice or even press for the passage or repeal of some law.

According to this, the session has the responsibility as a session to set up forums for every social, economic, and political issue of the day; to survey the community for housing and job opportunities for minority groups. But it is to do much more since the 1963 General Assembly passed this recommendation:

> The 175th General Assembly . . . alerts the church to other pressing metropolitan problems including methods of metropolitan government, mass transportation, equitable representation in state legislatures, suburban residential segregation, and chronic poverty of segments of our population [*Minutes of General Assembly,* Part I, p. 326].

This means that sessions must lead their congregations in a study of methods of metropolitan government and inform all cities of the nation what is the best type of metropolitan government. They must study mass transportation and inform, among others, the leaders of the city in which they live how to overcome traffic problems and how best to transport the working population to and from work. They must inform their state capitals as to what is an equitable representation in state legislatures. And they must come up with the solution to such poverty as may exist in certain segments of our population.

Since the congregation speaks as a Christian congregation, the assumption must be made that it knows the mind of Christ concerning metropolitan government, mass transportation, equitable representation, and so on. It must be able to declare to the various governing bodies: "Thus saith the Lord."

But to continue, sessions must be ready to send out members of the congregation to various cities, here and abroad, so that they can adequately study methods of metropolitan government. The problem of mass transportation has already cost millions of dollars, and still it remains unsolved. Must the church spend more millions, or does church affiliation equip individuals with greater knowledge and competence? Must the congregation engage political experts to help determine equitable representation in federal, state, and local government? And who can estimate the cost of eliminating chronic poverty? These are but a small fraction of the economic, social, and political problems about which the General Assembly, through its Committee of Church and Society, has already issued statements and made pronouncements.

But is this the mission of the Church? Does such a program square with the teachings of Christ, with the Scriptures, with the history and traditions of the Church, with the constitution of the United Presbyterian Church, and with reason and logic?

Even a superficial reading of Christ's words reveals that he did not interfere with civil affairs. This disappointed the Pharisees, who were looking for a political messiah. And in order to entangle Jesus in the political and economic situation of their day, they asked him whether it was lawful to pay taxes to Caesar. Jesus gave a classic answer that is timeless for the Church: "Render therefore unto Caesar the things which are Caesar's; and unto God the things that are God's" (Matt. 22:21). Christ definitely distinguishes between Caesar's kingdom and God's. There is a clear distinction between temporal kingdoms and the kingdom of heaven. The jurisdiction of the state and that of the Church differ. Jesus never concerned himself about Caesar's affairs. Job opportunities, methods of metropolitan government, mass transportation, equitable representation in legislatures are plainly problems for Caesar and not for the Church. And let us not forget that the economic, social, and political problems of Christ's day were just as serious as they are today, if not more so.

That Jesus refused to involve himself or the Church in economic situations even when they involved justice is borne out by Luke 12:13, 14. One of his followers said, "Master, speak to my brother, that he divide the inheritance with me." The brother was evidently cheating this follower of Christ out of his rightful inheritance. Here Christ had the opportunity to exercise justice and see that there was an equal distribution of wealth. But Christ refused to enter into a sphere that fell outside his divine calling. There are some church committees that feel that one of the functions of the Church is to bring about an equal distribution of wealth which they call justice. Yet Christ said, "My kingdom is not of this world" (John 18:36). What right has any court of the Church to cast the Saviour into a political role by involving his Church in civil affairs?

Most church pronouncements have to do with the material welfare of men. Now suppose someone would come and say to the Church: "Take no thought for your life, what ye shall eat, or what ye shall drink; nor yet for your body, what ye shall put on" (Matt. 6:25). One can readily imagine that a committee on social action would vehemently attack him. Yet these were the words of Christ to the Church in the Sermon on the Mount.

The modern-day Church justifies her invasion of economic, social, and political spheres on the ground of the Lordship of Christ. Is not Christ the Lord of all life? Then modern theologians, like Roman Catholic theologians, proceed from the Lordship of Christ to the lordship of the Church over all facets of life. Christ forbids the Church to enter into the sphere of Caesar. If the Church really takes the Lordship of Christ seriously, then she must listen to him as he defines the separate jurisdictions of state and church, as he declares that his kingdom is not of this world, as he maintains that he is not a divider of wealth, as he limits the Church to spiritual weapons. If the Church is not hypocritical in declaring the Lordship of Christ, she must follow both his example and his teachings.

In the Scriptures we find that the apostles followed the same principles as their Lord. They were interested in establishing a spiritual kingdom and refused to become involved in secular affairs. The Apostle Paul declared: "For the kingdom of God is not meat and drink; but righteousness, and peace, and joy in the Holy Ghost" (Rom. 14:17). The sixth chapter of the Book of Acts describes an incident that arose about the distribution of charity. The apostles said to the Church: "It is not reason that we should leave the word of God, and serve tables" (v. 2). So they asked for the appointment of seven laymen to handle this business and stated: "But we will give ourselves continually to prayer, and to the ministry of the word" (v. 4). Now if the apostles felt that prayer and preaching were of such supreme importance that they could spare no time for the distribution of charity, what would they say to denominational leaders of our time who seek to solve the problem of metropolitan government and mass transportation? The apostles knew that prayer and preaching the Gospel would bring a thousandfold greater benefit to mankind than even feeding and clothing the poor.

Calvin in commenting on this incident calls attention to the preoccupation of the Roman Catholic Church with secular business. He said: "They entangled themselves in divers businesses, which they were scarce able to overcome, though every one of them had had ten heads." If denominational leaders are going to solve all the secular problems they have taken upon themselves in this complex society, it would appear that they should be multiheaded.

The whole emphasis of the Book of Acts and of the Epistles is upon the preaching of salvation, the sanctification of believers, and the application of the Gospel in daily life according to the law of love. The apostles did not seek to reform society by external and political means; they used only the persuasive power of the Gospel. It was their conviction that the Gospel, and not legislative acts, would transform society. They did not discuss or become involved in economic, social, and political affairs, even though the society of their day was in a sadder state than ours.

Jesus Christ, the apostles, and the early Church knew that it was very important for the Church to adhere strictly to the Gospel, realizing that, should she become involved in non-ecclesiastical, controversial issues, those who opposed the position she took would question her competence to speak on ecclesiastical subjects.

During the Middle Ages the Church left the Gospel and entered into economic, social, and political spheres. By means of canon law the Church forbade the use of interest, fixed the amount of wages, and attempted to control the price of goods. The result was a period of poverty and stagnation. Society became corrupt because the Church neglected her spiritual weapons. Surely the example of the Middle Ages is sufficient to warn us against the folly of the Church's interfering in fields outside her God-given jurisdiction.

The Reformation brought the Church back to the preaching of the Gospel. Both Luther and Calvin confined the Church to spiritual functions. One of the first things Calvin did in organizing the new Protestant church in Geneva was to set up two groups: one he called the "Consistory"—this was composed of five ministers and twelve lay elders; the other he called the "Company of Pastors"—this was composed solely of ministers. Concerning the Consistory the constitution stated, "All this is to be done in such a way that the ministers have no civil jurisdiction and wield only the spiritual sword of the Word of God, as St. Paul commands them." The Consistory (which was the forerunner of what we know as the session) could reprove according to the Word of God. The severest punishment it could mete out was excommunication. It was denied any civil jurisdiction.

The ecclesiastical body, known as the "Company of Pastors," had in its constitution that the pastor's duty was "to preach the Word of God, to instruct, to admonish, to exhort and reprove in public and in private, to administer the sacraments, and, with the Consistory, to pronounce the ecclesiastical censures."

It is commonly thought that Calvin and the ministers of Geneva dominated the civil affairs of that city. That is contrary to the facts, as original records recently discovered and translated prove. Calvin himself wrote: "I know well that the impious everywhere cry out that I aspire with an insatiable passion to political influence, and yet I keep myself so strongly separated from all public affairs, that each day I hear people discoursing upon subjects of which I have not the least knowledge. The government has recourse to my counsels only in grave affairs, when it is irresolute or incapable of deciding by itself" (letter to Zurich in 1555).

According to an eminent Swiss historian, Anedee Roget: "We do not know that the Council ever consulted the Church for any subject in the offing, nor the assembly of ministers, nor the Consistory, a mixed body." Common sense tells us that the Reformation would never have proceeded from Geneva if the church had occupied herself with the civil affairs of Geneva. It was because the Geneva church concentrated on the Gospel that she came to have such an international influence.

John Knox and the Westminster Divines carried out the same policy and practice. Their belief found expression in the Westminster Confession of Faith, which forms part of the United Presbyterian constitution. Chapter XXXI, Section IV, reads:

Synods and councils are to handle or conclude nothing but that which is ecclesiastical; and are not to intermeddle with civil affairs, which concern the commonwealth, unless by way of humble petition, in cases extraordinary; or by way of advice for satisfaction of conscience, if they be thereunto required by the civil magistrate.

Many of the doctrines of the Westminster Confession were debated for weeks and months, but there was 100 per cent agreement on this section, which passed without debate. The Westminster Divines knew the damage the Roman Catholic Church brought upon Christianity by presuming to "intermeddle with civil affairs" and sought to safeguard the Presbyterian Church from such a proved folly.

Every time the Presbyterian Church as a corporate body becomes involved in economic, social, and political affairs, she transgresses both the word and the spirit of the constitution that elders and ministers sacredly vow to uphold.

When the Presbyterian Church in the U.S.A. was formed in Philadelphia in 1789, it adopted the Westminster Confession of Faith with its proviso that there would be no "intermeddl[ing] with civil affairs." One of the leading spirits in the formation of that church was Dr. John Witherspoon, the only clergyman to sign the Declaration of Independence. He separated his duties as a citizen from those of a minister. In a sermon he stated:

> The other direction I would offer upon this subject is, that ministers take care to avoid officiously intermeddling in civil matters. A minister should be separated and set apart for his own work; he should be consecrated to his office. . . . But it is still more sinful and dangerous, for them to desire or claim direction of such matters as fall within the province of the civil magistrate. When our blessed Saviour says, "My kingdom is not of this world," he plainly intimates to his disciples that they have no title to intermeddle with state affairs.

From 1789 to 1912 the Presbyterian Church kept out of the civil sphere, except for the slavery question. During this time it had its greatest influence and strength. During the nineteenth century Alexis de Tocqueville made these discerning comments in comparing the effect of religion in America with that in Europe: "There is no country in the whole world in which the Christian religion retains a greater influence over the souls of men than in America; and there can be no greater proof of its utility and of its conformity to human nature, than that its influence is most powerfully felt over the most enlightened and free nation of the earth. . . . They [clergy] keep aloof from parties and from public affairs" (*Democracy in America*, I, 314, 315). In other words, it was not by interfering in civil affairs and not by political pressures that the Presbyterian Church became such a powerful influence for moral good but by keeping strictly to her spiritual sphere and by employing the persuasive power of the Gospel of Jesus Christ.

From the year 1912 we find the beginning of an encroachment into civil affairs by the Presbyterian Church, chiefly through the influence of a united effort on the part of major denominations and centering in the Federal Council of Churches. It is obvious from history that in proportion to her engrossment with economic, social, and political matters, the spiritual and moral influence of the Church waned. The moral corruption and spiritual poverty of our day certainly stem in great measure from the neglect of the Church to carry out her spiritual mission. The social gospel has proved to be ineffective in lifting up the moral standards of our nation.

If the church as a corporate body should follow through with the economic, social, and political programs presented by the United Presbyterian General Assembly's Committee of Church and Society, she would find herself in opposition to the teachings of Christ and the apostles; she would ignore the lessons of history; she would despise the finest traditions of the Presbyterian Church and violate the constitution its elders and ministers have vowed to uphold.

Surely it is against all reason and logic that the congregation or the Church as a whole should enter into a program that can only prove divisive and weaken the spiritual witness of the Church. The program advocated is divisive. The Church has been known as an institution that proclaims the infallible truth of God, but when she issues pronouncements in fields outside her sphere, this can only bring shame, confusion, and disillusionment.

The great need of today is for the Church to be the Church and to manifest the spiritual power with which God had endowed her. Our people have a spiritual hunger; they desire the Bread of Life, not secular pronouncements. And if the Church proclaims the Bread of Life, she will, as has been proved in the past, so transform society that many of the prevalent social ills will disappear. She will infuse such virtues into society as to elevate all phases of human life. The mission of the Church is to redeem souls by the Gospel of salvation, and only as she redeems individuals will society be redeemed.

Article   July 3, 1964

31   *Five Marks of an Evangelical Preacher*

ANDREW W. BLACKWOOD

The man whom God calls to be a minister or a missionary should look on himself as the most blessed of mortals, and on the pulpit as the place of his highest joys. Even so, once in a while, alone on his knees, he should take stock of himself as leader of public worship, including the sermon. Here follow five marks of an evangelical in the pulpit. First and most, he stresses—

1. The Divine. The most beloved verse in the Bible starts with God's love for the world, centers around the Cross, and leads up to one person's belief in life everlasting. All divine! The Apostles' Creed first stresses God the Father, the Son, and the Spirit. In a day when preaching most often concerns many, why not assume that the friend in the pew comes to meet with God? Where but from the pulpit can he learn to put first "the manifold helpfulness of the Triune God" and to look at human sins and needs, starting with his own, in the light of the Cross?

2. The Bible. Other good books may help one to interpret life today, and thus provide a sermon with a portion of its woof. But God's written Word alone should supply the basic warp. So the evangelical preacher begins a sermon with a portion of the Book and devotes himself to making that text clear and luminous, in its own setting. At length he brings every hearer face to face with the central truth or duty and leads everyone to ask himself: "How am I personally measuring up to this revelation of God's holy will?" Ere long the hearer goes home with another illuminated text aglow in his heart, to guide him in doing the will of God here and now as it is ever done in heaven.

3. God's Free Grace. When the churchgoer beholds the glory of God he becomes aware of his sin, along with the sins of others (Isa. 6:3-5). Every Lord's Day he should likewise learn the heart of the Gospel: "By grace are ye saved by faith; and that not of yourselves: it is the gift of God" (Eph. 2:8). When such a pulpit master as J. H. Jowett looks back over all his past sermons, he finds that he has only one message: God's free grace, with the ideal response in faith, love, and good works. From such evangelical preaching comes the most Christlike character and the most effective service of the common

good, both here and beyond the seven seas, as well as the most radiant assurance of life eternal.

4. The individual. In the public utterances of our Lord, the stress often falls on one sheep, one coin, one son. Even amid a multitude of outcasts today, God still saves and transforms sinful hearers one by one, enlisting them for service and preparing them for eternal life. "Whosoever will!" In our day, perhaps more than ever, pulpit work tends to ignore the one sinner for whom the Redeemer died, and the one saint with a grief-stricken heart. Especially near the end of a message from God, why must his interpreter keep saying "we"? Is he addressing himself and other believers or the hearer most in need of God? "Thou art the man!"

5. Eternity. In the Gospels, "the center of gravity lies beyond the grave." If so, much preaching now must be eccentric. In dealing with the future, God's interpreter should pray for a sense of balance, lest he strive to make clear what God has not yet revealed (Deut. 29:29). Even so, every churchgoer should hear much about such holy mysteries as heaven and hell, the Final Advent, and the Judgment Day, so as to face the future in a holy spirit of "wonder, love, and praise."

In view of such lofty ideals, spokesman for God, what do you feel? Surely a sense of shortcoming and shame! Then get down on your knees and tell God how you feel. When he assures you of pardon, thank him anew for the call to preach. Rededicate to him all your God-given powers, as well as your human limitations. Then out through you as his earthen vessel will shine "the light of the knowledge of the glory of God in the face of Jesus Christ" (II Cor. 4:6b).

The Minister's Workshop   May 8, 1964

32 *Tomorrow's Task in Latin America*

R. KENNETH STRACHAN

Sidney James Wells Clark, for many years intimately connected with the World Dominion Movement, has been described as "the man who saw the truth about Foreign Missions." One of the guiding principles which he laid down was to the effect that the work being done had always to be carried out in the light of the work to be done. The unfinished task of tomorrow, he insisted, should always determine the activity of today. He defined and advocated the doctrine "that all missionary works ought to be done with 'the Big End' always in view, directed consciously to that end, and that whatever was done which did not assist directly to advance that end was wrongly conceived" (Roland Allen, *Sidney James Wells Clark—A Vision of Foreign Missions,* The World Dominion Press, London, 1937, p. 54). Time and the judgment of God upon missions in the Orient would seem to have vindicated his views.

We are entering into a new era in Latin America. Profound changes are taking place. The consciousness of these new directions invades all our missionary thinking, even as it also lies near the surface of the growing self-consciousness of the Latin American evangelical church. The bearing of this upon the missionary movement is of particular concern to those of us who serve in Latin America, because in this particular area the world's social and technological revolution is taking place amidst a population that is increasing two and a half times faster than the rest of the world.

We do not know what this will mean to us in terms of scientific advance, military and political alignments, economic conditions, and religious pressures. But in terms of evangelism, should the Lord tarry, it means that where today we are seeking to reach approximately 175 million souls, tomorrow—a mere 20 years from now—we shall be dealing with 420 million! And the day after tomorrow, 550 million! We are faced with a job that is larger than ever—and more complicated. It involves a much greater number of organizations and agencies, new media and new techniques, specialized ministries and operations. Tomorrow's task of evangelism, with all the follow-up it properly implies, must be carried out on a scale commensurate with the giant growth and radical changes that are taking place.

How, in the face of such an enormous task, are we going to fulfill the great Commission effectively?

That is why Clark's thoughts regarding missions are so important to us today. When we consider that of the total missionary forces in Latin America, 56 per cent belong to the Evangelical Foreign Missions Association and the Interdenominational Foreign Missions Association, and that approximately 75 per cent belong to what might be called the evangelical or fundamentalist wing of the Protestant Church, we must recognize the serious responsibility that weighs upon us.

Given this preponderance of evangelical forces, the future of Latin

American Protestantism may well rest in our hands. What we are and what we do now will have enormous effect upon the Church there tomorrow. That is why it is so vitally important that tomorrow's evangelical task be conceived and executed according to wise and scriptural principles in practical reference to the "Big End."

Evangelicals agree in affirming that the goal of missions is an effective gospel witness among all peoples that shall extend the Church of Christ, through which God's saving grace is to be made known to every creature, in every part of the earth.

This is all easily stated and serves as the basis for all public pronouncements as to mission goals and promotion. There seems to be no ignorance or confusion as to the ultimate aim. The trouble is—as many students of missions have pointed out—that most missionaries and most societies are so engrossed with the mechanics and the daily routine of the work immediately at hand—the program of their *own* particular group—that the long-range goals are lost sight of.

This becomes specially apparent when we break down the continent into national areas and examine the work being done in each. It becomes apparent that no coordinated effort is underway by the evangelical forces resident in the territory to complete the Commission in their area. Twenty-five, fifty, and in some cases seventy-five or a hundred years have gone by and, following initial waves of advance, their chief energies are now directed toward carrying on the existing work with limited possibilities of expansion. *And the most obvious deficiency of evangelical forces is the lack of a concerted movement to finish the job in their own territory.*

Data regarding the work carried on are generally available. The total number of missionaries, national workers, organized churches, evangelical communities in each given area is quite easily secured. But ask the Christian worker for the precise number of cities or towns that have not been adequately evangelized, and he is lost. There is abysmal ignorance of the work that remains to be done.

Costa Rica, for example, is a small country with an area of some 50,000 square kilometers and only a million inhabitants, and yet, to our knowledge, it has never been surveyed in terms of the work to be done.

What is responsible for the huge gap that exists between our professed aims and our actual activities? Why do we talk so big and do so little to accomplish it? I believe the main reason is our failure to mobilize our entire evangelical forces in constant evangelistic endeavor.

We have depended too much on the foreign missionary and too much on the full-time Christian worker. By and large we have founded static churches after the pattern in the homeland. Instead of the witnessing communities founded by St. Paul (cf. I Thess. 1:6-8) we have brought into being passive congregations to be waited on and ministered to by national pastors trained in the same static tradition.

As a result, we face a vast unfinished job which grows larger with each daily jump in population. And if we look a little more closely, it would seem that in every country there are four major areas of need.

1. There are the unreached multitudes in the big city areas. One phenomenon of Latin America's revolutionary transformation is the amazing growth of the cities. As in the times of St. Paul, these cities are drawing immense multitudes from the surrounding towns and villages. By modern means of communication and of transportation, the cultural and intellectual life and influence of the big cities inundate the surrounding countryside. Uprooted, overwhelmed by the new social and technological environment, the people are open to the Gospel as never before.

Nothing can equal the strategic importance of these big cities. The battle for Latin America will either be won or lost there. It is there that the social and technological revolution is taking place. In place of the former peon class with machete in belt, a labor class is rising, trained in mechanical skills, and politically conscious and vocal. And in place of the small minority of landed gentry, a growing middle class of professionals—engineers, technicians, small businessmen, lawyers, teachers—is emerging. The future of Latin America lies with them.

Apart from a few exceptions, the evangelical groups tend to be weakest in the largest city centers. Take the cities in Latin America with a population of over a million inhabitants—Mexico City, Havana, Caracas, Bogotá, Lima, Santiago, Montevideo, Buenos Aires, São Paulo, Rio de Janeiro, San Juan—and look for large evangelical churches. They are few and far between. In planning any advance for the future, careful thought and attention must be given to a more effective program of evangelism leading to the establishment of strong, active churches in the large city centers.

2. A second area of need is in the smaller towns and villages. Hundreds of these have never been effectively evangelized. Mission societies and national church bodies have tended to lose momentum in their evangelistic outreach and to expend their principal energies in maintaining established work.

The time has come for a new evangelistic push to occupy the towns and villages as yet unreached. Such an effort is not beyond the resources of the local forces, if carried out by a partnership of missionary personnel with the national leaders and the lay forces.

3. Thirdly, in keeping with the express injunctions of Scripture, a special effort should be made to reach the unevangelized Indian tribes still found within the national confines of almost every country. The fundamentalist missionary movement has carried out the principal efforts to reach these tribes. These agencies have succeeded as never before in focusing the attention of the churches at home upon the obligation and imperative of reaching the Indians for Christ.

But the work needs to be carried through to completion. And one of the requirements of the new missionary era is that in the approach to the Indians the national Latin American churches be encouraged to take more active part and assume greater responsibility. These tribes represent, after all, their home mission fields, and the Indian churches brought into being should be properly related to the national church.

4. While not a geographic area, there remains a fourth which is tremendously important. We refer to certain strategic classes of people.

Mention has already been made of the growing middle class of professionals which is emerging all over Latin America. Evangelical Christianity has most to offer them and most to gain from them. Professor John Gillin of the University of North Carolina tells us "they are men in search of a way of life, an ideology, and a social order that will justify and legitimize their still somewhat diffuse aspirations" ("Problems of Mestizo America: A Sociological Approach," by John Gillin, in *Civilization,* Vol. V, 1955, No. 4, p. 513). What the future will hold for them and for the evangelical movement in Latin America will depend largely on whether or not they are effectively reached for Christ. But no concerted effort has been made to reach them. Our evangelical message, worship service, literature, radio programming, are still geared almost exclusively to the less educated groups.

Of equal importance are the children and young people of Latin America. It is a truism that tends to fall on deaf ears to say that the future lies with the younger generation. But one factor in Latin America—not to be found to that degree elsewhere—makes it tremendously significant. That factor is related to the population explosion already referred to, and is brought out by one tiny statistic uncovered by the Friesen & Company Commission (a Canadian firm specializing in analyzing future hospital needs) in Costa Rica. Costa Rica, though tiny, is growing faster than any country in the world; recently it passed the million mark. *Of its million inhabitants, over 50 per cent are under 17 years of age!*

In the face of the immense task that looms ahead, we ask ourselves: Are our present methods effective? Is our present program adequate? Can we carry out our Commission satisfactorily at our present pace? The answer is No. It may hurt to say so, but we may as well face it honestly. If during 100 years of missionary efforts we have failed to complete the Great Commission for five generations, what hope do we have of completing it at a time when suddenly by the hand of Providence the population is doubled in one generation? At our present rate of progress and with our present manner of operation we are falling behind and will never get the job done.

What, then, is the proper method?

What South American missionary has not been intrigued by the amazing development of the Pentecostal movement in the Republic of Chile? The remarkable history of a small group that was forced out of a denominational church in Valparaiso, Chile, in 1910 and which has in the intervening years so multiplied that today it numbers over 70,000 baptized members and close to half a million adherents is something to make us think! Especially when it is contrasted with the relative stagnancy of the established denomination which they left, which today can muster only some 6,000 members in the whole republic! Why should one group experience such growth and the other not—in the same field?

The search for an answer is complicated by the fact that other religions and non-Christian sects are also experiencing similar success. What is the secret of their success? Are they closer to the truth than the rest of us? We should be loath to say so. The fact that groups with such varied emphases and contradictory doctrines are experiencing equal success would seem to prove that the message of each per se is not the key to their expansion.

What then? Superior man power? A stress on the emotional? Special methods? Organization? An examination will clearly reveal that the answer to their success does not lie in their doctrine, nor their peculiar emphases, nor their particular organization, nor their ordinances. One factor accounts especially for the growth of all these different groups. It is this: their effectiveness in mobilizing their entire membership in continuous propagation of their beliefs. The growth of each group is in direct proportion to its success in mobilizing its entire constituency in continuous evangelistic action. This was, humanly speaking, the key to the success of the apostolic church—and it is the key to success today.

We must buckle down to the task of mobilizing our entire membership in a continuous program of aggressive evangelism that is properly followed up. What does this mean? It does not necessarily imply that we must abandon the media and ministries presently employed, but it does mean a definite change in emphasis. It means an emphasis on the Latin American rather than the foreign missionary; an emphasis on the laity rather than the clergy; an emphasis on the local congregation as the chief unit for evangelism rather than on special organizations or individuals to do the job for them. It means concentrating on a teaching job, which is not at present being carried out, and of training the entire membership of our evangelical churches in the techniques and practice of witnessing. And it means developing a program of evangelism that will enlist the enthusiastic response of Christians and give direction and continuity to their efforts. And obviously both missionary and pastor will have to set the example.

If tomorrow's task of evangelism is so overwhelming, and if the only sound strategy which offers any hope of success is the one indicated, then it is imperative that we formulate some practical plan or program that will effect the needed reorientation in our present operations and enable us to cope with the challenge.

With full recognition of our necessary dependence upon the wisdom and guidance of the Holy Spirit and with full awareness that this wisdom and guidance must be sought in partnership with the Latin American church, we would submit the following propositions:

1. The time has come for the evangelical forces in each separate country to launch a concerted, coordinated drive, making full provision for adequate follow-up, that will have for its expressed and immediate goal to complete the evangelization of the entire national territory. We believe it is most practical to think in terms of national rather than general or continental areas, because it immediately defines the specific area to be evangelized and thrusts the main responsibility upon the local forces. Problems of fellowship and cooperation can generally be best tackled, and the approach to the congregations to mobilize their membership best carried out, on a local level.

2. A simple program should be drawn up to enlist and employ the total membership of each congregation in a continuous effort which could bring all forces together in a church-centered campaign of prayer, training in personal evangelism and follow-up, organized visita-

tion work, itinerant evangelism in the rural areas, and mass evangelism. Sparked and promoted by such a corps of outstanding workers as might be loaned and assigned by the cooperating bodies, effectively supported by such specialized media and ministries as literature and radio, and using all other means, such an evangelistic drive could be launched in one country after another and thus accomplish the goal of a stepped-up program that is commensurate with the demands of this growing continent.

3. The urgency of the times and the immensity of the task cry out to us to forsake our costly, overlapping, conflicting, competitive, independent ways of operation, and to determine to work together, lovingly respecting our differences of conviction and variety of gifts but ready to sacrifice our little ends for the sake of the "Big End." Our agreement on the fundamentals of the faith makes possible cooperation in evangelism if we but set our hearts on it. If we do not, we may well consider whether we are not sinning against the Lord and against the multiplying millions in Latin America for whom he died.

Given the revolutionary changes and the exploding population in Latin America and given the strategic position of the evangelical movement and the gigantic task of evangelism confronting us in that area, this is our one hope for meeting the challenge of tomorrow.

Article   December 22, 1958

33   *Parting of the Ways*

The congregation was listening attentively to the announcements. I was urging all to attend the evening service, the sermon being on Jesus' parable concerning the rich fool.

After a very brief preview of the content of the message I announced the topic: "A Fool and His Money Are Soon Parted."

Then in the next breath I said, "Will the ushers please come forward and receive the offering."—REV. RAYMOND L. COX, Corvallis, Oregon.

Preacher in the Red   November 24, 1958

34 *Crisis Evangelism in Latin America*

DAVID E. KUCHARSKY

During the missile crisis evangelist Billy Graham preaches to thousands in South America. The news editor reports from the scene.

Columbus landed in America with a theological thud that introduced Catholicism to the New World. Exactly 470 years later, in October, 1962, arms-laden flotillas were retracing his route and churning up a world crisis. Meanwhile, 4,000 miles to the south, the foremost evangelist of the twentieth century was reintroducing Christianity to South America in the spirit of the Protestant Reformation and on an evangelistic scale hitherto unparalleled.

The week of the big war scare found Billy Graham in the climactic event of his second Latin American tour of 1962: an eight-day crusade in sprawling Buenos Aires, one of the world's ten largest cities. Warm spring evenings saw turnouts of 20,000 eclipsing the nightly average of Graham's gigantic 1957 crusade in Madison Square Garden. Hour-long telecasts gave entrée to the Gospel in hundreds of thousands of nominally Roman Catholic homes in Argentina and Uruguay.

Graham made appropriate references to the crisis, but carefully avoided exploitation of fear. To a crowd of some 50,000 gathered for the closing service at San Lorenzo soccer stadium, he said:

"The problems of peace are sometimes greater than the problems of war."

At about the same hour that President Kennedy was delivering his arms quarantine address, Graham, unaware of the momentary gravity of the international situation, was announcing his sermon topic for the following evening: "The End of the World."

The next day he told a group of Southern Baptists that word of the blockade came as no surprise to him. He indicated support of Kennedy's action and disputed philosopher Bertrand Russell's statement that "we may all be dead in a week."

"We will not all be dead in a week, or a year, or ten years," Graham declared. "We may have war, but God has other plans for the universe."

Graham repeated the observation that night at Luna Park boxing arena, largest auditorium in the city, and subsequently on television. He cited biblical predictions of widespread fear and sudden destruction.

"But the Bible teaches that before man destroys himself, Christ will return and his kingdom will ultimately prevail," Graham added.

The basic problems of the world, he said, are spiritual. He urged Christians to intensify their efforts in spreading the Gospel, to exert leadership in such times of crisis, and to pray for world leaders. He suggested that the United Nations break precedent by calling delegates to prayer.

The overwhelming majority of the population welcomed Graham and his team wholeheartedly. The only thing resembling an incident occurred when a young tough beat the window of Graham's car with his fist. Once during the week a note was thrown into another car carrying team members. It read: "For God's sake, stop the blockade."

For years, missionaries to Latin America have been predicting a showdown there with worldwide impact. Few guessed it would come out of Cuba. Some mission leaders now have reason to regret that they did not take Cuba more seriously during the years of opportunity. They now realize that the island nation constituted their nearest foreign mission field, yet was neglected.

Graham himself has preached only once in Cuba—to a crowd of 500 at Camagüey. On the other hand, Protestant mass meetings have only recently become realistic possibilities in Roman Catholic lands. It is doubtful that Graham's reception into South America would have been as successful two or more years ago. In January and February he conducted crusades in Venezuela, Colombia, Ecuador, and Peru. In September and October he spoke in Brazil, Argentina, Paraguay, and Uruguay. Together he and his team addressed an aggregate of more than 750,000. More than 20,000 of these made public commitments to Christ.

Looking back, it was clear that this had been the opportune year for evangelistic penetrations into South America. Roman Catholic opposition was sporadic. Organized hostility was unthinkable in the ecumenical climate of 1962. Moreover, the latter part of the crusade probably was enhanced by the fact that the hierarchy was in Rome.

Graham's severest rebuke came in Asunción, Paraguay, where he encountered a boycott by the press and a competing Roman Catholic festival. By contrast, a high-ranking Roman Catholic prelate visited Graham in São Paulo and said he was encouraging people to attend the crusade.

The political climate also favored evangelistic endeavor. Graham paid personal calls on four heads of state: in Argentina, Paraguay,

Chile, and Ecuador. As he does at every such occasion the evangelist gave the account of his own conversion to each.

The crusade in Buenos Aires was the longest and probably had the greatest overall impact, although Graham said he felt the response in São Paulo was more marked.

Despite his weariness, the evangelist's health held up well. A flu attack felled him in Rosario, Argentina, however, causing cancellation of one of his rally appearances there. A recurrence of the illness confined him to bed for two days in Miami following the crusade.

Graham's Spanish translator was the Rev. Paul C. Sorensen, missionary of the Pentecostal Assemblies of Canada. Sorensen spoke with Graham at every point on the second tour except São Paulo, where Rev. Walter Kaschel interpreted the messages into Portuguese. A highlight of the São Paulo crusade for Brazilian evangelicals was the announcement of the nation's first Christian radio station, dubbed PRA-7 and owned by the Christian Cultural Corporation of Brazil and World Gospel Crusades.

Comprehensive and authoritative statistics are hard to come by, but there are believed to be at least 500,000 Protestants in Argentina's population of 21,000,000.

Although the Roman Catholic Church counts more than 20,000,-000 Argentines on its rolls, it is doubtful that more than 15 per cent attend church with any regularity. The vast majority of the population are religiously indifferent. They agree to belong to the church, but never take it seriously.

Nevertheless, the thinking of the people is Catholic-oriented, and Billy Graham took that fact into account.

"We're going to say a prayer," he would announce. It was a variation from his usual "We're going to pray."

Graham also referred to "the Blessed Virgin Mary," while he tactfully rejected the role assigned her in Catholic theology. In television appearances in which he answered telephoned questions, he stressed that the Scriptures did not warrant belief in a chance for salvation after death. Graham emphasized repeatedly that salvation comes by faith, not works.

Argentine evangelicals were heartened by the mass media opportunities. Said one: "Some of us could scarcely believe our eyes when we read expositions of John 3:16 and other texts in the daily paper."

Almost all Protestant churches in Buenos Aires gave their support to the crusade. In return they received new converts and a new sense of spiritual unity, not to mention the encouragement, instruction, and inspiration which mean so much to a minority element. The joint effort also went a long way toward healing cleavages.

News　November 23, 1962

35　*The Little Old Lady's Question*

ADDISON H. LEITCH

Little old ladies make good foils for preachers' stories. There was that little old lady (maybe in tennis shoes) on a guided tour in Westminster Abbey. And there, surrounded by noble and ignoble monuments and competing guides, she asked a ridiculous question. "Tell me," she demanded a little nervously and therefore a little louder than she had planned, "has anyone been saved in this church lately?" The question shattered things; it hung out there in embarrassed silence. "Anybody saved here lately?" My dear lady, have you noticed the beautiful architecture? Have you no feeling for history? Being "saved" is for the Salvation Army, or maybe sweaty tent meetings; this is a royal abbey. But there the question stood.

There are things hidden from the wise yet revealed to babes, and the foolishness of God is wiser than men. Apart from becoming like little children, we cannot even see the kingdom. I am not sure what *all* that means. But one gets the notion in theology today that both the questions and the answers are being set up and controlled by the deviously subtle experts, and that the questions people really ask are not being answered.

In a theological seminary where I once was the chairman of the question-and-answer period for a visiting lecturer, the famous guest rephrased every question to suit his theological slant. Finally I became blunt and maybe rude and said, "Why don't you answer the question the boy asked?" Well, he was clear enough, too: "Because he asked the wrong question, that's why." That simple questions can be very puzzling and lead to ambiguity or even mystery I should be the first to admit. But such answers as we know should fit the questions. And if the answers can be given and understood only by a man with an I.Q. of 185, then we are caught in a religion available only to people who are smart enough to get it.

The desperation in the Church regarding integration is both timely and overdue. A white Christian will accept a Negro as brother and indeed neighbor. But he is very naïve if he expects the other people on the street to act with him without his motive. The man who is saved has to find out how to act like a child of God. Those who deny God may be led to act the same way but from a different premise; they will be acting sociologically and not religiously.

Remember the time in the United Nations when the Arabs and the Jews were at each other's throats and a good American New England Congregationalist interrupted their wrangling to ask, "Why don't you people act like Christians?" Well, because they aren't Christians! Youth conferences are full of instructions about *living* for young people who haven't been *born* yet. "Are you saved?" Don't confuse the awkwardness of the questioner with the profundity of the question. We shall have to have some Christians before we have a Christian civilization.

All of which leads to the question of authority on such matters. If you want to put a theological faculty in a tizzy, write various professors and ask them a simple question: "Is the Bible *true?*" They will in most cases do one of three things: (1) not answer your letter; (2) give you an equivocal answer; (3) say that they do not care to be examined by someone improperly informed to ask such a question. So you have a question on salvation and you think the Bible ought to have the answer. But is the Bible true? The great and good Hal Luccock once wrote, as Simeon Stylites in The *Christian Century,* about the Philippian jailor. "What must I do to be saved?" cried the jailor. "Well," said Paul, "what do you think?" Maybe such questions are answered by committees or by majorities or, even better, by "What Are Youth Today Saying About Salvation?" Or maybe we need the woman's viewpoint.

Another little old lady on her deathbed once asked me about the future life and the promise of eternal life. I could only turn to the Bible. I could only turn to the words of Jesus Christ; with the authority of those words I had nothing to say. It did me no good to give her my opinion or even to ask her opinion in the light of her own existential experience.

How, indeed, does one get assurance existentially about something that is yet to happen and is only a matter of promise? Unless there is some assurance from the beyond, it is impossible for us to be able to say anything with any certainty at all. This, it seems to me, has been one of the terrible results of modern criticism. The ordinary person has been *taught* to be suspicious of the authority of what is said in the Bible. Can he possibly know what is being said with any assurance unless he first consults the experts? Thus in a very subtle way we have taken away their authority.

So here are the simple questions. Are we saved? If so, where shall we find this out? Then, is the Bible true? Is it true enough for one to rest his assurance of eternal felicity on what is said there in the very words of Jesus himself? And unless he says it, who will say it for us?

Hear what Markus Barth, in the recent book *Acquittal by Resurrection,* has to say about the Resurrection: "Canonical gospels and apostolic writings alike do not attempt to produce any proof of the possibility, rationality or respectability of the resurrection. They do not ask whether or when it may be opportune to speak of it. They are satisfied to tell that Jesus Christ was raised, to add narrative elements or doctrinal statements that explain the power and relevance and to call for repentance and faith." Again: "The gospels do not ask, What can we do with a risen Jesus? Rather they state what he, the resurrected, does and will do for them and all men. . . . A critical analysis or experimental testing of [the Resurrection] was not even attempted. It would have availed them little or nothing at all." Markus Barth goes on to make the interesting observation that the Resurrection was not something believed by believers but was a real event that made believers out of unbelievers.

Many churches have classes in lay theology. Perhaps the laymen will begin to ask again the plain, simple questions, which theology must learn how to answer.

Current Religious Thought   March 27, 1964

36 *Retarded Children and Christian Concern*

DOROTHY L. HAMPTON

My only child is a little girl of nine. She is tall for her age and extraordinarily pretty, with large dark eyes that sometimes seem to look right through you. So attractive is she that people have come to me in the supermarket and exclaimed over her—and then they have stopped in mid-sentence, for it suddenly strikes them that she is different. And indeed she is. My little girl is mentally retarded. Her I.Q. is between 50 and 60, classing her with the trainable group of the retarded.

I write therefore as the mother of a retardate, but more than that, as a mother who has put her heart and her life in Christ's hands. I have read articles by directors of Christian education or by volunteers teaching church classes for the retarded, but I have never seen an article by a parent of a retardate who is willing to speak openly to her fellow Christians about what it is like to mother a defective child.

Three out of every hundred persons are mentally retarded. Here is heartache. Only 3 per cent of the mentally handicapped are institutionalized: the remaining 97 percent are at home, many of them without adequate schooling, recreation, friendship, and church life. Some may say, "But I honestly don't know any retardates." Nevertheless they are with us—perhaps hidden, perhaps mildly retarded and "passing" in the community, but all needing the evangelical church and what it can offer.

There are several stages through which one goes upon learning that one's child is mentally handicapped. For those who do not know that Christ controls all that happens in their lives, there is usually a harrowing time of guilt and self-examination. Parents ask themselves again and again, "What did I do to give birth to such a grievously handicapped child?"

As a Christian I went through this for a mercifully short period, when it had to be all or nothing. Yet even with the most scripturally grounded believers, the human element of what may be called a built-in psychological mechanism is not wholly canceled. When a mentally handicapped child is born, this mechanism may lead to bewildered questioning. Parents cannot help asking, "Lord, why me? How can I live with this? What shall I do?"

Some unfortunate parents never progress beyond this stage. To the great detriment of themselves and their handicapped child, to say nothing of any other children in the family, they remain preoccupied with "I," "me," and "us." Most parents of retardates, however, pass out of this stage to a second, in which their thinking is all directed toward the child involved. Here the normal reaction is to ask, "What can I do to help *my* child, only *mine?*" Some parents, unfortunately, remain in this second stage, and are almost as useless to themselves and to the child as those still in the first stage. Hopefully, most parents pass into a third stage, that of asking, "What can I do to help *all* mentally handicapped children?" Only then, they realize, can they help their own child.

Some parents pass through these stages rapidly, others slowly, and some never through all three. Nor does being a Christian exempt parents from these experiences. But, as my husband and I know, many Christians are able through the grace of God to reach the third stage more rapidly than others. For ourselves, we learned that when parents are told their child is mentally retarded, they suddenly realize that if all they believe and have professed is really true, then it *must* be sufficient now in this moment of soul-searing truth. Christians who have faced with God this hardest of problems understand why their faith is powerful, why it is built on agony and sacrifice instead of upon mere platitudes and kind sayings.

If my faith offered only some practical guides to everyday living, I would not be able to write this. But for Christians who have such inescapable problems, it means everything to know that we have a hereafter to count upon for us and our children. We have a God who is all-loving, and in control. We know that our children are provided for in God's eternal plan, that not just a great man but the incarnate God himself said, "Inasmuch as ye have done it unto one of the least of these, my brethren, ye have done it unto me" (Matt. 25:40).

Surely among "the least of these" are the retarded, for who is more lowly than they? Perhaps the most comforting fact of all is that Christ loves the unlovely. Many retarded are unlovely; their features are ugly. Some have crossed eyes, some have heads malformed from birth injuries; others are palsied, and still others are so handicapped that they are living vegetables. What has helped most as I have felt the anguish of knowing that my little girl is retarded is to realize that the retarded are part of the Lord's plan and that his love encompasses them as much as it encompasses the most gifted children.

All of us (Christians included) have a great deal to learn about the problem of retardation. Every retardate has parents and often brothers and sisters who desperately need Christian friendship, Christian love, a church home, and genuine acceptance. How sad to hear it said in an open meeting about church classes for the retarded, when conservative evangelical churches are mentioned, "Oh, they don't care. They won't do anything but sit in their ivory towers and criticize!" How cruel it is to know that, with some exceptions, this is true.

Why is it true, not only concerning retardation, but also in respect to alcoholism, mental illness, and the underprivileged poor? Why are some evangelicals letting their liberal friends do most of the works of compassion, while they argue about immersion versus sprinkling and whether Christ will come before or after the tribulation—and all the time souls in the agony of despair over a mentally retarded child, an alcoholic or mentally sick relative, are perishing all around them? While Christians who have knowledge and understanding of the power that alone can save souls and ease burdens quibble over how separated they are, there is intense spiritual suffering going on in the very blocks where they live. And somehow they are strangely uninterested in helping. If this seems overly severe, let me ask this: Why is it only now becoming the "in" thing to assist the retarded and their parents? Where have we (and I include myself) been?

It is time to come down out of the clouds of theological controversy and spiritual pride and to take our share of responsibility for the unfortunates of society. Our great-grandparents did it for the slaves. We can do it for the "least of these," Christ's brethren.

What then should Christians do? Let me offer some suggestions based upon experience. First, they must realize that retarded children and adults need to feel wanted and that church life is important for them. "But," someone says, "their mentality in most cases limits their understanding of doctrine." Such a statement overlooks the wonder of the Gospel. Most retardates understand something about death; many can understand, to a limited degree, the concept of an all-powerful Being; many understand wrongdoing; virtually all can understand love —the quality they need more than any other. Thus many mentally retarded persons are able to understand something of the central truth that Jesus is God and that he loved them enough to die for them. And after all, what else is there? This is the magnitude of the Gospel and its magnificent simplicity.

I believe that my little child understands this great truth. Whether she is or ever will be at the age of discernment I may never know; but she loves Jesus, and she knows that he loves her. And if she could not grasp even this, I would still know that he loves her.

A teacher of a primary-level church class for normal children told me recently how a rather severely retarded child entered class the day the gospel story was told. Instead of being a behavior problem as the teacher feared, the child sat very still. At the end of the lesson, the teacher gave a simple invitation to accept Christ. The retarded child stood up, asking over and over, "Can I? Can I?" There were tears in that teacher's eyes as she said that she knows our Lord is as happy over that little one as over any other.

Secondly, Christians must understand that it is not enough to say, "Let's have a nice church class or Sunday-school class for the retarded," and then, after doing this, to think that nothing more is needed. Every retardate has a family, and these are often in greater need than the retardate. What about the parents and others in the family? This is what pastors and congregations must ask when they decide to do something for the retarded. What of the teen-age brother of the little mongoloid in the special class? Is this adolescent made welcome and shown that his church understands? Does the congregation realize that mongolism is not hereditary and is not the result of some hidden sin of the parents?

Churches must do more than begin classes for the retarded; concern must also be shown for their families. Evangelicals might well follow the example set by some of more liberal theology and start group therapy classes for parents, never forgetting that the greatest therapy comes through personal knowledge of Christ as Saviour and Lord.

Only those who have a defective child will ever know the terrible need for acceptance, the deep desire to be treated like other families. The cruel stigma against the retarded has been tolerated for too long. Human beings seem to accept any handicap so long as it does not limit the one thing we need above all else—the mind. The words of Milton's sonnet, "On His Blindness," apply also to mental retardation: Sight is not the only "talent which is death to hide." Even more essential is our ability to reason, to express ourselves in spoken and written language, to think.

Today in an inarticulate but eloquent plea the retarded are calling for help. It is to the lasting credit of our late President Kennedy, whose oldest sister is mentally retarded, that he heard that plea and led the movement resulting in the first legislation in our national history designed to help the retarded.

Emotional response is not in itself sufficient. Response must be informed. This means that Christians must take the trouble to learn the difference between retardation and mental illness. They should know what facilities their communities offer for therapy and schooling for all retarded. They should be aware of the need for greater educational opportunities, more job openings, additional legislation in the field of retardation, and institutional reforms. They should find out what parents' groups are available where fathers and mothers of retardates can meet others with similar problems. Above all, they should know that retardation can happen to *any* family, that it is no respecter of education, social position, or economic status. With such knowledge they will have something concrete to recommend when a young couple comes to church in the crisis of having just learned that their child is mentally handicapped.

Parents of retarded children can become victims of the most callous medical quackeries—money-draining schemes that claim miracle cures. The parents must be helped to realize that there is *no* cure. There can in some cases be great progress for the retarded child. Nevertheless, retardation is a condition, not an illness to be cured. Apparently our Lord meant for the retarded always to be with us, needing our help and understanding.

All children take their cues from their parents and the adults around them. Normal and gifted children must learn compassion for their unfortunate brothers or sisters. They should be told that handicapped children may be coming to church or Sunday school, that this is how God made these children, that they are to be helped and loved. Normal children will surprise parents and teachers with their matter-of-fact acceptance and eager willingness to help. The real hope for the retarded is regrettably not in this generation but in the next. If young people hear about retardation in the community and ask, "What can I do to help?" instead of saying, "Poor things, poor things," then progress will be made.

Retarded children have emotions. My child loves, she gets angry, she gets upset. She knows when people accept her openly for what she is; she also can tell when they feign sympathy. In addition to those who have already heard the call to help "the least of these," many more professionally trained persons—teachers, medical researchers, therapists, recreation directors, counselors—are needed. So much can be done for the retarded, many of whom, when trained and supervised, are able to lead useful and happy lives as part of the community.

Here is a call to Christlike service for evangelical youth. Such service entails more than professional skill; it can mean helping parents of retardates to a sure trust in Jesus Christ that will take them through the deepest valleys of despair.

The task of assisting parents who have older retarded children may be especially difficult; they will not always respond happily or even graciously. Perhaps years ago when they needed a church, none was ready to welcome them. They may ask, "Why is the church now opening its doors to us and our children?" The best answer is a positive program. It is important to schedule classes for the retarded at the same times as regular church services. Some churches offer classes for the retarded on Saturday or another weekday. This has two serious flaws. It prevents a group of parents from going to church on Sunday, because there is nothing on that day for their handicapped children; it also means that there are whole congregations of adults and children who will never see these mentally retarded children among them on Sunday as part of the Lord's flock.

Too long have most Christians lagged in assuming their burden for the unfortunate and the handicapped. We who have mentally retarded children need more than sympathy and tears. We need what committed Christians have to offer us in knowledge of sins forgiven, in courage for living, and in a blessed hope for the future. Let Christians to whom much has been given give of themselves and of their bounty to help the unfortunate. Let them give in love.

The second great commandment, "Thou shalt love thy neighbor as thyself," is part of the faith. Christians can no longer forget the young father and mother in that hospital room who have just been told that their baby is retarded and may always be a child in mind. To these can be given understanding and hope for eternity. While they cannot be offered immediate happiness, they can be shown that there are things more important than mere happiness.

We parents of the mentally retarded have heavy burdens. But when you free our souls by giving us the joyous knowledge that Christ is God, that he died for us and for our children, that he cares for us, that he is with us day by day, then there is nothing we will not strive to do for our children and all of "the least of these [Christ's] brethren."

Article   January 31, 1964

37   *Jonathan Edwards' Still Angry God*

From the American pulpit today one might easily conclude that the wrath of God is fiction. No longer are churches of the land aflame with a lively sense of God's anger against sin and sinners. Some churchmen still feel called upon to apologize for any stress on divine wrath, and many theologians are inclined to moderate or even to reinterpret it.

The Bible speaks often of God's intense wrath. If the Book of Revelation is from the pen of John the Evangelist, as evangelical scholarship has contended, then even the "apostle of love" warned of "the fierceness and wrath of Almighty God" (Rev. 19:15). And Jesus, who had more to say about hell than about heaven, himself declared: "Fear him . . . [that] hath power to cast into hell" (Luke 12:5). In this respect the Son of God confirms the uniform doctrine of inspired Scripture that God both disapproves sin and threatens sinners with eternal doom.

The doctrine that God's moral excellence demands punishment supplies the principle on which the Bible doctrines of satisfaction and justification rest. That Christ was set forth as a propitiation in order that God might be righteous in justifying the ungodly (Rom. 3:25 f.) is not only Pauline theology, but the unitary standpoint of the New Testament, which is that redemption from the guilt and power of sin comes through the sacrificial virtue of Christ's death. The Scriptures connect the salvation of men with the death of Christ, and to his death ascribe expiatory and propitiatory significance (Matt. 26:28, Mark 10:45, John 1:29). If pardon were possible without satisfaction, then Christ died in vain (Gal. 2:21). Mere "forgiveness" would not only leave the death of Christ unsatisfactorily explained but, contrary to a current tendency to regard faith as the ground of forgiveness (rather than the instrument of it), the sinner's pardon and justification in the absence of propitiation would contravene moral rectitude.

Modern theology has had trouble with the doctrine of the wrath of God ever since Hegelian pantheism brought into the Christian movement the notion of man's divinity. Liberal caricatures of an angry God, a "bully," as some writers have blasphemed, or a bloodthirsty tyrant demanding appeasement by blood, were in no sense proofs of the supposed fictitiousness of God's wrath, but rationalizations of modernism's unbelief. For liberal theology had originated a speculative and specious view of God that subordinated his divine justice to his love or benevolence.

Liberalism spurned the doctrine of the wrath of God as nothing but anthropopathy, or the ascription of human emotions and the variableness of them to God (like anthropomorphism, which is the ascription of bodily forms such as the "eyes" and "ears" of God); and the result was that divine wrath was dismissed as wholly figurative. Liberal theologians were hardly aware that they were ascribing a fictitious and sentimental view of love to God. Biblical writers had intended by their inspired statements of both God's love and wrath to express, after the manner of human analogy, real relations of God to the world—that is, not changes in God's eternal nature, but changed attitudes toward men conditioned upon their personal relationship to him. And their use of analogy did not imply theological fiction; the doctrine that man bears the image of God, and that God in some respects can be conceived analogously to man, lies at the foundation of theism, especially in its confidence that true reason, morality, and spirituality are ultimately of one order.

That the justice of God demands the punishment of the wicked, and that only Jesus Christ's mediation propitiates the wrath of God toward sinners and secures their forgiveness, was a great theme of Jonathan Edwards, the 200th anniversary of whose death is being observed this year. His clear exposition of the fact of divine wrath and the indispensable sacrifice of the Cross supplies an indirect warning that the ministry today, even when speaking of the forgiveness of sins, may obscure the justice of God and deprive anxious souls of the merits and comforts of the Cross.

In his famous sermon, "Sinners in the Hands of an Angry God," Edwards spoke unhesitatingly of "the wrath of the infinite God" and of "the vengeance of God on the wicked." He spoke of unrepentant sinners as exposed to destruction: "Thus are all you that have never passed under a great change of heart, by the mighty power of the Spirit of God upon your souls." Edwards' preaching might not prove "popular" today, nor was it in his day; indeed, the biblical doctrines of human corruption and supernatural redemption have never been welcomed by the natural man. But that is all the more reason for proclaiming them faithfully and zealously.

Modern men need to hear again the echo of Edwards' message, for in it they will detect the warnings and pleadings of the holy prophets and apostles: "Nothing . . . keeps wicked men at any one moment out of hell, but the [sovereign] pleasure of God. . . . They deserve to be cast into hell; so that divine justice . . . calls aloud for an infinite punishment of their sins. . . . They are already under a sentence of condemnation to hell. . . . The devil stands ready to . . . seize them. . . ."

These are strong words, but they reflect the biblical teaching of man's precarious position outside of Christ, and the fervent utterance of this warning will stir some to repentance as no other appeal does.

Jonathan Edwards also stressed that justification is not the bare remission of sins and acquittal from wrath, but freedom from guilt and desert of punishment rooted in the substitutionary and propitiatory work of "a mediator that has purchased justification." He stresses: "If Christ had not come into the world and died to purchase justification, no qualification in us could render it a meet or fit thing that we should be justified: but . . . Christ has actually purchased justification by his own blood for infinitely unworthy creatures. . . . It is not . . . on account of any excellency or value that there is in faith . . . that he that believes should have this benefit of Christ assigned to him, but purely from the relation faith has to the person in whom this benefit is to be had, or as it unites to that mediator, in and by whom we are 'justified' " (from Edwards' sermon on "Justification by Faith Alone").

The Protestant pulpit today is tending to evade the subjects of human guilt and penalty, while concentrating on the depravity of man. Hence, in expounding the cure for man's illness, it emphasizes the forgiveness of sins, the new birth, and sanctification. But because it ignores guilt and penalty, it ignores also the corollary doctrines of justification and imputation. Yet God does not regard the act of faith and man's submission to obedience as sufficient basis of forgiveness, for that leaves man's guilty past uncovered. Whoever ignores man's guilt and exposure to punishment must reckon further with Jonathan Edwards' still angry God.

Much of the preaching on the Cross today modifies and even twists the biblical plan of salvation. For it implicitly denies that Christ vicariously bore the penalty for the broken law of God as the sinner's substitute, that the Mediator's righteousness is imputed to the believer as the ground of his justification, and that saving grace involves the justified sinner's resting in the person and work of Christ alone.

Neo-orthodox theology has been somewhat more deferential to the reality of the wrath of God than classic liberalism, but the difference is largely a relative one. Emphasizing the wrath of God as it does, in view of man's sinfulness and God's righteousness, neo-orthodoxy nonetheless subordinates God's anger to his love in refusing to make any ultimate distinction between God's wrath and his benevolence. That is why Karl Barth's doctrine of last things veers toward universalism, and Emil Brunner's toward conditional immortality. And that is why neither can admit the doctrine of propitiatory atonement (which Barth dismisses as pagan); for were God's wrath but a corollary of his love, there would be no necessity for propitiation antecedent to his forgiveness of sinners.

Modern philosophers may give sophisticated respectability to these mollifications of divine wrath. God is always subject, never object, some would say, and hence the Father cannot be an object of the Son's work upon the Cross. The essence of Christ's atonement, others would affirm, is his victory over evil powers, into which he incorporates those who put their trust in him. Hence incorporation, not substitution, is considered the key to the meaning of atonement.

But the witness of Scripture still stands. Righteousness and love are perfections, equally ultimate in the Godhead. The wrath of God, mediation, atonement, sacrifice, propitiation, are part of the biblical doctrine of redemption. Sinners with hearts uncleansed by the purifying blood of Christ will discover polluted blood unwashed from their guilty hands. Jonathan Edwards' God is still angry.

Editorial   January 6, 1958

38 *Nightwalker*

To keep a weekend engagement, I arrived by train at a country station 11 miles from Reading on a Saturday evening in December. I found Mrs. Green's cottage two miles from the station.

"Take off your wet shoes and put my late husband's slippers on. He died 12 months ago tonight."

After supper, during which a detailed account of the good man's homegoing was recited, Mrs. Green showed me to my bedroom from which her husband passed away. "I don't sleep here since that sad occasion," explained my hostess. "I go to my neighbors. You are not afraid?"

She went with a sombre "Good night." I heard her lock the door. In bed and almost asleep, I heard shuffling footsteps on the stairs. The door opened and a tall, gauntly draped figure appeared in the pale moonlight. The bedclothes at the foot of the bed were lifted. A bony hand gripped one of my feet, released it, gripped the other, and then pulled the clothes back over and left the room. Was I dreaming?

How pleased I was to hear Mrs. Green humming, "Brief life is here our portion," as she poked the fire the next morning. "Ah!" she said as I entered the kitchen, "I do hope you passed a good night." Then she added before I could answer, "Last night I had forgotten to put a hot water bottle in your bed, so I came over and felt your feet. They were warm, so I was content."

"Ah! Sister Green," I said, "you are kind."

—REV. J. WILLIAMS, Cinderford, Gloucester, England.

Preacher in the Red   October 26, 1959

39   *The Church and Awakening Groups*

S A M U E L   M .   S H O E M A K E R

The relationship that is to prevail between the organized Church and the informal groups which arise from time to time, seeking to bring about deeper spiritual experience, is an important subject. The voice of the organized Church has often warned that such groups do not constitute themselves a church, that they check their plans and work with leaders in the church, that they remind their people how important it is to join a church, and in general treat the church as the final authority. Undoubtedly there is wisdom in all this. But I think it is high time that someone remind the Church how important it is that she treat these groups with understanding and welcome, and remember how the organized Church stands in continuous need of awakening, and realize that the small group may be both a judgment and an answer from God.

Exception must be made, of course, in the case of groups that become deliberately inimical to the historic Church, or patently disloyal to her basic ethos. But that is something quite different from being dissatisfied with the ways and customs of some one local parish or minister that may be falling down in giving people what they need spiritually. It is right for the Church to "try the spirits whether they be of God." Now and then a group arises that is not basically in line with historic Christianity; or it may begin so, but veer in unhealthy directions. Its leaders can become too much impressed with their own inspiration and importance, and the movement tends to become "the Church." The awakening group may evince more power at some given time than the historic, accepted Church; but it has no more right to "unchurch" the organized Church than the organized Church has a right to "unchurch" the informal group. Untrue and unhealthy signs may appear in the utterances and from the leaders of movements that claim unique powers and do not see themselves in the long stream of Christian history.

But many of these groups are not heretical in any sense. They are doing Christ's work, honoring his Name, and winning people to him. They are trying to be loyal to his Church, not only because hostility to the churches can go a long way towards putting them out of business but because they are aware that the conserving job of the churches cannot be overemphasized. My experience is that most of these movements lean over backwards to keep the good will of an organized church (which often has not enough spirituality to discern the working of the Holy Spirit in the groups) because they happen to be personally distasteful to the church leader or the ethos of his group. It is dangerous ground to forbid men "because they follow not with us." Every year I live, I am more impressed with the way God greatly uses some people that I question whether he ought to use at all! My own tastes, even the predilections of my own denomination, may not be sufficient grounds to rule out someone who is being blessed and used by God.

Perhaps I can say something on the whole question. I have dedicated my own services to that of being a parish minister and an evangelist. I have never felt any impulse to go out with a suitcase and travel around making speeches. I have wanted the Church, the old, organized Church, to be part of any awakening in which I was involved. I have wanted the continuous impact of the Church's history and stored wisdom to be on my own work. I know that in the end the Church should be the conserving force for anything that evangelism turns up; and that, while the Church will seldom start an awakening herself (the settled clergy and people are not good at this), she can easily pour cold water on what the awakening does accomplish. I know the value of a local "laboratory," where spiritual research is being done, and that what is said elsewhere is validated principally by what is happening at home. I know the need of spiritually new-born people for what the Church can give them, as, for example, the responsibility of Christian leaders to see people through, not only the early stage of new birth but the later stages of growth and spiritual habits which sustain the new birth, and the applications in life which give it contemporary validation.

However, I know that the local church and denominational exposure are not enough. If some kind of urging had not sent me, as a school boy and college student, to Northfield and there to come under the spell of the giants of those days (Speer and Mott especially), I suppose I should have been as churchy an Episcopal parson as could be imagined. I needed to learn something of the size of the kingdom, its scope, and to see some of its great leaders in other communions. I needed to discover the constant influence in the direction of awakening which such conferences, with their steady evangelistic impact, represented vis-à-vis the old, settled Church. In constantly emphasizing the priestly and pastoral aspects, my own church is always in danger of minimizing the evangelistic and prophetic ones. Yet Anglicanism means both, or it means nothing: it has always claimed to be both, and we are ministers "of the Word and of the Sacraments." More and more clergy of all communions recognize this double nature of our calling and task. But many of them drift too easily into those aspects of the ministry which fail to emphasize evangelism. It is because the genuine awakening power of the churches is so rare that these cell groups, prayer groups, life-changing groups, are becoming widespread.

Sometimes these groups are local and unknown, and meet in houses and offices as well as churches. Although they often are out of touch with any other groups, they feel the need for fellowship between groups, as individuals have felt the need of fellowship between themselves. Sometimes these groups are of a different kind, large and necessarily organized, like the Yokefellow Movement, International Christian Leadership, the Fellowship of Christian Athletes, Faith at Work, Young Life, and many more that might be mentioned. Wherever men or women are given the charismatic gift of evangelism and can speak to large numbers of people with decisive spiritual results—like Graham, Peale, Sheen, and others whose names are yet more controversial to ultra-conservative, settled churchmen—the same need is evidenced and begins to be met. (When I say "ultra-conservative," I refer, of course, not to doctrinal conservatism, but to plain stuffiness of spirit.)

Let me say that the clergy, especially those in settled parishes, are inclined to think their own strictures and objections to the informal group as pure concern for upholding the Church's true message and the faith. But in many cases I am sure that the origin of their criticism is not so lofty. Frequently their censure arises from (1) jealousy that the movement is able to win and begin to change people who have not been changed by the routines of parish life, and (2) stung and troubled consciences over these things that happen elsewhere but do not happen with nearly enough regularity in the old organized Church. Let's face it: we do not do very much in a spiritual way with the rank and file of our people, and the fruits of the average "young people's groups" are certainly nothing to brag about. When one of our official "children" goes out and finds a shining and enlivening faith and experience, the home clergyman just does not like the judgment implied upon his own ministry. He retreats stuffily behind his ecclesiastical defenses, and talks about his people being "taken away" from the church! It is a shabby and contemptible rationalization. They have not been "taken away" from the Church if they have been brought nearer to Christ. And what is more, when a person with such an experience comes back to the church, the minister may subtly or openly undercut what has happened to the person, which is another instance of his own jealousy and stung pride. I have seen it too many times not to recognize it and call it by its right name. I remember going to an opening night of a play in New York and sitting behind a large company of actors. Their clapping and comments proved they were so generous and appreciative of the play, that it made me ask myself why the reverend brethren were not more often generous about what some other brother (or sister) has been enabled to do.

The old, organized Church needs the challenge of the small group. Theories about the Holy Spirit do not constitute an experience of him. While he works through official channels, he is certainly not confined to them; and there are times when he must work through something other than the established channels if he is either (1) to awaken the people in the churches, or (2) to reach those outside who are often disappointed and let down by the want of spiritual power in the churches. What he finds usable may be something or someone who is anathema to the old, plodding, organized Church. I often feel that any spiritual lash sharp enough to whip the sluggish beast of ecclesiastical organization into any semblance of spiritual life will also be so sharp that the organized Church will seek to retreat beyond its reach. What true awakening has not started in a despised individual or group on whom the Church turned thumbs down? How many such have been scheduled before they never got anywhere because the Church lacked imagination and sympathy? The Church often prays for awakening, but when God actually sends it in a form which the organized Church finds uncongenial, it is repudiated. The Holy Spirit is wider than we, more democratic, more "functional." He seems to look rather for faith and dedication and expectancy than for right formulas and proper ecclesiastical ancestry.

If Irenaeus was right, that the Church is where the Holy Spirit is, we may need to revise some of our notions about the spiritual priority of the organized Church. What we think is the Church, and what God thinks is the Church, may be very different. I should greatly suspect that any person or group to whom he can get through and use to reach his world is probably considered by God to be a genuine part of his Church. Punctiliousness about historical continuity and careful ecclesiastical arrangements sometimes have to give way to immediate usability. I know this can lead to anomaly at times; but I know also what failure in reckoning with this truth has done again and again in the life of the Church. When the Church does nothing but sit on her prerogatives and criticize the emerging group or movement that demonstrates the Holy Spirit, and when subsequently she refuses to accept the challenge and the judgment of God upon her own powerlessness which the fresh group represents, then the group tends to be driven outside the Church, all contact is lost with the authentic elements in the organized Church which the group needs for growth and sustenance, and the Church loses the value of new life which might have been infused into her.

It is a loss both ways, and a loss to the world. The fresh movements need the breadth, balance, wisdom, and sacraments of the ancient organized Church. That same Church needs the new fire of fresh awakening. Both constitute the Church, really. The organized Church cannot stand back and wait to be sought for and courted by the new movements, as if they were upstarts and the organized Church alone were the authentic thing: this is pride, and cuts the power of the Spirit. Neither can the fresh movement go on alone, critical and indifferent to the Church, as if itself were now the authentic thing, and the old Church outworn: this, too, is pride, and cuts the power of the Spirit. They have something for each other. I believe they are two sides of the same shield—the "ecclesia" and the "koinonia." The mark of the true Church is always the presence and power of the Holy Spirit.

It is always the high hope of those who help to initiate a new movement of the Spirit that this one may never drop to the level of routine and organization. Yet we know of no movement in history that has not to some extent suffered this fate. There seems to come a "hardening of the arteries" with age, and it appears to occur within about two decades of the real beginnings of the movement. When the Church proposes herself as the agent to prevent this deterioration, one is inclined to ask whether the accepted and familiar arteriosclerosis of the organized Church is any real improvement upon that which crops up in the new movement.

Dr. Henry P. Van Dusen of Union calls it "the logic of spiritual vitality," and says we have seen it "re-enacted again and again in the pilgrimage of the Christian Church, whereby a period of intense and creative religious renewal is unfailingly succeeded by an aftermath of diminishing spiritual vigor but increasing theological and organizational rigidity, then by a time of comparative sterility—until revival bursts forth afresh, and the curve of descending life and power is re-enacted" (*Spirit, Son and Father,* Scribner's, p. 27). In this remarkable book he gives a summary of "the fate of the Holy Spirit at the hands of the theologians and Church officials across the centuries," and calls it "on the whole, a pathetic and tragic story" (*op. cit.,* p. 125). He goes on to explain something of why this happens: ". . . the Holy Spirit has always been troublesome, disturbing because it has seemed to be unruly, radical, unpredictable. It is always embarrassing to ecclesiasticism and baffling to ethically-grounded, responsible durable Christian devotion. And so it has been carefully taken in hand by Church authorities, whether Catholic or Protestant, and securely tethered in impotence . . . professional ecclesiasts constitutionally distrust the novel, the unconventional and, even more, the reproachful and the challenging."

I find it hard not to believe that much of the ecclesiastical fear and suppression of emerging groups is due not to greater wisdom or deeper realization of the meaning of the Gospel and even of the Church but more to spiritual snobbishness, shallowness, and pique. It is not as if we had a counter full of awakenings from which we might take our pick. Real awakening is rare. It never comes unmixed with the temperamental and theological limitations of its first stimuli and its leaders. The "ideal" awakening, temperamentally congenial and theologically satisfactory, only exists in somebody's wishful imagination. But wherever we see genuine spiritual awakening, whether or not it falls in with our own predilections, we do well to welcome it warmly. Only a Church which takes that attitude towards the struggling group deserves respect and loyalty from the group, or is likely to receive it. Much of the loss which often follows the first fire of awakening is due to the fact that a church unfamiliar with conversion in her own daily life will tend to be all fingers and thumbs when it comes to ministering to converted people. When a person, especially a young one, who has been exposed for years to the rather lifeless routines of a church, without anything approaching a personal spiritual experience, meets individuals or groups that lead him into an experience that is dynamic and meaningful, though such may occur within a framework ecclesiastically or theologically uncongenial to his clergyman, he will, if he has any spiritual gumption, put his first loyalty where the challenge is greater and the experience deeper. If his fresh experience is greeted by his home church and minister in the attitude that he must have got caught in the toils of a bunch of fanatics from which he needs to be rescued as a brand from the burning, then I think the church is stupid enough to deserve to lose his loyalty. If on the other hand, the person's new experience is treated with seriousness and respect, and the home pastor has grace enough to ask and seek humbly for something that may have been missing from his own ministry, but which the young person found in the other group, the church runs little risk of losing him at all. In such a situation, the two work in harmony, which I believe is God's will.

The fresh group which brings about awakening is like an obstetrician who is needed at birth. The Church which nourishes the new life of the convert is like a pediatrician who takes care of the child after it is born. One has the feeling that the Church is very busy trying to act as pediatrician to large numbers of people who have never been born again at all. But both functions are essential, though they are different. The happy arrangement is for each to fulfill his function well. Surely the whole Church needs to be engaged, both in bringing about the new birth and in nurturing that new life with the "means of grace" of which she is the custodian.

Dr. Hendrik Kramer has said (*A Theology for the Laity*, p. 86), ". . . the whole Church is constantly called to renewal. As we have got into the habit of not (as the Bible insists) considering renewal the perennial and constant rule for the Church, but regard it as a miraculous episode which befalls us from time to time, self-assertion and self-affirmation are still very prominent in the confrontations of the churches with each other. . . ." The small group, not being primarily doctrinal nor liturgical, may be, and I think very often is, the ecumenical movement at its grass-roots levels, bringing people into fellowship in Christ across the barriers of denominations. And they are at least an honest effort to keep the Church mindful that renewal should be "the perennial and constant rule for the Church."

Article   October 10, 1960

40   *Avoiding the Abstract*

PAUL S. REES

"When preaching is dull," said Morgan Phelps Noyes in his Lyman Beecher Lectures, "or when preaching fails to be helpful, the chances are that it has gone off into abstractions." It isn't that abstractions are always under ban. Lecture rooms can do with them—but not pulpits.

How to avoid the abstract?

For one thing, be biblical. The world of the Bible in certain external particulars is not our world of astronauts and countdowns and blast-offs, our world of vitamins and cholesterol and Salk vaccines; but it is, for all this, a real world peopled by magnanimous Abrahams and greedy Lots, by cunning Jacobs and transparent Josephs, by moody Elijahs and lying Ahithophels, by hot-blooded Davids, and treacherous Judases, and winsome Johns, and adventurous Pauls, and by a host of others who, like these, are capable of acting "out of character," so that the noblest of them, eyeing the worst of them, are obliged to say, "There, but for the grace of God, go I!"

The Bible is full of ideas, but they are not primarily ideational: they have skin on their faces and a glint—good or bad—in their eyes.

Closely linked with the wisdom of being biblical is a second piece of counsel for the preacher who would cultivate the concrete: be imaginative. This, we should be warned, is not the same as letting one's fancy run riot or one's rhetoric run purple and gold.

In the service of the preacher imagination is a kind of coagulant by which ideas, held in intellectual and theological suspension, are "precipitated" in the form of images. What, for example, is God's bearing toward any prodigal who is sick of it all and ready to return in chastening and penitence? "Merciful," we may say. Or "forgiving." True enough! But is that the only way to say it?

One night, years ago, a preacher said, "Right now, if you will listen, you can hear the looms of Heaven weaving new robes for prodigals who, having wandered far, are coming home." And suddenly the world of reconciliation, God's world of grace, was lit up for me by the flash of an image I have never forgotten.

"First of all," wrote Gustave Frenssen, in comment on his own homiletic method, "I take the text out of its ancient setting and plant it in our own life, and in our own time. My text, so to speak, saunters up and down the village street once or twice with thoughtful eyes and meditative mind. It becomes accustomed to the village, learns to feel at home in it."

Here, obviously, is homiletical harnessing of the imagination, the effect of which is to pull the sermon through many an otherwise dull stretch where interest would flag and time would hang heavy.

One other suggestion: be word-conscious. Said that pulpit craftsman extraordinary, Charles Jefferson: "Words have moods as people do. . . . There are reverent, kneeling words, warm, tender, and affectionate words, open-handed, open-hearted, hospitable words, laughing, shouting, hallelujah words—words which are so rich in human experience, so saturated with laughter and tears that if the preacher breaks them upon his congregation, they fill with perfume, like precious alabaster boxes, all the place where he is preaching."

Let the preacher go back over his notes or manuscript and prune severely those words that are torpid rather than lively, dull rather than bright, abstract rather than specific.

The *Saturday Review* reports that when British children were asked, "What are the twelve loveliest things you know?" one boy answered:

"The cold of ice cream.
The scrunch of dry leaves.
The feel of clean clothes.
Water running into a bath.
Cool wind on a hot day.
Hot water bottle in bed.
Honey in your mouth.
Smell of a drug store.
Babies smiling.
The feeling inside when you sing.
Climbing up a hill, looking down.
Baby kittens."

Note the specific situations. Mark the simple language. Catch the overtones of words like "clean" and "cool" and the sense-suggested-by-sound effect of a word like "scrunch." Then think, if it isn't too utterly beyond belief, of the distinguished clergyman who, according to the London *Times,* once preached a sermon to the ordinary people living in Wordsworth's Lake District in which he assured them they were surrounded by "an apokdeiksis of theocratic omnipotence." A garrison like that must have seemed more oppressive than protective.

But Jesus would have caught the eye and ear of that English lad.

He would have done it with his "city set on a hill," and his "salt of the earth," and his "candle" on a "candlestick" and not "under a bushel," and his "sower" going forth "to sow," and his "five sparrows" in the market place, and a hundred other pictures-in-words which he painted with a deftness never surpassed.

The lesson is for all of us: our hearers are dulled and distanced by abstractions. What captures them is the concrete.

The Minister's Workshop   November 8, 1963

41   Supreme Court Prayer Ban: Where Will It Lead?

The U.S. Supreme Court evoked a tidal wave of criticism and but mild commendation when six of its justices ruled "it is no part of the business of government to compose official prayers . . . as part of a religious program carried on by the government." New York public schools abruptly terminated daily teacher-pupil recitation of the "non-denominational" prayer approved by the State Board of Regents: "Almighty God, we acknowledge our dependence upon Thee, and we beg Thy blessings upon us, our parents, our teachers and our country."

Would the ruling of the highest judiciary lead eventually to a godless state? Most critics thought so. They contended that the Supreme Court virtually exchanged the nation's traditional "freedom of religion" for "freedom from religion," thereby anticipating the removal of "In God We Trust" from our currency, "one nation under God" from the oath of allegiance to the flag, the Bible from the courtrooms, chaplains from the armed services, and cessation of opening prayers in Congress and in state legislatures. They noted that atheists or agnostics are often in the forefront of minorities appealing cases to the Supreme Court, and that legislation increasingly tends to promote the preferences if not of subversives, at least of those more interested in religious detachment than in religious commitment.

Few critics explored the other alternative; that is, just where political approval or stipulation of prayer patterns in the public schools might lead. In keeping with their church's traditional objective of union of Church and State, and their current desire to narrow the contrast between public and parochial schools, Roman Catholic spokesmen deplored the Supreme Court action as leading to godlessness in education. Many evangelical Protestant leaders—even some usually alert to issues of church-state separation—found little if any good in the Supreme Court decision. Some noted that since the Regents' prayer was not specifically Christian, the Court's action could not be deplored as anti-Christian. Did they thus imply, it may be asked, that the Court would have acted agreeably to Christian (Protestant rather than Romanist) conscience if a specifically Christian prayer were legislated upon the public schools? Doubtless their point was well made that the Regents' prayer originated as much in Protestant-Catholic-Jewish compromise as in the overarching faith of the founding fathers as expressed in the Declaration of Independence (however offensive to agnostics the emphasis on dependence upon a personal deity might have been). One vocal Protestant churchman dismissed the Regents' prayer as innocuous because it included no reference to the Mediator. Christians adhering to the New Testament view of prayer, that God's answer is pledged only to petitions offered "in Jesus' name," might further have deplored the promotion of a religion-in-general doctrine of intercession implied in the New York devotional. Biblical Christians therefore could have considered themselves discriminated against as much as atheists.

A second look should lead all critics to second thoughts about the Supreme Court decision. It can be defended, and commended, as compatible both with a proper Christian attitude toward government stipulation of religious exercises, and with a sound philosophical view of freedom. It does not preclude anyone's private prayers in the classroom; it does not even exclude group prayers; what it does exclude is government-approved prayers in the public schools. If free-thinkers fear that government-approved prayer may lead to religious coercion, the devout and the godly ought to fear lest it lead to government-disapproved prayer (as in Russia).

It must be granted also that public education does not really exist for the exercise of spiritual devotions. Its prime purpose, however, is presentation of the whole body of truth. Unfortunately, the growing climate of academic and legal prejudice against American religious traditions makes it increasingly difficult to confront the younger generation in our public schools with truth about God and the moral world. The Bible has a proper place in the curriculum, not simply as literature, but in the dialogue about truth. If God is banished from the class periods, and survives only in some nebulous form in corporate prayer, then the inference is not remote that the notion of deity, while emotionally significant, is intellectually dispensable. The Communists could not wish for more.

Yet it must not be ignored that minority pressures have become increasingly effective in shaping the American outlook. The sharp grass-roots reaction has served notice that a long look is needed at the vanishing religious and moral traditions in public life. American policy-makers have been hitting toward left field so sharply (if we may borrow a metaphor from baseball) that more and more citizens are now crying "foul!"

A comprehensive insight into the Supreme Court's views on church-state separation cannot, however, be drawn merely from this narrow strip of decision. The nation's highest judiciary must yet rule on important cases originating in Maryland and Pennsylvania. Most imperative will be an enunciation by the Supreme Court of guiding principles that will prevent both anti-religious government and sectarian government. If the Supreme Court is unable to draw a consistent line between the wholly godless state and a state religion, then the nation needs a new team of umpires.

Editorial   July 20, 1962

42 *Measurements*

LESLIE SAVAGE CLARK

How poor, how paltry seems the goal
Of a missile's little span,
When the heights of heaven may be scaled
By the prayers of man.

April 28, 1958

43 *Resurgent Evangelical Leadership*

HAROLD JOHN OCKENGA

What the Communist party is in the vanguard of the world revolution, the evangelical movement must be in the world revival.

What is an evangelical? An evangelical is a Christian "holding or conformed to what the majority of Protestants regard as the fundamental doctrines of the Gospel, such as the Trinity, the fallen condition of man, Christ's atonement for sin, salvation by faith, not works, and regeneration by the Holy Ghost." A subsidiary definition is "in a special sense, spiritually minded and zealous for practical Christian living, distinguished from merely orthodox." Another secondary definition is "seeking the conversion of sinners, as evangelical labors or preaching."

The doctrinal position of an evangelical is that of orthodox or creedal Christianity. This doctrinal basis is stated in the incorporation papers of the Church, namely the New Testament, and in the great creeds and confessions of Christendom. It is the Chalcedonian Creed and the later Reformed confessions such as those of Heidelberg, Augsburg, and Westminster. Only those who embrace these objective truths have the right to the name evangelical.

Evangelical Christianity should be differentiated from other movements. First, it must be differentiated from Roman Catholicism, or sacerdotal Christianity, which emphasizes a salvation mediated by sacraments and erected on tradition rather than on the Word of God. Second, it must be distinguished from liberal or modernist Christianity. Many modernists appropriate the name evangelical merely because they are non-Roman Catholic, but do not embrace the basic truths of historic orthodoxy. It is a misnomer to call a modernist an evangelical. Third, an evangelical must be distinguished from a fundamentalist in areas of intellectual and ecclesiastical attitude. This distinction was made by Dr. J. Gresham Machen, who was often called a fundamentalist. Said he, "The term fundamentalism is distasteful to the present writer and to many persons who hold views similar to his. It seems to suggest that we are adherents of some strange new sect, whereas in point of fact we are conscious simply of maintaining historic Christian faith and moving in the great central current of Christian life" (cf. *Valiant for Truth,* by Ned B. Stonehouse, pp. 40, 337, 343, 405, 428).

The evangelical depends upon the Bible as the authoritative Word of God and the norm of judgment in faith and practice. This brings him into tension with Romanism which, while giving lip service to the Bible, exalts tradition and papal infallibility above the Bible; with modernism which exalts the autonomy of the human mind; and with neo-orthodoxy which identifies the Word of God with something above and beyond the Bible but witnessed to in the Bible.

Has evangelicalism fallen into eclipse? The history of the last five decades has been largely under the aegis of a triumphant modernism. Basically, modernism is evolutionary naturalism applied to the Bible and to Christianity. By it the supernatural in the origins and nature of Christianity was sacrificed by the accommodation of Christian theology to the data of the scientific method and the dicta of the scientific mind. Hence, by presupposition, there could be no Virgin Birth, no miracles, and no Resurrection as the Bible taught. Modernism was based on higher criticism's view of the Bible. The books are redated in accordance with evolutionary naturalism; ethical monotheism is tolerated only later than polytheism, and the writing of the prophetic sections is placed after the events. Modernism developed a new theology concerning Christ, man, sin, salvation, the Church, and the Church's mission.

Against this came the fundamentalist reaction. The name fundamentalist was derived from a series of treatises written by leading orthodox scholars on various biblical doctrines and published in 1909 by the Bible Institute of Los Angeles with the aid of Lyman and Milton Stewart. The contributors to *The Fundamentals* were men like Melvin Grove Kyle, James Orr, George Robinson, W. H. Griffith Thomas, F. Bettex, George Frederick Wright, and others, all recognized biblical scholars of their day. The resistance to modernist attack upon biblical Christianity precipitated the modernist-fundamentalist controversy which raged for several decades following publication of *The Fundamentals.* This reached its height in the successful effort of the Presbyterians, led by Clarence Edward Macartney, to oust Harry Emerson Fosdick from the pulpit of a Presbyterian church in New York City. In the controversy there arose the emphasis upon the essentials or fundamentals of the Christian faith, such as the inspiration of the Scriptures, the Virgin Birth, the miracles of Christ, the vicarious atonement of Christ, and the bodily resurrection of Christ. What happened in the Presbyterian church repeated itself in almost every other denomination, and the Protestant Church was divided between modernists and fundamentalists.

Time revealed certain weaknesses in the fundamentalist cause. First was the diversion of strength from the great offensive work of missions, evangelism, and Christian education to the defense of the faith. The fundamentalists were maneuvered into the position of holding the line against the constant and unremitting attacks of the modernists or liberals. Gradually the liberals took over the control of the denominations and began a series of acts of discrimination, ostracism, and persecution of the evangelicals. Many evangelicals suffered at the hands of ecclesiastical modernism. This reduced fundamentalism to a holding tactic, impotent in denominational machinery and indifferent to societal problems rising in the secular world.

The cause of the fundamentalist defeat on the ecclesiastical scene lay partially in fundamentalism's erroneous doctrine of the Church which identified the Church with believers who were orthodox in doctrine and separatist in ethics. Purity of the Church was emphasized above the peace of the Church. Second Corinthians 6:14-17 was used to justify the continuous process of fragmentation, contrary to the meaning of the passage itself. Emphasis was upon contention for the faith rather than missions, evangelism, education, and worship. The number of competent scholars declined in evangelical ranks as the decades passed.

Then came the rise of neo-orthodoxy under the influence of Karl Barth and Emil Brunner, in which theology professed a return to biblical concepts without the acceptance of biblical authority. Neo-orthodoxy accepted the Word of God as revelation but differentiated this from the written Word. It spoke about the creation of man but repudiated the historical Adam. Due to the aridity of modernism and a nostalgia of people for biblical ideas concerning God, man, sin, and redemption, the influence of neo-orthodoxy grew rapidly. Nevertheless, its attitude toward evangelical Christianity is essentially hostile because of its refusal to accept the biblical authority as the ground of its theology. The watershed of modern theology remains one's attitude toward the Bible as the ultimate and final authority for faith and action.

Is evangelicalism reviving? Is it emerging to challenge the theological world today? A new respect for the evangelical position is evidenced by the emergence of scholars whose works must be recognized. The younger orthodox scholars are repudiating the separatist position, have repented of the attitude of solipsism, have expressed a willingness to re-examine the problems facing the theological world, have sought a return to the theological dialogue and have recognized the honesty and Christianity of some who hold views different from their own in some particulars.

Simultaneously, all branches of theological thought have felt the impact of mass evangelism under Billy Graham. In him we have seen the phenomenon of an evangelical who crossed all theological lines in his work while maintaining a strictly orthodox position. His work has not been disregarded by those of other theological convictions and has compelled them to rethink the basis of their approach.

Evangelical theology is synonymous with fundamentalism or orthodoxy. In doctrine the evangelicals and the fundamentalists are one. The evangelical must acknowledge his debt to the older fundamentalist leaders. It is a mistake for an evangelical to divorce himself from historic fundamentalism as some have sought to do. The older leaders of the orthodox cause paid a great price in persecution, discrimination, obloquy, and scorn which they suffered at the hands of those who under the name of modernism repudiated biblical Christianity. For decades these fundamentalists were steadfast to Christ and to biblical truth regardless of the cost. They maintained the knowledge of orthodox Christianity through Bible schools, radio programs, Christian conferences, and Bible conferences. In the true New Testament sense, they were witnesses, or martyrs. Most of these leaders, men such as James M. Gray, Lewis Sperry Chafer, Arno C. Gaebelein, Harry Ironside, J. Gresham Macheu, J. Alvin Orr, Clarence Edward Macartney, Walter A. Maier, Robert Dick Wilson, W. B. Riley, and Oswald T. Allis, were known to me. They were great defenders of the faith.

The evangelical defense of the faith theologically is identical with that of the older fundamentalists. The evangelical believes in creedal Christianity, in the apologetic expression of Christianity, in the revelational content and framework of Christianity. Therefore, he stands by the side of these fundamentalist leaders. He differentiates his position from theirs in ecclesiology. These men were driven by controversy and discrimination to various shades of separatism. Some were compelled to leave their denominations, some operated as autonomous units within their denominations. Through controversy, in suffering, they sired a breed of fundamentalists who, in following them, confused courtesy in contending for the faith with compromise of the faith;

academic respectability with theological apostasy; and common grace with special grace. They developed the theory that any contact, conversation, or communication with modernism was compromise and should be condemned.

Let it be repeated that there is a solidarity of doctrine between fundamentalism and evangelicalism. Moreover, they have a common source of life, for they belong to one family. Christian life comes from the Christian faith and cannot be divorced from it. The repudiation of Christian truth cannot eventuate in a Christian life. In this the evangelical stands with the fundamentalist. But the evangelical goes a bit further and condemns doctrinal orthodoxy which does not result in a life of love and service. The test which Jesus gave to his disciples was that of brotherly love but it was given in the framework of an acceptance of his Deity, his miracles, his Messiahship, and his imminent death as Saviour. If, therefore, the fundamentalist criticizes the evangelical or vice versa, that criticism should be within the family relationship and demonstrate the spirit and attitude of love which is a test of true discipleship.

The evangelical has general objectives he wishes to see achieved. One of them is a revival of Christianity in the midst of a secular world. The world is helpless in the presence of its problems. Its attempt at solutions totally disregards the orthodox message and answer. The evangelical wishes to retrieve Christianity from a mere eddy of the mainstream into the full current of modern life. He desires to win a new respectability for orthodoxy in the academic circles by producing scholars who can defend the faith on intellectual ground. He hopes to recapture denominational leadership from within the denominations rather than abandoning those denominations to modernism. He intends to restate his position carefully and cogently so that it must be considered in the theological dialogue. He intends that Christianity will be the mainspring in many of the reforms of the societal order. It is wrong to abdicate responsibility for society under the impetus of a theology which overemphasizes the eschatalogical.

The specific goals of evangelicalism are definite. It seeks evangelical cooperation. This was expressed in the formation of the National Association of Evangelicals in 1942. The NAE insisted on a positive position toward the then Federal Council of Churches and later National Council in distinction from the position later adopted by the American Council of Christian Churches. The NAE gathered evangelicals in fellowship for articulation of the evangelical cause in a score of different fields without attack upon other cooperative movements of diverse theology. It summoned together a fellowship in action of many of those denominations not in the Federal Council, and for the first time it gave them a sense of unity and strength. Many individual congregations whose denominations were in the Federal Council of Churches were received into the NAE in order to articulate their convictions and give them an opportunity of cooperative action on an evangelical and orthodox base. The influence of this movement was great. While the parent organization of the National Association of Evangelicals has not reached a numerical strength which some had expected for it, it nevertheless has stimulated many subsidiary movements which originated as commissions within the National Association or were bound together with the National Association. Many of these are powerful organizations and movements in their own right, such as the National Sunday School Association, the National Radio Broadcasters, the Evangelical Foreign Missions Association, Youth for Christ, World Evangelical Fellowship, and other related movements such as Child Evangelism Fellowship and Inter-Varsity Christian Fellowship. It was the parallel organizations to the NAE in England, India, and other areas that sparked the great Billy Graham campaigns in other parts of the world. Thus, the influence of the NAE has been far greater than its numerical strength.

Another objective was the training and feeding of evangelical ministers into the churches. Since the seminaries determine the course of the Church, it was felt necessary to fortify existing evangelical seminaries with additional professors and funds. As a result, several new evangelical seminaries were established. Here was adopted a positive attitude in inquiry, teaching, and proclamation of biblical Christianity. The students who passed through this training came forth with a certainty and knowledge expressed by "Thus saith the Lord" and with a practical program joined with a passion. In addition, there was inculcated an understanding of the connection of Christian principles with political and economic freedom.

It was the intention of evangelical strategy to reach evangelical churches who were pastored by ministers uncertain in their theological conviction. To reach these ministers with the rationale of biblical Christianity is the objective of *Christianity Today*.

An up-to-date strategy for the evangelical cause must be based upon the principle of infiltration. We evangelicals need to realize that the liberals, or modernists, have been using this strategy for years. They have infiltrated our evangelical denominations, institutions, and movements and then have taken over the control of them. It is time for firm evangelicals to seize their opportunity to minister in and influence modernist groups. Why is it incredible that the evangelicals should be able to infiltrate the denominations and strengthen the things that remain, and possibly resume control of such denominations? Certainly they have a responsibility to do so, unless they are expelled from those denominations. We do not repudiate the Reformation principle, but we believe that a man has a responsibility within his denomination unless that denomination has officially and overtly repudiated biblical Christianity.

Evangelicals need a plan of action. The pressing demand is for an over-all strategy instead of piecemeal action by fragmentized groups. The younger evangelicals are determined to join hands with evangelicals everywhere in testimony and in action. They want to defend and maintain the institutions, endowments, and organizations which remain within the evangelical theological position.

It demands that each one of us make a personal commitment. We should examine our activities to make sure that we are engaged in intelligent service. Let us ask ourselves: What is this organization accomplishing? Does this organization fit in with God's plan? Is this movement advancing God's cause? We must take an inventory of our investment of money. It is folly for businessmen and foundations to support institutions, movement, and individuals which subvert that for which the businessmen and foundations stand. This is paramountly true in Christian organizations. It is our responsibility to implement the strategy of evangelicalism by personal commitment.

An evangelical makes no apology in asking the help of convinced and committed Christians. This commitment is essential in developing evangelical leadership. Every evangelical should find his place in the implementation of the modern evangelical resurgence in Christianity.

Article   October 10, 1960

44 *The Assassination of the President*

A shot came out of nowhere and changed a thousand things around the world. An unknown assassin brought sudden and tragic end to the life of a world-renowned figure; John F. Kennedy was dead by the hand of an evil man whom nobody knew, and who will be known only as long as his infamy is remembered. Three months before a father laid his infant son to rest; he now lies down to rest beside him.

In one tragic moment, an unexpected event changed the plans and hopes of many people and of a nation. Strategies devised with an eye to next year's presidential elections were suddenly obsolete. The whole civil rights issue at once took on new but unknown dimensions.

Lyndon B. Johnson, who had hoped for the office of President and had seen his hopes vanish like a bubble in the rough conflicts of politics, was by unforeseen tragedy and no plans of his own the President of the United States. So little, one shot, by one unknown man, changed so much. The President's death was not only a national tragedy but an event of great international significance. The fragile fabric of personal diplomacy patiently built up by Kennedy and Khrushchev was broken by the same evil that broke his life.

While the news that President Kennedy had been shot was flashed around the world, the White House paradoxically appeared as quiet as the eye of a storm. The usual traffic moved slowly on Pennsylvania Avenue and the usual number of people walked the broad sidewalks in front of the White House. During the 35 minutes that the fallen President lay dying in a Dallas hospital, three men gathered dead leaves and leisurely loaded them into a truck that stood on the circular drive that fronts the White House. The whirring blades of a helicopter could be seen above the grass in the back of what was the Kennedy home. Here of all places everything looked normal on this warm, gray, November day. But suddenly a flag was quietly lowered to half mast above the white mansion. Others on surrounding public buildings were similarly lowered, and the eye received the message that the mind found impossible to believe. The President was dead.

America lost a man of great intellectual gifts, a President of strong courage and of great political imagination. Kennedy had kept his promise to the nation and had held the line on the church-state issue. And whatever one may feel about his civil rights stand, he held it with integrity and undeviating moral conviction, even when it threatened to be politically disadvantageous. Men of good will long will pay him tribute and the nation long will sorrow for such a man, cut down in the strength of his years and the height of his service.

As night fell on the Capital, the shriek of a traffic officer's whistle arose from the now snarled traffic, and the White House loomed in the deepening night, all dark within, the only lights those illuminating the portico outside. A similar darkness fell over the hearts of a nation. For the moment there is no light within, only sadness at such tragedy, and a dumb perplexity at so absurd and ugly an evil.

One of the eye-witnesses to the assassination was a 25-year-old senior at Dallas Theological Seminary, Malcolm Couch, a television cameraman who was riding in one of the cars following the President's. Couch saw the President slump as a rifle was pulled in from a window overlooking the street. The President's car then sped to a hospital.

Concerned Christians sympathize not only with Mrs. Kennedy and the two youngsters, but with the late President's father and mother, his brothers and sisters. The Joseph P. Kennedy family, known to be so closely knit, has through the years experienced many deep sorrows, including the World War II deaths of Joseph P. Kennedy, Jr., and a son-in-law, the Marquess of Hartington, and only last summer the death of the infant Patrick Bouvier Kennedy.

Seven blocks away from the White House is old Ford's Theater, now a Lincoln museum, which yet stands as mute testimony to the hazards of public service—particularly in times of national division and strife. Lincoln, Garfield, McKinley . . . and now John Kennedy. Believers in man's upward progress could be tempted to point to the lessening frequency of U.S. presidential assassinations as symbolic of their dreams, for the last instance was the 1901 shooting of William McKinley. But before one could relegate such phenomena to the shadows of the nineteenth century—giving way to the "glorious light" of the twentieth—he would have to ponder the attempts on the lives of Franklin Roosevelt in Miami and Harry Truman at Blair House.

The assassin represents the temporary breakdown of the democratic process. With a single move of his index finger he annuls the decision of millions of voters. A dark spot in his brain vetoes carefully thought out decisions of national leaders.

But the democratic process makes allowances for the exigency. We now have a new President. We are grateful for belated progress in our system which has resulted in more careful thought being given to the qualities of vice-presidential candidates. A recent example is the warning that President Eisenhower's illnesses carried for the 1960 conventions of both major political parties, who nominated eminent and politically-experienced candidates for the vice-presidency.

Thus an illness has left us a legacy. Such a turn of events could also well leave us a reminder of the providence of which our forefathers so often spoke. We sing of a God who is both sovereign and loving, a God who brings good from evil, a God who moves in a mysterious way, a God who rides upon the storm:

> Behind a frowning providence
> He hides a smiling face.

Let Christians pray for the bereaved; let them pray for the recovery of Governor Connally; let them hold up the arms of President Lyndon B. Johnson in prayer, that the nation may experience a new unity in time of crisis. There are cruel foes without; there are agonizing problems within. God grant that the Psalmist's affirmation become our own: "Some trust in chariots, and some in horses: But we will remember the name of the Lord our God."

Editorial   December 6, 1963

45 *Lee Oswald: His Mother's Story*

J I M M I E   R .   C O X

A *Christianity Today* news correspondent was the first to obtain an extended interview with the mother of Lee Harvey Oswald. No effort was made to evaluate her statement, which is left to the verdict of history.

Mrs. Marguerite Oswald, mother of the man accused of the assassination of President Kennedy, tried under difficult circumstances to provide religious training for her three sons.

Her own parents were of different faiths. Her father, a Roman Catholic, permitted her mother to oversee the religious upbringing of the family. Her mother, a Lutheran, had Mrs. Oswald baptized in a Missouri Synod Lutheran church in New Orleans where she also was confirmed at the age of twelve.

When Lee Harvey Oswald was born on October 18, 1939, his father, Robert E. Lee Oswald, had been dead for two months. Although the elder Oswald had been an insurance salesman, he had insured himself for only $3,500. The only other money available to the widow was a small sum from the sale of the equity in the family home.

Like his mother, the infant Lee was baptized in a Missouri Synod Lutheran church in New Orleans. He was never confirmed.

Mrs. Oswald attempted to stay at home and rear her family but eventually was forced to go to work. She paid a maid to care for the children for a time, but when World War II came, she had to make other arrangements. The older two sons she placed in a Lutheran institution which accepted children having only one parent. She said she was expected to pay whatever circumstances would permit.

But Lee was too young to enter the church home. Mrs. Oswald said she had no choice but to leave him to the care of a sister, who also lived in New Orleans, and to hire other attendants for him whenever possible.

"The older boys received a wonderful religious education," Mrs. Oswald declared, pointing out that Lutherans also operated a school in connection with the children's home. But Lee was not accepted until he was three and remained in the institution only two years.

At this time, Mrs. Oswald remarried and moved with her second husband to Fort Worth. She took Lee with her and had the other two sons enrolled in a military academy. But the second marriage ended in divorce after only eight or nine months.

Mrs. Oswald remained in Fort Worth, working and sending her sons to school until Lee's next oldest brother, Robert Oswald, entered the service. She then moved to New York to be near Robert and his wife.

"I wanted to have someone in the family to care for Lee while I worked," she said. Lee then was eleven.

Immediately on moving to New York she enrolled Lee in a Lutheran school. It was an hour and a half, subway time, from their home, however, and she later moved to the Bronx, where Lee attended public school. A psychiatric report at that time is said to have considered Lee "dangerous," but Mrs. Oswald refused to discuss it.

Mrs. Oswald moved back to New Orleans with Lee toward the war's end, again so that she could be near a relative, her sister. When Robert Oswald received his discharge from the service, he wanted to return to Fort Worth, and Mrs. Oswald, with Lee, moved there, too, in July, 1956.

In October of the same year, Lee, then seventeen, joined the Marine Corps, thus beginning the turbulent career that ended in a tragedy which stunned the world.

"In every place we lived," Mrs. Oswald insisted, "I always tried to be with my children. I was an active worker in my church in New Orleans before Lee was born, and as he was growing up I would try to see that he attended Sunday school and church."

She said she was not able to attend regularly because of the necessity that she work for her children's livelihood. At this point she commented somewhat bitterly on the attitude of some professing Christians toward her during her struggle to provide for her family.

"I don't remember ever being visited by a minister or anyone representing a church during all that time, as we moved from one city to another." She allowed, however, that perhaps church people were unable to contact her because she worked long and irregular hours.

Nevertheless, she added: "Some good people were very thoughtless and inconsiderate. They wouldn't think of missing church on Sunday, but they would expect me to have Sunday dinner ready for them when they returned."

In spite of this, and all that has happened, however, Mrs. Oswald asserts that her own faith in God has remained unshaken, and if anything, has been strengthened.

In the week following Lee's arrest for the assassination of the President, she received more than 400 letters from all parts of the United States and even from foreign countries. Many of the letters have been from Christians—some quoting Scriptures of comfort to the distressed, others offering sympathy and material assistance both to the mother and to her dead son's Russian-born wife and two children.

"I know that my son was not an atheist," Mrs. Oswald declared. She recounted an incident that occurred shortly after his return to the United States after three years in the Soviet Union. His wife, who could speak no English, brought a double picture frame to his mother. One side held a picture, taken in Russia, of the young couple with their child, June. In the other side was a print of "Christ and the Child." Pointing to her daughter, then to the painting of Jesus, she indicated in sign language and broken English that she wanted the child baptized.

Mrs. Oswald said Lee asked her to make arrangements for the baptism to be performed at a Lutheran church in a public ceremony. He later decided not to go through with the ceremony on grounds that a financial contribution usually was expected from the parents of children when they were christened.

"At the time," said Mrs. Oswald, "he didn't even have money to buy food and clothing for his family."

Lee Oswald's wife later had the christening performed in an Eastern Orthodox church in Dallas. The clergyman who performed the rite has been quoted as saying that it was done without Lee's knowledge.

Mrs. Oswald said that on returning to her apartment in Fort Worth after her son's burial, she found cards in her door from ministers of many denominations offering to make themselves available to assist her in any way possible. She said she was disappointed and grieved by the attitude of some persons, however, among them close acquaintances who remained aloof and showed no concern for her during her moment of greatest trial. A few persons were reportedly upset because her son was buried in the same cemetery with their deceased kin.

Mrs. Oswald still maintains that her son was innocent of the murder of the President, despite the evidence compiled against him.

She says, too, that she has no worries about the future. She recalls the words her minister spoke to her at the burial of her first husband. In answer to her question about why her husband had been taken, the minister replied, "You know that we can't ask such things. Never question the will of God."

"I did not question his will then and I do not question it now," says Mrs. Oswald. "I know that things will be worked out according to God's purpose."

News   December 20, 1963

46 *As It Would Look from the Wall*

During the last days of November the American people had a singular opportunity to see what a wall of absolute separation of government and religion would be like in actual practice. What a cold and bleak thing it would have been if no religious act or sentiment could have come from men in high places of government!

In the academic halls of debate aloof from the actualities of life, the proponents of absolute separation of government and religion achieve a persuasiveness more doctrinaire than real. Had all religious expression been prohibited, how remote the government would have been from the deep grief of the Kennedy family, and how far from the hearts and feelings of the American people.

It is easy to theorize oneself out of existence. A heady reflection can propose positions that are credible only in the cool realms of abstractionism. Hegel was a worthy opponent in debate; yet a single fragment of existence could fell his system, as Kierkegaard annoyingly demonstrated when he pointed out that Hegel denied his system every time he reached for his handkerchief to cover a sneeze.

Had the proponents of absolute separation chosen to urge their interpretation of the First Amendment upon the American people while the late President lay dying in a Dallas hospital, they would have found an unsympathetic audience. Had they insisted that religion must be wholly excluded from government at the time President Johnson assumed the awful responsibilities of his office and on television requested Americans to pray God to sustain him, they would have put their position to the test where America lives. This is a question, not of sentiment, but of testing a theory in the realm where its supporters propose to make it operative.

Raise the question where Americans actually live and few would agree that a prayer in Congress, or a congressional appeal for prayer for a dying President, is something that the Constitution forbids.

Forty-five minutes on the afternoon of November 22 shattered the theory that the American people want every religious dimension shut off from government by an absolute wall of separation. When they respond out of the actualities of their national life, they do not believe that the Constitution requires absolute separation for the protection of the rights of those who believe there is no God.

It is rarely recognized that only atheists and those who deny the efficacy of prayer can urge an absolute separation of government and religion. He who believes that God hears and answers prayer, by his very prayer invites the Almighty to enter the area of government.

Editorial   December 20, 1963

47   *A Time for Moral Indignation*

Americans are having sex thrust upon them every waking hour of their day. This is not done by "the girl next door." Whoever she may be, her power to project sex was never equal to the massive bombardment that hits Americans today before, after, and between meals. In the judgment of Malcolm Muggeridge, America is the most sex-ridden country in the history of the world (*Esquire,* February, 1965).

Our modern media of communications—newspapers, magazines,

books, movies, advertising, radio, and television—have made possible this unparalleled degree of mass saturation. Sex precipitates from the national atmosphere and drips into every nook and cranny of the land. Modern technology has made sex omnipresent; there is today no escape from it. Even if a person takes wings and flies to the other side of the land, he will behold the movie offerings on the seat ahead, or at the end of the cabin.

Without this massive projection of sex by our impersonal media of modern communications, we would not have our national, impersonal sex symbols. When the projection of sex depended on the girl next door, sex was not divorced from the human person. Under these circumstances sex could never be a mere symbol. But thanks to modern communications, we now have national, impersonal sexual images that are mere sex symbols; the nameless nude, the fictional Lady Chatterley or Candy, the television and movie actress whom 95 per cent of the viewers have never really seen, let alone spoken to. This or that segment of a woman's body, divorced from her person and known only impersonally on paper or screen, becomes the mental image of what sex is or can be. Although such people are often not in their private lives what their public image suggests, this does not prevent millions of Americans from pursuing these faceless, fleshless symbols. Our expansive technological amplification of communication has done what the girl next door could never do: project an omnipresently haunting, but always elusive and retreating, sexual attraction.

Nor was the girl next door ever able to impart to sex a symbolic religious significance. The very presence and limits of her personality prevented her from becoming a sex symbol with religious dimensions and aura. Only an impersonal projection of sex can turn it into such a religious symbol, into a goddess. Muggeridge suggests that the ultimate experience of sex "has replaced the Cross as the focus of longing and the image of fulfillment."

This separation of sex from the human personality and its impersonal projection through modern modes of communication has produced what has become an object of pagan veneration. "Instead of the cult of the Virgin Mary, we have," says Muggeridge, "the cult of the sex symbol . . . a Marilyn Monroe or a Jean Harlow, displayed in glossy photographs, on cinema and television screens." That these women are dead does not destroy the symbol; the symbol was always ephemeral. The person dies but the symbol lives on, for the symbol was always impersonal. This provides the motive for the current attempt to return Jean Harlow to the screen in a new movie. Had she not been an impersonal symbol, the public would find it repulsive to find entertainment in the charms of a dead woman.

Dangle the impersonal, emptied sex symbol before the modern sex-ridden mentality and it is pursued like a tin rabbit on a dog track. One result is that no society pursues sex more than our own and yet none enjoys it so little. No normal sexual experience manages to catch the elusive pleasure the symbol promises. The accumulated disillusionments consequently send the unsatisfied devotee into more frantic pursuit, passing from one sexual conquest unfulfilled to another, from one husband or wife to the next, ever goaded on by a sense of having missed that religious fulfillment the impersonal sex symbol always promises but never gives. When the disillusionment is complete, the heterosexual is often abandoned for the homosexual experience in the sordid, forlorn hope that perhaps the never-never exquisite experience has been sought in the wrong place.

A second result of this exaltation of depersonalized sex into what can only be regarded as an idolatrous religious symbol is that while the allurement of sex is enhanced, the arrestive restrictions are removed. When sex is confronted in the girl next door, its very embodiment in her person acts as a restraining influence upon sexual abandon; no matter how uninhibitedly she projects her sexuality she, by the very fact that she is a person, arrests what she induces.

In short, all the next-door girls in America could not achieve that mass sex saturation of our national mind which has now been brought about by the application of technology to sex.

Americans have become victims of their own media of communications. Victims, because sex is not a symbol; sex is what we are: "Male and female created he them." We have raised sex to the status of an idol; by impersonalizing sex we have depersonalized ourselves. As the Psalmist said long ago about idol makers: "They that make them shall be like unto them."

This process of self-victimization with all its untallied human misery, frustration, divorce, crime, and dirtying of the human spirit will not stop of itself. There will always be more than enough people willing to commercialize sex and exploit it to whatever degree serves their financial purposes.

If we are to free ourselves, we must recognize first of all that the freedom to project sex upon the public mind, whether by author, publisher, advertiser, or movie or television producer, is a limited freedom. Both sex and freedom of expression are good, but when stripped of all limitations, they become fetishes that are destructive of society. Unless we recognize that there are limits, we render ourselves helpless. When "anything goes" in sex and freedom of expression, it is society that finally goes.

It is doubtful that additional legislation would be helpful. Nevertheless we must rid ourselves of the ridiculous notion that because no one can define obscenity with absolute legal precision, no legal regulation of obscenity is possible or enforceable. No one can precisely define a cow either; yet we have laws regulating the buying, selling, and keeping of cows. Indeed, there are few things that can be so precisely defined by law that frequent recourse need not be taken to the courts for precise application and judicial decision. Is indeed obscenity so hard to recognize that even in its baldest forms we cannot detect it? Large piles of *Candy* are currently on sale on many newsstands. Have we become so sophisticated about the legal niceties of freedom and about the academic precision of moral definitions that we are unable to protect the youth of America from a book that, while ostensibly satirizing the sex novel, contains an extended and minute description of the process of seduction? It is often pointed out that in the last analysis the laws of our society embody the standards that the people accept. Yet there are many publications on the market that the great majority of Americans would reject as utterly vulgar; common decency can often make better moral judgments than we are able to codify in our laws and enforce in our courts. Admittedly, the line between law and freedom is a delicate one. Yet delicate though it is, there are many areas of life in which we recognize limitations upon freedom of expression, and there is no principal reason either in law or in freedom why a delicate balance of these two cannot be achieved in the area of freedom of sexual expression.

What America's present moral situation requires even more than laws and their enforcement is the arousal of a tidal wave of righteous moral indignation against a wanton exploitation of sex. There are signs that such an indignation is smoldering beneath the surface. Every American dedicated to common decency must become morally indignant and let this indignation burn righteously in an articulate protest against an exploitation of sex that is unparalleled in the history of the world. Never before in human civilization has sex been so pervasively prostituted to financial gain, for the technological possibilities were not present until our time. Public opinion is still a powerful force for public righteousness. It can outshout all the sounds of modern communication if it finds its voice and in moral indignation lifts it high.

The millions of Christians in America have a special duty. They know that when anything becomes a national idol, it is because God has first been displaced and his moral law set aside. The final resolution lies with God, who alone can give purity of heart. But until such a time, Christians are summoned to reflect his holy wrath against every unclean thing. It will be a shameful thing if the secular moral conscience voices its indignation against a glaring evil first and is belatedly joined by the millions of Christians in America, who will then sound only like an echo.

Editorial   March 12, 1965

48 *To John Knox*

SHERWOOD ELIOT WIRT

Gentler spirits have lived
in Christendom,
More gracious messengers preached
The Word of Christ
without a-dinging the pulpit,
But God knew what He was doing
when He chose you
to build his Church.

He knew the temptations to compromise,
the dulcet voice pleading in tears
the soft hand of scheming sovereignty.
You were keen as steel,
As deaf as ice:
God's man
for God's work
in God's time.

April 25, 1960

49 *May It Not Die in Vain*

JAMES DAANE

A review of *The Gospel of Christian Atheism,* by Thomas J. J. Altizer (Westminster, 1966).

This book goes a long way toward clarifying what is meant by the death of God, and what radical theology is asserting in its attempt to formulate an atheism within the possibilities of the Christian perspective.

God once existed; but he created a world, became incarnate, and died in our history, and this divine self-annihilation for the sake of man was not followed by a resurrection. There is, therefore, no longer a transcendent sovereign Lord above and beyond the movements of life and history, no God to whom we can return, no Eternal who is our eternal dwelling place. He once was, but he actually died and is no more. This is the meaning of the name of Jesus, which the radical theologians want to retain. The traditional idea of a Christ who is God, who rose again from the dead, and who by granting forgiveness of sin and guilt returns us to God and to the primordial state of innocence, carries with it a No-saying to the movements and vitalities of life and history. This Christ must therefore be surrendered. But the name of Jesus, which bespeaks an incarnation, an authentic kenosis, and the death of God, releases us from that repressive sense of a Fall from an initial state of innocence and opens up the possibility of a Yes-saying both to the self and to the vitalities and movements of the history and world in which we live.

Altizer, of course, has no true knowledge or hearty confidence that God has actually died, and he admits it. One must assume the risk of life, he says, and take a chance either on the classical Son of God, the Christ of the historical Church, or on the Jesus who bespeaks the actual death of God. Altizer takes his chance on this Jesus. Why? Does his sense of guilt, of damnation and hell become more bearable if the final Judge is dead? This is not a facetious question, for Altizer is no smiling liberal who sees no evidence of hell and damnation. He recognizes that artists and poets today speak more about damnation and hell than do most men of the pulpit—a fact he bitingly adduces to show that even the Church does not take seriously the old view of God and the world. Altizer, however, wagers on the Jesus-of-the-death-of-God as the more likely winner, since the Church's image of the traditional Christ returns man to an antecedent living God and to a primordial state of innocence, thereby demanding a negation of life and of the forward movements of history.

Altizer urges that mankind's historical consciousness is only two hundred years old and that the awareness of what this consciousness means has progressed from Blake, Nietzsche, and Hegel to the point where today men are beginning to see that God is truly dead and that traditional Christianity is utterly meaningless to the modern man. "Ours," he says, "is the first form of consciousness and experience that has evolved after the full historical realization of the death of God." The Christian who today "chooses the orthodox image of Christ is making a wager in which he stands to forfeit all the life and energy of a world that is totally alien to the Church's Christ."

Needless to say, the Christian atheism of the radical theologians does not emerge in continuity with the Christianity of the past. Altizer's radical theology is as new as the affirmation within Christianity that God is dead. It is essentially anti-Christ, a quite new, free-wheeling, and impulsive syncretion of psychology, oriental mysticism, and an inverted definition of Christianity's kenotic incarnation. Altizer's point of departure is not revelation but wager, a wager dictated by the current common error of allowing human existence to formulate the questions to which revelation must perforce give the fitting answer. Evangelicals should realize much more than they do that this method, made impressive by Paul Tillich, is followed not only by today's radical theologians but also by those confessed Christians of the pulpit who reduce Christianity to nothing more than a remedy for human need.

In classical Christianity, God came in the form of a servant to serve human need but in becoming a servant remained God. In radical theology, God serves man and in so doing dies and ceases to be. In some liberal versions, Christianity is merely something that meets all human needs and solves all human problems. Some more "orthodox" versions say that man must first learn to know that he is a sinner before Christianity's Saviour has relevance. In both kinds—as in the radical theology of Altizer—God is meaningful only within a life-situation and must therefore be reduced to the terms of the situation's demands and needs. In Altizer, and in these liberal and conservative views, God must serve man, even if he must die to do so.

Robert McAfee Brown says that *The Gospel of Christian Atheism* is neither gospel, nor Christian, nor atheism, and that its attempt to celebrate the death of God only demonstrates the "death of the 'death-of-God theology.' " But before it dies one could wish that liberal and conservative ministers and theologians who have unwittingly succumbed to its method would see the reflection of this method within their own theologies. Its balder expression in Altizer could serve to enlighten both. If it does, the death-of-God theology will not have lived in vain. For all who reduce the truth of God in Christ to a mere remedy for human need are unwittingly committed to a theological method that leads to the death of God. For the God who is no more than a servant of human need is not God.

Book Review   June 24, 1966

50   *Ecclesian: Lesson 1*

EDMUND P. CLOWNEY

This is your first language lesson in Modern Ecclesian. (Dialectical Eglisais and Kirchendeutsch are available also.) You may supplement these exercises by attending selected churches and by reading journals written in Ecclesian.

1. Translate from the Ecclesian:

a. By developing new perspectives in creative tension we shall gain fresh insights into the dialectic of our situation.

b. Our fundamental concern must always be the existential expression of our common solidarity in the ambiguity of the human condition.

c. Openness in history to the judgment upon history from beyond history when the historic becomes historical demands a meaningful encounter with mythological symbolization.

d. This is deep. This is big. This is man in his predicament. Today. Here. This is you. Now.

2. Render these in simple Ecclesian:

a. I have a headache.

b. You can't get there from here.

    c. Peace, it's unbearable!
    d. Fairy tales are really true.

3. Vocabulary
Develop: to rarefy ambiguities in thought or discussion. Loan-word from Business Eng.; used especially for committee reports.
Perspective: the horizontal structure from a given viewpoint. An invaluable term for reconciling contradictions. The plurality of perspectives is the structuring figure for unitive prose.
Dimension: see perspective. To give further perspective to all perspectives, add another dimension.
Insight, invaluable: the force of the prefix seems to be without, as in the term income.
The Human Condition: the mess we take pride in being in.

4. Notes
    a. Observe the shift in style in 1.d. above. This is Low Ecclesian. The staccato rhythm of this dialect gives it the relevance and immediacy of a dentist's drill.
    b. To enter into competition for the Babel Medal in High Ecclesian, send your completed lesson to this magazine, addressed to the undersigned.

Eutychus   September 16, 1957

51 *Outburst of Tongues:*
The New Penetration

FRANK FARRELL

In ancient Corinth today, seven Doric columns look down upon the tumbled debris of a once great city. At Caesarea marble pillars lie desolate on the shore of a formerly magnificent harbor. Above the ghostly streets of Ephesus soar the skeletal remains of a tremendous theater. No Greek drama disturbs the silence. Rather, the silence is the drama. Not far away the base of a column protrudes above swamp water just enough to whisper the transient glory of Diana of the Ephesians and her mighty temple.

The three cities slumber on, sharing a common silence. But the cities share something else, which centuries after their death is causing men to look to them once more. Each of them, with Jerusalem, holds a common memory of that strange and lively phenomenon of the early Church—the practice of speaking in tongues other than those commonly heard in their streets. And today Bible scholars, theologians, ministers, and laymen are scrutinizing the New Testament passages dealing with these occurrences. Not many months ago these same people showed relatively little interest in the subject despite a half-century of aggressive promotion on the part of the Pentecostal movement. For the movement was outside the historic, main-line denominations. Now it is within, and clergy and laity have been driven to a probing of the Scriptures and church history for answers to questions and explanations of phenomena pressed hard upon them by fellow ministers and parishioners. And assessments are about as varied as the phenomena.

Ecumenical leaders have shown increasing interest in the Pentecostal movement, known as the fastest growing segment of Protestantism in the Western Hemisphere, where approximately one of every three Latin American Protestants is Pentecostal. While many of these churchmen have favored courting Pentecostal churches on behalf of ecumenism, they had never dreamed of the possibility of considerable numbers within their own denominations incorporating Pentecostalist experience and doctrine. They are reacting quite gingerly to this—the new penetration.

Nearly all the major denominations have been affected by what is called the charismatic revival, Episcopalians and Lutherans preeminently so. Greatest strength of the new penetration is in southern California, but reports of developments have come in from across the nation:

Two ends of the ecclesiastical-cultural spectrum come together in Springfield, Missouri, as officials of the Protestant Episcopal Church and the Assemblies of God converse on the work and ministry of the Holy Spirit in the Church today; some 2,000 Episcopalians are said to be speaking in tongues in southern California; also speaking in tongues are upwards of 600 folk at the First Presbyterian Church of Hollywood, world's largest Presbyterian church; James A. Pike, Episcopal Bishop of California, confronts the practice in the Bay Area; a journal relates that in the entire state of Montana only one American Lutheran pastor has not received the experience of speaking in tongues; Dr. Francis E. Whiting, director of the Department of Evangelism and Spiritual Life of the Michigan Baptist Convention (American Baptist) speaks in support of present charismatic works of the Spirit, declaring the choice is Pentecost or holocaust; a Minneapolis Evangelical Free Church splits over the issue; members of the Inter-Varsity Christian Fellowship at Yale speak in tongues, as does also a Roman Catholic student, a daily communicant at St. Thomas More chapel; and echoes of penetration come from evangelical institutions and organizations such as Fuller Seminary, Wheaton College, Westmont College, Navigators, and Wycliffe Bible Translators.

In the midst of all this, the question is increasingly heard: Do we confront a new Pentecost or a new Babel? Most common response is: Neither one.

On the day of Pentecost when the assembled disciples were filled with the Holy Spirit, they "began to speak with other tongues [*"lalein heterais glossais"*—cf. the term "glossolalia"], as the Spirit gave them utterance." Jews of the Dispersion then gathered in Jerusalem were amazed to hear God's praises in the languages and dialects of their own lands (Acts 2:1-13). In Caesarea, tongues accompanied the outpouring of the Holy Spirit upon the first Gentile converts (Acts 10:44-46; 11:15), and was perhaps one of the external manifestations of the receiving of the Spirit by the earliest Samaritan believers (Acts 8:17, 18). In Ephesus, the phenomenon appeared again among a group of disciples who had apparently not heard of Pentecost (Acts 19:6).

Protestants often interpret this visible evidence of the giving of the Holy Spirit after Pentecost as an endorsement of the reception of new classes of believers into the distinctly cautious young Jewish-Christian church. Most commentators, though not all, believe that the tongues spoken at Pentecost were foreign languages. And many believe this to be so in the other references in Acts because of parallels in terminology.

But when it comes to the Pauline treatment of the subject in relation to the Corinthian church (I Cor. 12-14), the weight of biblical scholarship favors identification of tongues not as foreign languages but rather as ecstatic ("glossolalics" themselves differ as to the propriety of this word) and unintelligible utterances: "For if I pray in an unknown tongue, my spirit prayeth, but my understanding is unfruitful. . . . Yet in the church I had rather speak five words with my understanding, that by my voice I might teach others also, than ten thousand words in an unknown tongue" (14:14, 19). Thus, for instruction tongues were valueless apart from interpretation (v. 13)—

an added gift not required at Pentecost. In Acts the phenomenon appeared to be an irresistible, initial experience which was temporary, while at Corinth its nature was that of a continuing gift controlled by the recipients, not all Corinthian Christians possessing it (14:27, 28; 12:10, 30).

Paul spoke in tongues himself and valued the practice as a gift of the Spirit, primarily for worship but also for a sign to unbelievers and, when interpreted, for edification of believers (14:2, 5, 14-17, 18, 22, 28).

But commentators have generally concluded that the total effect of Paul's instructions in chapters 12 through 14 is to play down the relative importance of this gift, despite vital appeals to this passage of Scripture by Pentecostals. For the Corinthian church was in trouble—spiritually, theologically, and morally. Corinth had become synonymous with vice. A wealthy commercial center, its pleasures and high cost of living were famed. The summit of Acro-Corinth bore a temple of Aphrodite served by a thousand priestesses. To describe an evil life, the ancients coined a new word: "Corinthianize."

The church at Corinth had not risen heroically to the challenge of its environment, nor had it fully withstood the pervasive temptations. And though rich in gifts (1:5-7), the saints there had indulged themselves in the more spectacular of these, notably tongues. Their excesses perhaps echoed a pagan background wherein Greek oracles made ecstatic utterances with consciousness of priest or priestess in complete abeyance and subsequent explanation being needed. A gift of the Spirit could thus be abused by the immature Christians of Corinth to serve as a vehicle for their divisiveness, pride, and self-glorification, the result being confused scenes of profit neither to believer nor to unbeliever.

So the great Apostle to the Gentiles lays down guidelines that "all things be done decently and in order" (14:40): Not more than three are to speak in tongues at a single service; they are to speak not simultaneously but in turn; in the absence of an interpreter, they are to remain silent; women are not to speak tongues in the church (14:26-36).

Paul's de-emphasizing procedure does not stop there, for he compares the gift of tongues and the gift of prophecy to the disadvantage of the former (14:1-6). He seems to strike at Corinthian axiology as twice he puts tongues last in his listings of the charismata, the "grace-gifts" (12:4-10, 27-30); in a similar listing in Romans 12:6-8, he omits tongues completely. And soaring above all the gifts of the Spirit is agape, celebrated by Paul in his great hymn to love (I Cor. 13), introduced by the words: ". . . covet earnestly the best gifts: and yet show I unto you a more excellent way. . . ." He speaks of the fruit of the Spirit (see Gal. 5:22, 23—love is first named), which has precedence over the gifts of the Spirit. Love remains even when the gifts pass away (13:8).

The question being echoed today, as in every period of glossolalic manifestations, is: How long do the gifts remain? Answers vary greatly. Perhaps the most common view relates the gifts of the Spirit to the founding of the New Testament Church, their cessation during the fourth century taking place after it was well established under the authority of the completed New Testament canon. Presbyterian theologian B. B. Warfield believed the charismata to be given for authentication of the apostles as God's messengers, a sign of apostleship being possession of the gifts and the ability to transmit them. Gradual cessation of the gifts thus came with the death of those who had received the gifts through the apostles (see his *Miracles: Yesterday and Today*). For W. H. Griffith Thomas, the charismata constituted a testimony to Israel of Jesus' Messiahship and thus ceased at the end of Acts with the Jewish rejection of the Gospel (*The Holy Spirit of God*, 1913, pp. 48, 49).

Other scholars respond that these theories fly in the face of history. But then to darken matters further, commentators duly remind us that *the degree of similarity between the New Testament phenomenon of glossolalia and later manifestations (e.g., current ones) is uncertain.* Leon Morris points to the obscurity of present-day understanding of the exact nature of some of the gifts, such as "helps" and "governments" (I Cor. 12:28): "We may make . . . conjectures. . . . But when we boil it all down, we know nothing about these gifts or their possessors. They have vanished without leaving visible trace." On tongues he says: "Despite the confident claims of some, we cannot be certain of exactly what form the gift took in New Testament days." (*Spirit of the Living God*, 1960, pp. 63, 65, 66.) Even as early as the fourth century, Chrysostom expressed puzzlement at Paul's account of the Corinthian situation: "The whole passage is exceedingly obscure and the obscurity is occasioned by our ignorance of the facts and the cessation of happenings which were common in those days but unexampled in our own."

Any tracing of tongues phenomena through church history faces the common lack of clear-cut distinctions between tongues and prophecy, and between use of foreign languages and ecstatic utterances. Before the apparent cessation which Chrysostom mentions, Irenaeus in the second century makes reference to some who speak "in all kinds of languages," and there is evidence of glossolalia among Montanists in the same period, when the practice was attacked by Celsus. This Platonist wrote of Christians who spoke gibberish and claimed to be God. In the third century, Origen associates the phenomenon with the Gnostics.

Some occurrences are reported in the Middle Ages, but to G. B. Cutten the surprising thing in "this age of wonders" was their infrequency (*Speaking with Tongues, Historically and Psychologically Considered,* 1927, p. 37). It is recorded that Francis Xavier and others possessed the gift of languages, used in missionary labors.

In the modern era, prophecy and languages are claimed for persecuted French Huguenots called the Little Prophets of Cevennes—very young children sharing the gifts. There were also outcroppings among Jansenists and Shakers. Mother Ann Lee, founder of the latter sect, which regarded her as the "female principle in Christ" with Jesus being the "Male principle," is said to have testified in seventy-two different languages before Anglican clergymen who were also noted linguists. Certain emotional phenomena among early Methodists and Quakers have been linked to glossolalia. In contrast to the twentieth century, with its fast-expanding Pentecostal movement, the nineteenth century was relatively quiescent, presenting only the Irvingites and the Mormons, the latter tending to discourage tongues because of ridicule thus provoked.

The trail of glossolalia through church history is slender and broken. It is generally absent from the mainstream churches, but rather tends to be found in enthusiastic sects particularly in times of persecution. An apocalyptic aura is often present, and the trail leads frequently to heretical byways.

Glossolalia is not to be thought confined to Christian groups and offshoots. This emphasizes the fact that the practice is not self-authenticating. It occupied an important place in ancient Greek religion. Plato discourses on the phenomenon. Many Asian and African cultures afford examples of the practice.

The modern Pentecostal movement is often traced from an eruption of tongues in a mission on Los Angeles' Azusa Street in 1906, though Pentecostals also point to origins in revivals of the late nineteenth century. Due to common emotional excesses, Pentecostals were frequently made unwelcome by the old-line denominations and formed their own groupings which often fragmented. Their virility, in recent years particularly, has aroused the wonder of the church world, and they form the largest segment of what has become known as the "Third Force in Christendom." Apart from Pentecostalism's largest group, the Assemblies, the movement encompasses such bodies as the numerous independent Churches of God, and the International Church of the Foursquare Gospel—founded by Aimee Semple Mc-Pherson. (There are well over a hundred sects in America which practice glossolalia, not all Pentecostal, e.g. Father Divine's Peace Missions.)

Common to all Pentecostals is the one basic belief that "the baptism in the Holy Spirit" is an experience subsequent to conversion—all believers should have it, and the initial physical evidence of this baptism or infilling is the speaking of tongues. For proof, one is pointed back to Jerusalem, Caesarea, and Ephesus. Tongues as initial evidence is distinguished from the gift of tongues (I Cor. 12:10), which was not granted to all.

Exponents of classical Protestantism counter that: (1) The few historical accounts of tongues in Acts, in comparison with the other Scriptures, provide a flimsy foundation indeed upon which to erect a doctrine of the Christian life; no directives for normative Christian experience are contained in these passages. (2) Not all references in Acts to the outpouring of the Holy Spirit speak of an accompaniment of tongues. (One could as well argue from the accounts the necessity of laying on of hands of an apostle, as recorded in Acts 8:17 and 19:6.) (3) Pentecostal use of the terms "infilling" and "baptism" of the Spirit in connection with tongues is unsupported by the texts cited. Only one of nine references to the terms "filled with" or "full of the Holy Spirit" in Acts (not to mention four references in Luke's Gospel) is directly connected by Luke with the expression "speaking with (other) tongues." This referred to Pentecost, where the tongues were apparently foreign languages. Key passage for baptism of the Spirit is I Corinthians 12:13: "For by one Spirit are we all baptized into one body, whether we be Jews or Gentiles, whether we be bond or free; and have been all made to drink into one Spirit." All Christians are thus by definition baptized into the body of Christ, being thus constituted members of the body regardless of race or social status. Unlike the filling of the Spirit (Acts 4:31), there is no second baptism. (4)

There are indications that tongues are associated with spiritual immaturity (see I Cor. 13:11; 14:20). Those recorded as speaking in tongues were recent converts. Paul possessed the gift in great measure but stated his preference for intelligible words (14:18, 19), and there is no record of a specific instance when he used the gift. (5) New Testament tests of the Spirit's presence are the glorification of Christ (12:3) and the ethical fruit of the Spirit, preeminently love. (6) Dearth of Pentecostal biblical scholarship highlights an overshadowing of exposition by experience.

Traditional Pentecostal fears regarding higher education are slowly waning in some quarters. For example, evangelist Oral Roberts has announced the opening in 1965 of the Oral Roberts University, a $50 million liberal arts institution in Tulsa, Oklahoma, for 3,000 students.

Of significance to current discussion of Pentecostalism is the presence in the United States of a single copy of an M.D. dissertation, *Glossolalia,* by L. M. Van Eetveldt Vivier for the University of Witwatersrand, South Africa. Temporarily in possession of New York's Union Seminary, the sympathetic treatment contains results of a number of psychological tests taken by a test group of Pentecostals who had spoken in tongues. Two control groups of similar educational and vocational standing took the tests as well. One was comprised of Pentecostals who had not spoken in tongues, the other of Reformed Church members whose pastor believed tongues had ended with apostolic times. Psychologically the latter group ranked highest, followed by the Pentecostals who had not spoken in tongues. The glossolalics were discovered to have had, psychologically, a poor beginning in life characterized by insecurity, conflict, and tension, which led to a turning from the orthodox and traditional to "an environment of sensitiveness for emotional feeling and a group of people . . . clinging to each other for support" toward the goal of being freed from themselves.

But what of the new Pentecostals who remain within their mainline denominations and purpose to make these Pentecostal in experience? They are generally recognized as standing on a much higher plane intellectually and culturally than the old Pentecostals. Spearheading the new penetration is The Blessed Trinity Society, whose leaders travel indefatigably to spread the message of charismatic revival. Chairman of the Board is Dutch Reformed minister Harald Bredesen of Mt. Vernon, New York, who testifies to a transformation through a Pentecostal camp meeting. He has spoken in tongues over

California television and claims to have witnessed to foreigners in their own languages, unknown to him (such as Polish and Coptic Egyptian). But he believes most of the current glossolalia is unknown languages. A group of government linguistic experts sought to analyze for *Christianity Today* a tape of his glossolalia but found it unrecognizable, though one said it sounded like a language structurally.

A director of The Blessed Trinity Society is David J. du Plessis, Pentecostalist from South Africa who believes he has a call to take the message to ecumenical leaders. In his opinion, the "Pentecostal revival" within the ecumenical movement may become greater than that outside it. His ecumenical activities have led to a severing of his ministerial relationship with the Assembles, by the latter.

Personable Jean Stone, wife of a Lockheed Aircraft executive, is a board member and the editor of the society's attractive, Episcopal-tinted quarterly, *Trinity* (paid circulation: 4,000; print order: 25,000, many of which go to churches by the hundreds), published in Van Nuys, California. Episcopalian Stone contrasts the new penetration with the old Pentecostal movement as follows: less emotion in receiving the gift of tongues after which they are spoken at will—their private use more important than public, more oriented to clergy and professional classes, more Bible-centered as against experience, not separatist, more orderly meetings with strict adherence to Pauline directives, less emphasis on tongues.

The new penetration as a definitive movement is usually traced to Sunday, April 3, 1960, when the Rev. Dennis J. Bennett, rector of St. Mark's Episcopal, Van Nuys, told his congregation of his Pentecostal experience which had its roots in the October previous. He was asked to resign, did so, and the event gained national publicity which drew attention to beginnings of the penetration already under way.

But apart from tongues, leaders cite evidence to support their claim that all nine of the gifts of the Spirit listed in I Corinthians 12:8-10 are manifest in the movement, including miracles and healing. Episcopal leaders are divided in their response to the penetration, but the general mood is one of caution and forbearance, which is generally true of most other denominational leadership—there being little desire to force the new wave of Pentecostals from the churches as was done half a century ago. Yet they are somewhat fearful of divisiveness resulting from glossolalia.

Conservative Protestant reactions range from participation in the movement to warnings that tongues can be Satanic. Some tell of the love, joy, and peace found in meetings, and the increased zeal for Bible study and power in witnessing manifest in those who have "received" the manifestation of glossolalia. Accounts multiply of nominal Christians, casual churchgoers, being transformed into vital believers, many experiencing conversion. *Christian Life* magazine is actively promoting the charismatic revival.

Some approve of the tenor of the movement in certain places but speak of excesses in others, along with divisiveness and pride of possession. Criticism has been directed at the commonly used method to induce tongues in after-meetings: those wishing to receive the fullness of the Spirit are told to offer their voices and make noises, during the laying on of hands. It is feared that the physical sign is unintentionally given priority over the infilling of the Spirit.

Critics point also to self-confessed spiritual immaturity of the majority of those heard from by way of testimony. Prior to their experience of tongues, many were formalistic Anglo-Catholics, church members in name only, or backslidden evangelicals lacking a warm devotional life. Echoes of Corinth?

There is also a confessed lack of theological leadership, and evangelicals have been disappointed to note a resultant drift to the Pentecostal doctrine that tongues are the outward manifestation of the baptism of the Spirit. Possibly the majority in the movement now believe that non-glossolalics have yet to receive the baptism or fullness. When one reflects upon the work of such non-glossolalics as Calvin, Knox, Wesley, Carey, Judson, Hudson Taylor, Jonathan Edwards, Moody, Spurgeon, Torrey, Sunday, Graham, he would perhaps, if desiring to do a great work, ask the Lord to excuse him from the baptism of the Spirit—which is of course unthinkable save on Pentecostal terms.

Probably most evangelicals who are informed on the subject are sympathetically waiting to see the fruit of the new movement, not wishing to quench the Spirit, but sensing a need to try the spirits. They generally believe God is working in and through the movement but are questioning how close it may be to the biblical ideal. They are grateful for spiritual awakening.

And a salutary facet of the whole phenomenon is renewed and widespread study of the doctrine of the Holy Spirit; if his ministry is properly fathomed, the issue is the exaltation of Jesus Christ, glorious fruition indeed.

Article   September 13, 1963

52 Did Khrushchev See America?

DAVID E. KUCHARSKY

The news editor was the only representative of a religious periodical to accompany Soviet Premier Khrushchev on a tour of the United States.

Minutes after his silvery TU-114 appeared on the blue Maryland horizon, Khrushchev—one of the most celebrated international visitors since the Queen of Sheba—was reflecting his high priority for economics.

"I will be glad to talk with statesmen, representatives of the business world, intellectuals, workers and farmers, and to become familiar with the life of the industrious and enterprising American people," said Khrushchev in response to President Eisenhower's initial welcome at Andrews Air Force Base.

"It is true that you are richer than we are at present," the Red leader said at a state dinner in the White House the same evening. "But then tomorrow we will be as rich as you are, and the day after tomorrow we will be even richer."

The next 12 days bore out clearly what his first utterances hinted at: that Khrushchev was toeing the Marxist line which merges the dialectic with economic determinism as the comprehensive key to reality.

Preoccupation with economics characterized Khrushchev's entire tour of the United States. Absorption in material things shaped an itinerary, moreover, which raises the question whether he really saw a true cross-section of America.

Khrushchev viewed little during his stay that was distinctively Christian or that would underscore America's great spiritual heritage. This turn of events could be attributed largely to Khrushchev himself. U.S. State Department spokesmen said the course of the tour depended to a great extent upon decisions of the little man whose country had just placed its coat of arms upon the moon.

It was left to Eisenhower to salvage something for the cause of Christian witness, and many clergymen feel his deeds on the final day of Khrushchev's stay represented the most devout gesture during his entire term of office. Eisenhower not only broke into top-level talks with Khrushchev to attend a Sunday morning worship service, but invited the Red leader to accompany him. Khrushchev declined, explaining that an acceptance would shock the Russian people. But the impact of the President's spiritual priorities was firmly registered.

"I am personally an atheist," Khrushchev had said earlier in Los Angeles. Yet nobody could deny his religionlike devotion to Red materialism. His natural religious inclinations seem diverted wholly to the thesis that man's basic need is economic, and it was precisely this concern which dominated his interest in America.

Business leaders made up the large bulk of his private dinner guests throughout the trip. In New York it was the Economic Club which got to sponsor a banquet for him. In Washington it was the *Journal of Commerce.*

Economic interests vitalized many of Khrushchev's U.S. speeches, too. In his oft-repeated *mirnoe soshuschestvovanie*—peaceful coexistence—the trade angle was prominent. Even when he spoke of disarmament, the Soviet chief revealed that he was thinking of its significance in channeling Soviet defense funds to consumer goods. He remarked publicly in San Jose, California, that the most amiable contacts of his U.S. tour were with business leaders.

The economic overtones were evident despite Khrushchev's insistence that he had not come here to beg. "Trade is like a barometer," he said in New York. "It shows the direction of the development of policy."

One of the more surprising aspects of Khrushchev's approach was his use of references to deity. He used far more Christian expressions than he heard from Americans. The fact that this practice contradicted his professed atheism illustrates his willingness to brush aside logic for convenience.

Clergy reaction to Khrushchev's pious pronouncements dismissed them as (1) a tactic to establish common ground, and (2) Russian expressions which no longer imply belief in their truthfulness.

Whatever the merits of his visit, many U.S. Christians seized the opportunity to promote special prayers for Khrushchev. And who can say, they will ask, that the Holy Spirit did not deal with his heart?

Some quarters nonetheless lamented the fact that, in the framework of his own preferences, the influences of American Judeo-Christian tradition were not presented in a more favorable light.

Most distressing was the episode at 20th Century-Fox studios, where the Khrushchev party was exposed to three *Can-Can* scenes, featuring a wild dance with suggestive skirt-flipping climaxed when a male runs off with a leading lady's bloomers.

The Russians were detained at the studios beyond time allotted while movie producers, eager for expanded markets, were making their impression. The bid backfired.

"We don't want our people to see that kind of trash," Khrushchev was reported to have remarked later. He publicly referred to the dance as "immoral" and called it a form of pornography. The development had played into his hands and Khrushchev had come out as the apparent champion of a high morality.

In a private audience with seven top labor leaders the following evening in San Francisco, Khrushchev was said to have mimicked the dancers by stooping over and flipping his coat tails.

Khrushchev spent Sunday, September 20, on a train traveling up the California coast and here again he failed to see the real America where some 63 per cent of the population belongs to a church. Morning church hours found hundreds of persons, most wearing leisure togs, lining the tracks for a glimpse of the Red leader. The image of families dressed in Sunday best, Bibles under arm, was conspicuously absent.

It was in San Francisco that the Premier attributed a portion of Communist philosophy to the teachings of Christ. His audience took the remark at face value and applauded him enthusiastically.

Khrushchev, while in San Francisco, visited the Top of the Mark, "probably the world's most famous bar," but he made no attempt to view a church there or elsewhere or to meet any of the nation's religious leaders. Not until he got to Pittsburgh did he hear an invocation (by Dr. Howard C. Scharfe, prominent Presbyterian minister).

Of all questions publicly addressed to Khrushchev during his U.S. visit, the very last was the only one which evoked anything even approaching a serious discussion of religion under communism. It was asked by Edward P. Morgan of the American Broadcasting Company at the end of a news conference held in Washington just a few hours before Khrushchev left to return to Moscow.

MORGAN: "Those of us who went to the U.S.S.R. with Vice President Nixon were surprised at the number of young people in church. If there is an increasing interest in religion, what will be your attitude towards churches?"

KHRUSHCHEV: "Well, first of all I believe the question itself confirms the fact that we do have a full freedom of conscience and religion in our country as we have been saying all along.

"Furthermore, I would like to say that this is partly explained, the large number of young people in churches, perhaps is partly explained by the feeling of curiosity. Young people are curious. I was telling the

President the other day that immediately after the war when our Marshal Tolbukhi was returning from Bulgaria, I invited him to my home in Kiev. My grandchildren were very curious to see how a real marshal looked like. They hid and looked from around the corners to see what he was like, what a live marshal was like.

"Many of our young people hear about religion, about God, about saints, about church ceremonies, and they have a curiosity about this. Even if each one of them goes to church only once, they are so numerous that the doors of our churches would never close.

"This feeling of curiosity is very important. For instance, I am sure that many people in this country ran out to see me because they wanted to see a living Communist from the Soviet Union. It is the same way in our country. If a capitalist comes to our country, our people, our young people, want to take a look, to see if he has a tail as an attribute to his person.

"So there is nothing surprising about these things."

Though gesturing dramatically, Khrushchev replied evasively. He cited what presumably he believes is the reason for the religious interest of Russian young people, but he failed to face up to the heart of the question, which inquired of his attitude toward such interest.

News   October 12, 1959

53 *Peripheral Christianity*

L. NELSON BELL

One of the gravest dangers to contemporary Protestantism is its obsession with the periphery of Christianity. We see many spokes to the wheel and much emphasis on the rim of Christian activity, but we are in danger of neglecting the hub of the Christian faith itself.

For a long time I have been reading the voluminous daily reports supplied by a religious news service that tell of church activities at home and abroad.

It becomes depressingly obvious after a while that much of our activity in contemporary church life is on the periphery—around the rim of a wheel—and that these activities represent the spokes of innumerable councils, commissions, committees, and organizations.

We would hardly imply that the rim is an unintegral, unimportant part of the wheel. It is at the rim that contact is made with the road and the wheel becomes effective. In like manner, the Church must make effective contact with the world if its own usefulness is to continue.

However, just as a wheel collapses unless its spokes are firmly centered in the hub, so too the wheel of church activity ceases to make an impact unless it is firmly centered in the doctrinal content of Christian truth.

By some strange conspiracy of silence, doctrine is almost an ugly word in Protestant circles today. There seems to be almost an obsession against any reference to the revealed truths basic to the Christian faith. Facts having to do with the person and work of our Lord are shunned. So long as an individual, a congregation, or a denomination is active, the reason for that activity seems to be a matter of secondary importance.

We hear a great deal about the "prophetic role of the Church." This is good insofar as that role is concerned with sin, individual and corporate, and where the message of the cleansing blood of Calvary is proclaimed as God's way of redemption.

Only too often this prophetic role has become enmeshed in the symptoms of personal and social disorder, while the cause of man's distress—his separation from God through sin—has been ignored in this day and generation.

Some time ago a discerning Christian went to hear one of America's most publicized young ministers speak. He came away with this remark: "He can say nothing the most beautifully I have ever heard it said." Little wonder that that ministry fizzled and sputtered out in the ashes of lost convictions. The periphery collapsed because the hub of vital faith was not there.

The Church is in gravest danger of saying nothing beautifully. Unless there is a positive message of redemption from sin—in God's way and on God's terms—what is there to preach? Unless the Christ who is preached is the Christ of the Scriptures, whom shall we preach? And unless the correct diagnosis of sin is made and God's remedy in the sacrifice of his Son on the Cross is stressed, why preach at all?

In our obsession with the peripheral things of Christianity, we cater to the pride and restless energies of the flesh, while we suppress that which could keep our activity from becoming so much beating of the air. Concern for the human predicament is no more than humanism, unless it centers on the divinely ordained way out of that predicament.

Again we stress that Christianity does have a periphery. Without an outward demonstration of the Christian faith, the inward becomes a mockery. No amount of emphasis on the doctrine of the Holy Spirit can be effective unless the fruits of the same Spirit are evident in the lives of those who profess to have him. A wheel consisting of only a hub is a caricature. A hub with projecting spokes alone would wobble and disintegrate. A true wheel is a perfect combination of hub, spokes, and rim.

When we consider the great emphasis in Protestantism today on the spokes of organization and the rim of activity, and note how much the hub of Christian doctrine, which moves the wheel of Christianity, is disregarded, we wonder at the difference there was in those who went out to establish the early Church. These men had a burning faith in the crucified and risen Christ—a Christ about whom certain things were true; a Christ who had performed certain specific acts for man's redemption, the central one being his death on the Cross.

Small wonder that so many church-sponsored activities result in little more than consuming the time of those engaged in them! Small wonder that the average church member, lacking indoctrination, finds himself at a loss to give a reason for the faith he professes! Is it strange that the Church makes such a limited impact on the world as a whole?

How different it is with the Communists who, thoroughly indoctrinated in their evil philosophy, go out to win the world to their beliefs.

The analogy between a wheel and the Church is a valid one. Just as a wheel must have a sturdy hub to be strong and effective, so a church must have an intelligent doctrinal faith as the basis on which to build effective Christian living, both personal and corporate.

But by and large Protestantism eschews the strong meat of Christian doctrine because it is regarded as "divisive." It seeks a unity of organization and activity based on a willingness to play down those Christian doctrines upon which the Christian faith must be built if it is ever to be translated into Christian living.

"Saying nothing beautifully" may soothe the conscience and involve us in a multiplicity of activities. But to say: "Christ died for our sins, according to the scriptures; and that he was buried, and that he rose again the third day according to the scriptures" is the message of the Church to a lost world.

Do we preach that message? If not, we are leaving out the hub of the Gospel.

Let us suppose that from every pulpit in America there should begin a new emphasis, a return to the simple preaching of the basis of the Christian faith. Suppose that study books, programs, and activities out on the perimeter of Christianity were dropped for the time being and church members were indoctrinated with the facts of the Christian faith.

Should all of this happen, the problems of the individual and of society as a whole would remain; but people would begin to look at them in a new light—in the light of Holy Scripture and by the Spirit of the living God. Lives would be transformed and these transformed people would do more to evangelize and right the ills of the world than all the hosts of unregenerate people whose concern is a reformed rather than transformed society.

For a change let us go back to the hub of Christian doctrine and begin building the wheel of Christian conviction, organization, and program firmly on it.

A Layman and His Faith   July 20, 1959

54 *"What If . . ."*

JOHN LAWING

LAWING

What I hear you saying, Paul, is that you feel powerless to do the things you'd like.

December 18, 1964

55 *Evangelicals and the Right-Wing Renascence*

A revival of conservative political thinking captures the American headlines. How does it fit in with theological thought?

Some 50 radio stations linked with the Mutual Broadcasting System added a 30-minute weekly broadcast this month featuring the voice of Dr. Billy James Hargis, founder-director of Christian Crusade, "largest anti-communist ministry in America." Hargis was already being heard on 15-minute daily broadcasts carried by some 76 stations and on 30-minute weekly broadcasts heard over 66 stations. He also has a 15-minute weekly telecast seen in 12 U.S. cities and in the Virgin Islands. The added outreach for the 14-year-old Hargis organization takes advantage of a rightist revival now sweeping the United States. Assorted new organizations, all thriving on bad publicity, are springing up almost daily.

The right-wing renascence is basically a political phenomenon, but some of the motivations are religious, as are some of the repercussions.

The Hargis organization and the Christian Anti-Communism Crusade of Dr. Fred C. Schwarz both have a large following among fundamentalists, but their scope long ago transcended theological lines. Schwarz was catapulted to national prominence this fall through widely telecast public rallies in southern California. Retraction of a critical story in *Life* magazine also helped the cause, inasmuch as *Life* publisher C. D. Jackson actually took the platform at a Schwarz rally to concede the magazine's "oversimplified misrepresentation" and to praise the Schwarz enterprise.

Responsible evangelicals applaud the initiative of genuinely sincere anti-Communists. But some observers record their reservations over an excessively negative approach. They agree that the public ought to be more aware of Communist strategy, and that the ideological transition from socialism to communism is well worth publicizing. But they question whether some of the hoop-la rallies provide much ideological orientation. More important, these observers are disturbed at preoccupation with communism to the neglect of positive Christianity. The question is asked: Would we not be more profitably engaged if we indoctrinated the masses in the fundamentals of the Christian world-life view and called for personal commitment and for aggressive cells of workers?

Some anti-Communists and anti-liberals have become so irresponsible in their accusations and blanket denunciations that they hurt their own good cause. They have even leveled accusations at people who share their own convictions but who exercise more restraint. Extremists fail to see that they are being used as decoys by the liberals: smoke swirls about right-wing extremists while left-wingers quietly go about peddling their influence.

The aggressive liberal attack on right-wingers gives the liberals the initiative, keeps the right on the defensive; it raises questions about the right, while making the left seem respectable and normative; it enables the liberals to achieve their ends while discrediting those who would call them to account.

Many right-wingers are highly sensitive to the conspiratorial facets of contemporary Communist strategy, a fact which causes some to trace all socialistic trends back to the Kremlin. Thus the socialistic overtones in liberal church pronouncements are interpreted as continuing evidence of the presence of "Communist clergymen" in the United States.

Anti-Communist extremists who saw a Red in every other committee went into virtual hibernation at the demise of McCarthyism. They came to life again when the National Council of Churches made a big affair out of an obscure Air Force Reserve manual which warned of clergy subversion. Some Protestant anti-Communist extremists also came to new life in the wake of the Roman Catholic issue in Kennedy's election campaign because they happened also to share a genuine concern for church-state separation. Almost to a man they supported the candidacy of Vice President Richard M. Nixon, and Nixon's narrow-margin loss was a bitter blow.

Political discontent in America today largely follows one of two general courses. To the left are pacifistic critics of nuclear testing. To the right lie a myriad of complainers ranging from George Lincoln Rockwell and his self-styled Nazism to the arms-carrying Minute Men of southern California.

Liberally-oriented news analysts continually do the public a disservice by lumping all together under the right-wing forces under the same umbrella and assigning them a common identification. Washington correspondents largely regard the right-wing bloc as a laughing-stock, and their bias is readily discernible in news stories. Thus far, however, this adverse treatment (even President Kennedy's denunciation) has worked to the advantage of the extremists. It seems to win them friends, and most certainly spreads the word to persons of like convictions eager to line up behind a cause.

Two tactics currently used to discredit right-wingers are the same as those long decried by liberals: guilt by association and arbitrary labeling on the basis of isolated quotations removed from context.

News   December 22, 1961

56 *Bultmann's Three-Storied Universe*

GORDON H. CLARK

Rudolf Bultmann claims that the New Testament teaches a three-storied universe which modern science has made incredible. Therefore, to preserve Christianity in our day, the New Testament "mythology" must be reinterpreted.

Bultmann writes, "The cosmology of the New Testament is essentially mythical in character. The world is viewed as a three-storied structure, with the earth in the center, the heaven above, and the underworld beneath. . . . Supernatural forces intervene in the course of nature. . . . Miracles are by no means rare."

This introductory statement to his essay *New Testament and Mythology* Bultmann expands in considerable detail. The idea of a Holy Spirit, or spirits generally, the mysterious cleansing effect of baptism and the still more mysterious Eucharist, the doctrine that death is a punishment for sin, and the resurrection of Jesus—all these are mythical and incredible. Bultmann locates the source of this mythology in Jewish apocalyptic literature and in the redemptive myths of Gnosticism. Indeed, from Gnosticism came the idea that Jesus was not a mere human being, but a God-man. All in all, Bultmann considers the New Testament to be pervasively mythical.

Therefore, the New Testament as it stands cannot be accepted. Modern science has now discovered the real truth about nature, and the scientific laws of causality prevent modern man from believing in any divine intervention. "All our thinking today is shaped irrevocably by modern science. A blind acceptance of the New Testament mythology would be arbitrary. . . . It would involve a sacrifice of the intellect which could have only one result—a curious form of schizophrenia and insincerity."

Fortunately (as Bultmann sees it) "there is nothing specifically Christian in the mythical view of the world as such." The real gospel, which even the modern man needs, can be obtained by reinterpreting and demythologizing the New Testament. Then we can leave behind the fairy tales of a divine Christ and a bodily resurrection and preach the pure, powerful gospel of Heidegger's existentialism! (When accused of imposing Heidegger's categories on the New Testament, Bultmann should rather be startled by existentialism's independent discovery of biblical truth!)

Bultmann's view is open to criticism both with respect to the "mythology" of the New Testament and with respect to the state of modern science. First, his picture of the mythical world, allegedly found in the Bible, depends for some of its details on Gnostic sources. Apparently Bultmann takes over the theories of Bousset and Reitzenstein, who claimed that many Christian ideas were borrowed from the mystery religions and Hermes Trismegistus. But while these theories were popularly received in the early years of this century, when Bultmann was a student, they are today completely exploded (see for example *The Origin of Paul's Religion,* by J. Gresham Machen, chapters VI, VII). If, now, the New Testament does not in fact teach the mythology of Gnosticism, this latter cannot be used as an objection to accepting the New Testament. No doubt Bultmann would reply that even so the New Testament teaches the existence of spirits, the occurrence of a resurrection, and the doctrines of heaven and hell, and this is mythology enough. To this point we shall return in a moment.

The second and more important criticism strikes closer home: Bultmann's view of science is defective. His repeated allusions to a "causal nexus" indicate that he conceives of science in terms of eighteenth-century, or, at best, nineteenth-century mechanism. But science dropped the concept of causality more than a hundred years ago; and in the twentieth century Heisenberg's indeterminacy principle seriously called in question even the idea of mechanism.

No doubt some popular evangelical writers have made too much of indeterminacy by trying to find room, as it were, for God, miracles, and free will in the random motion of the ultimate particles. But at least mechanism can no longer be confidently used as an insurmountable objection to miracles. Indeed, contemporary science cannot be confidently used in objection to anything in the New Testament because contemporary science is in a state of confusion. With the destruction of the Newtonian gravitational mechanics and the introduction of quantum theory, the splitting of the atom, the mutually incompatible formulas for light, and all the wizardry of relativity research, the result has been and still is chaos. The basic concepts of mass, inertia, energy, and the like are no longer well defined; and an accepted scientific world view, to be used either for or against the New Testament, simply doesn't exist. Bultmann's confidence is outdated.

Furthermore, the most recent philosophy of science, operationalism, denies that science has the purpose of describing nature. According to this theory scientific laws are directions for laboratory procedure and do not give any information at all on the constitution of the world. If therefore operationalism be accepted, there could never be scientific knowledge of nature to compel abandonment of the actual New Testament picture of the world.

This is not to say, however, that no problem remains. After Bultmann's Gnosticism is removed from the interpretation of the New Testament, the New Testament picture of the world is still not that of the "modern mind." Indeterminists and operationalists, for all their abandonment of Bultmann's antiquated view of science, are not about to acknowledge the Holy Spirit, or Jesus Christ as true God and true man, or angels, or devils. They still oppose the teaching of the New Testament, even if they can no longer logically oppose it on the basis of science.

To accommodate these who disbelieve in spirit, who dislike vicarious atonement, who ridicule the Lord's return, Bultmann proposes to reinterpret the New Testament so as to accord with modern existentialism. But sober thought, whether Christian or not, must reject this fanciful reinterpretation. No better reason exists for finding Heidegger in the New Testament than for finding Hegel there. Bultmann's method of reinterpretation is on a par with the old allegorical method. If Bultmann finds Heidegger in the New Testament, so did Philo find Plato in the Old.

Honest examination of the text disallows demythologization. The Bible plainly teaches that the Almighty Spirit created the world, that mankind disobeyed God's commands and became guilty of God's wrath and curse, that the second Person of the Trinity was born of the Virgin Mary in order to satisfy divine justice by his death, and that he rose from the grave the third day for our justification.

This message is offensive to the modern mind. But this is nothing new. It was offensive to the Pharisaic and Epicurean minds as well. And it will remain offensive no matter what new philosophies of science may become popular in centuries to come.

It goes without saying that the sincere Christian wants to communicate with the modern mind. But the question how to communicate is not to be answered by substituting a different message. Heidegger is not Paul or John. And however much we agonize over the difficulty of reaching our contemporaries, we want to reach them, not with the message of a passing philosophy, but with the eternal New Testament message of Christ's satisfaction for sin.

Article   March 2, 1962

57   *Miracle*

HELEN FRAZEE-BOWER

God does not change the courses of the stars,
    To satisfy man's whim;
Nor will He chart a pathway through the sky
    Up which to climb to Him.

He views man's frantic foraging in space
    With condescending eye,
And, with the majesty of tolerance,
    Permits the brave to try.

But when on earth one contrite spirit bows,
    Acknowledging His grace,
God sweeps the stars aside and, with one move,
    Sublimely cancels space.

The heavens may continue to evade
    Man's scientific art;
But faith in Christ, at any moment, will
    Bring heaven to the heart.

January 30, 1961

58 *Coronation: Paul VI and East-West Tensions*

DAVID E. KUCHARSKY
The news editor covers the visit of President Kennedy to Rome and the coronation of Pope Paul VI.

Has the East-West struggle reached an unpalatable stalemate? Is it time to introduce a third party, an intermediary to break the deadlock?

In sweltering Rome, these questions gained surprising relevance this month—in fact and, curiously enough, in fiction.

The fact lay in what may have been, according to the American newspaper in Rome, "the biggest double feature here since Nero fiddled while the city burned": the coronation of Pope Paul VI and the visit of President Kennedy.

The fiction lay in a new novel, *The Shoes of the Fisherman,* wherein a Ukrainian pope becomes the go-between for the United States president and the Soviet premier. The book was released just seven days after the death of Pope John XXIII and was an immediate U.S. best-seller. It was written, not by an alarmist bigot seeking to arouse anti-Catholic sentiment through fear of papal power, but by a veteran Vatican correspondent turned novelist. The author, Morris West, formerly of the London *Daily Mail,* previously wrote *The Devil's Advocate,* which also was a sensation. West's early years were spent as an apprentice of the Christian Brothers, an Australian teaching order.

Adding still more fuel for speculation was the audience with Paul VI, just four days before that of Kennedy, of the President's 1960 election opponent, former Vice President Richard M. Nixon. Nixon and his family were on a vacation trip. They spent about half an hour with the Pope.

West's novel will never come true altogether. Some of its lines border on the ludicrous. But it may well prove historic as an accurate portrayal of the spirit of the times, that is, a yearning for more normal world conditions.

Moreover, the elevation of Giovanni Battista Montini to "the chair of St. Peter" probably spells additional participation for the Vatican in world affairs. The Vatican has long been reputed to be a diplomatic listening post for the world, and Montini brings to it extensive experience in political affairs. He is widely recognized as a first-rate diplomat and served for years as Vatican secretary of state under Pope Pius XII. He has already indicated that he will follow up the conciliatory overtures made toward Moscow by John XXIII.

Beyond that, opportunities may indeed be forthcoming whereby the Vatican, as a morally prestigious and politically neutral force, assumes the role of international arbiter. Most distinct possibility of this would probably come in a grave crisis when button-pushing is imminent.

Several years ago, there was some feeling that the Afro-Asian neutralist bloc might emerge as the reconciling third party in world affairs. But these nations now appear to be content with promoting their own ends, sometimes even playing the two world powers against each other for rather narrow purposes.

It is obvious to informed observers that the timing of the papal audiences so near the coronation was coincidental. Kennedy's schedule originally provided for a meeting with the late John XXIII at about the same time that, as it turned out, he saw Paul VI. The trip to Rome at one point was called off altogether, then reinstated. One important change in the President's schedule was made following the announcement by the Vatican that the coronation would take place June 30. Kennedy was due in Rome that day. He spent it in Milan instead. The United States was represented at the coronation by a four-man delegation headed by Chief Justice Earl Warren.

Rumors circulating in Rome while John XXIII was still alive spoke of a possible summit meeting in Rome of the pontiff, Kennedy, and Khrushchev. But these were largely discounted. A trip to Rome by Khrushchev, however, is probably only a matter of time, if only as an effort to offset the Kennedy trip. The Soviet leader's hastily conceived jaunt to East Berlin was widely interpreted as just such a maneuver.

Kennedy concluded his ten-day European tour on a spiritual note. In a speech at NATO headquarters in Naples he quoted some phrases uttered by Italian patriot Giuseppe Mazzini 115 years ago. Mazzini was described as having said at a mass meeting in Milan: "We are here . . . to build up the unity of the human family so that the day may come when it shall represent a single sheepfold with a single shepherd—the Spirit of God."

Kennedy's comment was that "the unity of the West can lead to the unity of East and West until the human family is truly a 'single sheepfold' under God."

Earlier that day Kennedy had made his much-celebrated trip to the Vatican. As usual the Vatican laid on all its majestic pomp. Remarked one sweating newsman, " 'Tis like a page out of Gilbert and Sullivan."

The Palatine Guard band struck up "The Star-Spangled Banner" when Kennedy's car pulled into the San Damasus courtyard. The President and his party, including Secretary of State Dean Rusk, were escorted to an elevator which brought them up to the richly muraled Clementine Hall. This was as far as the 100-odd newsmen covering the event were allowed to go. The only exceptions were several "pool" reporters and photographers.

Kennedy, the United States' first Catholic President, went on through a series of anterooms and was introduced to Paul VI at the threshold of the pontiff's library. The President bowed but did not kiss the Pope's ring as Catholics normally do.

Asked why Kennedy did not kiss the ring, Presidential Press Secretary Pierre Salinger replied that he did not wish to discuss the matter publicly. Salinger said shortly afterward that a Roman Catholic monsignor was available to interpret, but he did not know whether the interpreter was actually in the room at the time or whether the audience was completely private. About fifteen minutes later Rusk was ushered into the private library, and subsequently other members of the White House staff entered. Kennedy was reported to have said to the Pope: "I hope to see you in the United States."

The Pope was described as replying with a non-committal gesture.

After the President left, the Pope greeted visiting newsmen in Clementine Hall. He was clad in a white robe, white skull cap, and red shoes. His first words were drowned out by the Palatine Guard band's send-off for the President.

"You know what we discussed," said the slightly built Paul VI. "Above all, the peace of the world." Kennedy's next stop was at Pontifical North American College on Janiculum Hill overlooking the Vatican. He was greeted there by a kiss from his own long-time archbishop, Richard Cardinal Cushing of Boston. Kennedy's sister, Mrs. Stephen Smith, also was on hand. "Hi, Jean," said Cushing. "My, you look good."

He then shook hands with Kennedy and jokingly poked him in the chest.

For a moment, the President looked startled. Cushing put up his fists in a boxing pose, and they broke into laughter.

What kind of era will Paul VI usher in? Vatican observers are straining for clues. One even saw in the Pope's new lightweight crown an apparent determination "to face the challenge of this anxious modern age." Perhaps the safest generalization is that Paul VI will gear his program around the priority of peace in keeping with the growing world feeling that absence of hostilities is a desirable end in itself. The prospect that perhaps deserves the most attention is how he might try to implement the proposal made in John XXIII's "Pacem in Terris" encyclical for a new global authority to guard the peace.

News　July 19, 1963

59 *Evangelicals in the Church of Rome*

The worn, tired, sterile apologetic of many Protestants that nothing can change in the Roman Catholic Church, at least nothing that makes any real difference, is being soundly disproved today and exposed for what it always was, an all too easy defense of Protestantism. Big changes are occurring in the church of Rome, and many of these changes are wholesome, the work of the Holy Spirit and a source of joy to Protestants who are learning that easy slogans long used to characterize the other side are only half true. Protestants are also learning that many of the theological problems engaging Roman Catholic thinkers should also engage Protestant thinkers. The question of Scripture and tradition is surely one of these. Protestants, with their strong belief in the power of the Word of God, are heartened by the current renewal of interest in Scripture reading, teaching, and preaching among Roman Catholics. And, conscious of the power of the Word, they realize that no one can safely predict the possible extent of reform and renewal within the Roman church.

At no time since the Council of Trent in the sixteenth century has the church of Rome faced so many internal and external pressures toward action and reform. Within that church today, forces are at work that are in many ways similar to those at work in the church before the Reformation, though the problems of the two periods are etched against sharply contrasting backgrounds.

Since the time of Luther the papacy has been reformed so that recent popes have lived exemplary lives. There are no modern Tetzels hawking indulgences, promising buyers that the souls of their loved ones will fly out of purgatory even before their gold coins fall to the bottom of wooden chests. Simony and nepotism are not a grave problem, and red hats are not handed out to teen-agers or to those of royal blood. While there still is persecution of non-Catholics in some parts of the world, the days of the Inquisition are over. The church does not hand over heretics to the secular authorities to burn at the stake. The rack, the strappado, and the "iron lady" are no more. Thus the church of Rome in the twentieth century, faced with new pressures and problems, approaches them from within a situation vastly better than that in which the Reformers rose in the sixteenth century.

In the church of Rome before 1500 there emerged men like John Wyclif and the Lollards, John Huss of Bohemia, Jerome of Prague, and Savonarola. Some of them bore witness to their religious convictions as they were burned at the stake. They were succeeded by Luther, Calvin, Beza, and Knox, and the Reformation was born and grew. Surely it served a useful purpose even for the church of Rome. But the Counter-Reformation followed the Reformation, and one of its chief instruments was the Council of Trent, which convened intermittently from 1545 to 1563. There the Roman church was renewed, its witness consolidated, and its forms settled for four hundred years.

Now the Roman Catholic Church is at a major crossroads once again. From scores of sources around the world reports filter in of priests, nuns, and laymen who have experienced the same kind of religious experience as their counterparts of Reformation and pre-Reformation days. Unlike the Reformers, who were forced out of the church, these modern disciples remain within the fold. Yet they have come to know Jesus Christ in an intimacy that sometimes surpasses the devotion of many Protestants. The reality of their experience we cannot question; the depth of their commitment and the open expression of joy in their newfound faith are good to behold. This movement of God within the church of Rome comes at a time when it faces grave problems, some common to all faiths in the Christian tradition and some peculiar to that church. Atheism, higher criticism, the spread of Communism, the population and knowledge explosions, and the need for organizational updating to meet the challenge of the times are common problems. But the Roman church also faces knotty difficulties rising from an internal surge toward democracy, a marked interest in the priesthood of all believers, the question of the relevance of archaic church forms in modern society, the cry for religious liberty for all men, and a desire for academic freedom in educational institutions.

Undoubtedly, dissent and discontent within the Roman church were in some measure responsible for the calling of Vatican Council II. That council is over now. But the church will never be the same. The council opened windows through which refreshing breezes will continue to blow for many decades. There were the statement on religious liberty; the acknowledgment that the Jews are not unilaterally guilty of the death of Christ; the movement toward ecumenism and dialogue with other faiths; the reorganization of the church; a return to the Scriptures and the emphasis on biblical theology; the putting of the mass into the vernacular; and many others.

But amid these many changes one must recognize that the church of Rome has not changed and will not change in its essential theological position. Pope Paul is an intelligent man who knows who he is, what his office signifies, and what he must preserve. He must "reconcile the spirit of change . . . with the protection of the office he has inherited," says Sanche De Gramont in *Dominion* (January, 1966). Paul's definition of the papacy is unacceptable to Eastern Orthodox and Protestant alike. As late as two years ago he said to an assembly of the faithful: "This, dearest sons, is what an audience with the Pope should leave in your souls: the impression, indeed the stupor and the joy, of a meeting with the Vicar of Christ" (*ibid.*).

Now that the church of Rome has begun to reform itself once more, and will continue to do so in the future, we must ask what the outcome will be. Can the church contain the new revolutionary forces and tame them? Will those who press for change be satisfied if the church moves slower than events warrant? Will there come another schism in which spiritually vital elements of the church will be drawn off into new channels or into already existing but non-Catholic structures? Surely to meet the challenge of the spirit of change and at the same time maintain the papacy in its historic forms is a formidable task for Paul VI and his successors.

In the midst of change and renewal, evangelicals should reach out with heart and hand to those who, though they are in the church of Rome, are our spiritual brothers and sisters in Christ. Substantive changes have taken place within Protestantism, too. There are conflicting currents and opposing viewpoints. And it is unmistakably clear that Protestant evangelicals are far closer, in theology and commitment, to many within the church of Rome than to many liberals in the Protestant tradition.

History has its own sifting process. Therefore evangelicals must not isolate themselves from those of evangelical conviction within the Roman Catholic Church. Indeed, Protestant evangelicals have nothing to fear and much to gain by frank dialogue with the church itself. Bridges can and must be built and more intimate contacts made. If there is risk in encounter, so is there risk in any of life's relationships. And conversations with Roman Catholics pose risks for them as well as for evangelicals. Whatever the risks, they are minimized when Protestant evangelicals test all opinions (even their own) and sustain all doctrines by fidelity to the Word of God and insist that all fellowship and all conversation start and end with the Scriptures. In line with this principle, evangelicals can talk to anybody, at any time, and about any subject anywhere.

Editorial   March 18, 1966

60 *Depth Psychology*

EDWARD JOHN CARNELL

A review of *Theology of Culture,* by Paul Tillich (Oxford University Press, 1959).

Tillich has synthesized German speculation and American pragmatism. Depth psychology, with its roots in the Viennese school, is the key to this synthesis. Freud recovered the symbolism of common grace by accepting people who were unacceptable. Grace communicates a sense of worth. "You cannot help people who are in psychosomatic distress by telling them what to do. You can help them only by giving them something—by accepting them."

Within this pragmatic climate Tillich dilates the more speculative aspects of his system. Christology, for example, answers to man's search for self-realization. "There is a power from beyond existence which for us is verifiable by participation. This gives quite a different type of Christology. Christ is the place where the New Reality is completely manifest because in him every moment, the anxiety of finitude and the existential conflicts are overcome. That is his divinity." To separate the threads of biblical truth from this skein of speculative error will require considerable patience and theological skill.

Tillich evacuates Scripture of its dogmatic rights by contending that philosophy enjoys autonomy in "the description of the structures and categories of being itself and of the logos in which being becomes manifest. Any interference of theology with these tasks of philosophy and science is destructive for theology itself." One could only wish that the matter were this easy. Tillich, it would seem, has made an unfortunate concession to worldly wisdom.

Relieved of dogmatic theology, Tillich seldom misses a chance to depress those elements in Scripture that fall outside his system. The account of the virgin birth, for example, is "a most obviously legendary story, unknown to Paul and to John. It is a late creation, trying to make understandable the full possession of the divine Spirit of Jesus of Nazareth." This hypothesis may be fashionable in critical circles, but it is void of accuracy. Some enterprising reader ought to send Tillich a copy of J. Gresham Machen's *The Virgin Birth of Christ*. If we neglect the historical elements in Christianity out of a zeal to defend the transcendent elements, we exhibit a very poor understanding of Christianity.

When we ask Tillich why he builds his system on those parts of Scripture that he himself considers important, he replies in a somewhat disarming tone. First, he takes refuge in Protestant liberty. "There is no pope in Protestantism, and if the Bible speaks, it speaks to us. Not only is there no pope, there is no council of bishops, no presbyters, no voting of church members on these matters." Second, he appeals to the way in which the Church has conducted itself in previous cultures. Culture, he believes, dictates the Church's attitude toward the Gospel. "In the medieval church, it was the anxiety resulting from the social and spiritual chaos following the breakup of the Roman Empire which produced the transcendent-sacramental foundation of a hierarchical system to guide society and individuals. In the Reformation it was the anxiety of guilt and the message of justification which was decisive for every formula of all the Reformers. In modern Protestantism it has been the message of a religious cultural unity in view of a more personalistic—and in America, more social—conception of the Kingdom of God as a religious cultural unity."

For the benefit of readers who are nervously waiting to learn whether Tillich is propagating heresy, a consolatory announcement can be made with dispatch. By no stretch of Christian charity can Tillich's theology be considered consistently biblical.

When we place Tillich on the Index, however, have we really accomplished anything constructive? Hardly. Christ did not shed his blood that we should spend our days as spiritual vultures, feeding on the carrion of other people's shortcomings.

The fact remains, and no orthodox remonstrance can change a line of it, that cultured people will continue to read Tillich, and with no small profit, either. Tillich, for example, defines sin as estrangement— "estrangement from oneself, from the other man, from the ground out of which we come and to which we go." At first blush this seems to contradict the confessional definition of sin as "any want of conformity unto, or transgression of, the law of God." But it may turn out, on more careful inspection, that the two definitions are quite friendly. Estrangement is a want of fellowship, and a want of fellowship is sin. Love is the law of life.

Although Tillich prefers speculation to exegesis, he yet is one of the most stimulating thinkers of our day. He is energetically trying to make faith relevant. And that is more than can be said of many who boast possession of the divine oracles.

Tillich challenges culture on the analogy between the gift of God's grace and the expressions of kindness in therapeutic psychology. God accepts people who are unacceptable. "This, of course, includes the reformation point of view, a view which has also been rediscovered by medicine, namely, you must feel that you have been accepted. Only then can one accept himself. It is never the other way around. That was the plight of Luther in his struggle against the distorted late Roman Church which wanted 'that men make themselves first acceptable and then God would accept them.' " The Church has been culpably tardy in applying Freudian insights to the biblical doctrines of original sin, common grace, and justification.

Since confessional Christianity tends to be anachronous in its thought forms, Tillich may seem more radical than he really is. In any event, Tillich is here to stay. Even if a critic rejects everything Tillich says—an almost impossible situation—Tillich will nonetheless force the critic to do some very serious searching of soul. And who knows what may come of this? For if the critic were to show a little more concern for Tillich's truth, Tillich might show a little more concern for Tillich's error.

Book Review   July 6, 1959

61   *"What If . . ."*

JOHN LAWING

Say this to the people of Israel, "The ground of all being has sent me to you."

May 31, 1965

62   *Modern Theology at the End of Its Tether*

A spate of books and articles is currently appearing on "the problem of God," assuring us, in the name of the modern intellectual, that God is indeed an enigma to the man of our times. The alien cultural setting of the late twentieth century, we are told, demands a "contemporary understanding" of the Gospel because of the special stance of the "godless" man of our times. In certain seminary classrooms and in the writings of certain churchmen, one now finds supposedly serious proponents of the Christian religion assuring us that mankind is now too adult to take the theology of the Bible literally.

Anybody familiar with the history of philosophy will recognize this so-called gospel of modernity as antique rationalism. What is new in this recent turn is (1) that some widely publicized theologians and churchmen are saying it; (2) that they are saying it not after openly forsaking the Church for the world but rather within the Church itself; and (3) that at the same time they are welcomed as authentic Christian voices in denominational and ecumenical dialogue.

These theological faddists reject the right of revealed religion to disclose how reality is objectively constituted and proceed to construct an anti-metaphysical or non-metaphysical "Christianity." The way for an acceptance of their views was prepared, sometimes unwittingly, by recent modern religious thought from Kant to Kierkegaard to Bultmann. Although the dialectical and existential theologians reasserted the reality of the transcendent and insisted on special divine revelation, these theologians were anti-intellectualistic in that they denied the ability of conceptual reason, even on the basis of revelation, to provide objective and universally valid knowledge of transcendent Being. The net effect was to undermine confidence in orthodox Protestant theology as an authentic exposition of supernatural realities.

In the post-World War I ferment, Rudolf Bultmann made a spectacular effort to conform Christianity to the modern scientific world view. His existential theology insisted on the reality of the transcendent but spoke of the supernatural as myth. The biblical account of the supernatural, the Bultmannians contend, aims to promote our self-understanding and need of spiritual decision, not to give us objective truth about God or to inform us how ultimate reality is constituted. Bultmann minimized the importance of the historical aspects of Jesus' life as unimportant for faith and stressed the centrality of the kerygma —the apostolic preaching of Jesus Christ. But supporters of this pseudo-Christian ideology have split into rival camps, and its foundations are now so widely viewed as tottering that most religious frontiersmen are consciously seeking an alternative. The Bultmannian forces are decimated; the movement lives on in "the new hermeneutic" sparked by Fuchs and Ebeling in Germany and by Robinson and Michalson in America; and Conzelmann, Dinkler, and even Käsemann retain significant loyalties to the dethroned monarch of Marburg existentialism. But the Bultmannians have ascribed to the Bible positions and meanings the New Testament does not validate. The New Testament Gospel includes the total public ministry of Jesus Christ; Mark's account opens with the declaration that Jesus' baptism is the beginning of the Gospel, even as the Resurrection is the climax. Moreover, the New Testament includes affirmations about the transcendent nature of God and the historical character of his acts.

Ever since Karl Barth and Emil Brunner exposed classic modernism as a rationalistic heresy, many British and American liberals have been eager to fly a new flag. The breakdown of Barth's influence, however, and the evident decline and decay of Bultmannian theology, have herded American liberals of anti-metaphysical temperament into the expanding fold of analytical philosophy as a refuge from historic Christian faith. Analytical philosophers regard the function of philosophy neither as the construction of a metaphysical theory embracing ultimate reality nor as the provision of answers to persistent questions about man and the world, but as the clarification of all assertions. Analysis of concepts has always been an essential preliminary task of philosophy, but linguistic analysis is now asserted to be its main, even its exclusive, function.

After A. J. Ayer's *Language, Truth and Logic* (London: V. Gollancz, 1936) lifted logical positivism to prominence beyond the attention commanded by such earlier proponents of analytic philosophy as G. E. Moore and Bertrand Russell, empirical verifiability gained acceptance as the criterion of meaning. The patent fact that metaphysical, theological, and ethical statements are intrinsically nonsensical and empirically unverifiable came to signal a radical assault on the truth-character of religious assertions.

Such theological innovators now find the secret of "up-to-the-minute" accommodation of Christianity to "empirico-scientific reality," not in mythical interpretation of the Bible alongside an existential philosophy of self-understanding, but rather in a speculative view of "the function of religious language." Contemporary linguistic analysis becomes the open-sesame of religious intelligibility and acceptability. Whereas the Bultmannians built on the pervasive academic influence of Heidegger's existentialism, and in this context sought to vindicate a permanent role for Christianity by existentializing the New Testament message, the "linguistic theologians" seek to vindicate religion in the current climate of analytic philosophy by secularizing

Christianity. To authenticate religious experience on this universal basis, the linguistic theologians dismiss even Bultmann's attenuated interest in the kerygma of Jesus Christ.

While the linguistic theologians, over against the logical positivists, deplore the restriction of meaning to empirically verifiable statements, they nonetheless defend the validity of religious language on other grounds than truth. The value of traditional religious affirmation is not preserved as conceptually significant; instead, the verificational analysis is functional. Ludwig Wittgenstein's insistence on a variety of "language-games" has encouraged some analysts to defend religious affirmations as "meaningful assertions of relationships" not empirically verifiable. Religious beliefs are assigned therapeutic significance, or are viewed as meeting a psychological necessity in human life, or as providing experience with creative human models akin to working models in the scientific world. Such validation of religious belief nowhere answers the modern mind's insistent question whether or not religious beliefs are true, not simply useful or helpful.

If the realm of cognitive language must be denuded of all trans-empirical concepts, then no affirmations about the supernatural are rationally verifiable, and no reason can any longer be given for preferring one metaphysics or ontology above another, nor for regarding any view of ultimate reality as right. If all religious concepts are banished beyond the realm of verification, no reason can be adduced for choosing one faith or set of religious beliefs over its opposite, or, for that matter, for choosing any at all on rational grounds. But regardless of the piety, prominence, or presumption of theologians who insist merely that religious views are pragmatically or psychologically serviceable, twentieth-century men can be counted on swiftly to abandon beliefs they can no longer cherish as true.

Among some theologians, the empirical validation of Christianity leads not to a special role for religious language as much as to a deliberate restatement of Christianity and of the Gospel in secular this-worldly terms. The secular theologians all reject objective ontological and dogmatic language about a transcendent Deity, and include within the category of myth even the kerygmatic elements on which recent European theology has insisted.

Secular theology is post-existentialist and post-European in that it summons contemporary Protestant theologians to end their "crying out to God." Theological language is tapered to statements about Jesus of Nazareth and human self-understanding. These secular theo-

logians are not concerned simply because supersensible realities are
without effective force in modern life; they boldly aim to make religion relevant by erasing its supernatural aspects entirely. From the
objective-transcendent personal God of Judeo-Christian theology,
therefore, neo-Protestant interpreters have moved in recent generations to the nonobjective-transcendent personal God (Barth and
Brunner), to the nonobjective-transcendent impersonal Uncondi-
tioned (Tillich), to the nonobjective-mythological-transcendent personal God (Bultmann), to nonobjective-nontranscendent religion.
Thomas J. J. Altizer views "the death of God" as a "historical event"
datable in our own lifetime, and offers his religious speculations as an
example of relevant theologizing in the time of "the death of God."
Paul M. Van Buren obligingly informs us that "the word 'God' is
dead" (*The Secular Meaning of the Gospel,* Macmillan, 1963, p.
103); what remains is the man Jesus—his life and death and availa-
bility for others, his values, and the contagion of his perspective, urging us to freedom from self-concern and to self-surrender for others.
But skillful critics observe that, on the one hand, Van Buren's "secularized Christianity" perverts the essence of New Testament Christianity no less than does Bultmann's existentialism, and that, on the
other hand, by championing the ethical centrality of Jesus as one who
calls us to serve in the world, "secularized Christianity" espouses a
selection of values fully as unintelligible and offensive to the modern
empirico-scientific outlook as the traditional concepts Van Buren proposes to replace.

On the assumption that modern knowledge renders unintelligible
the scriptural formulation of the Gospel, the secular theologians elim-
inate the invisible, transcendent, absolute God of the Bible. All references to the supernatural God, to supernatural relationships, even to
dependence on the supernatural, are spurned. The metaphysical and
cosmological aspects of revealed religion are thereby eliminated and
the relevant subject matter of theology reduced to the historical, human, and ethical.

If this maneuver were ventured frankly as an open and avowed
repudiation of revealed religion, confusion would be lessened and
truth and fact advanced, since God and Christ and redemption and
the Church lose their biblical actuality in these contemporary fabrica-
tions. But Bishop J. A. T. Robinson promulgates his "Honest to God"
as an authentic revised version of biblical Christianity, while Van
Buren seeks to assure us that his secularized Christianity omits "noth-

ing essential" to Christian faith. Yet these and similar efforts—among them William Hamilton's *The New Essence of Christianity* (Association Press, 1961) and Altizer's *Mircea Eliade and the Dialectic of the Sacred* (Westminster, 1963)—not only violate the essential spirit and substance of historic Christianity but radically alter the role of religion in human life.

The most obvious defect of this contemporary theological faddism is its mislocation of the problem of modern man. It is always falsely implied that no view of Christianity is possible for modern man other than one screened through empirical categories. But the modern problem is not the transcendent God but rebellious man—not modern man in some peculiar way but man as fallen. Even in our time we are not dealing with a man who is wholly "godless," although we are dealing assuredly with a man who is ungodly, with a creature in the grip of sin and death, for whom sin and death are such inescapable concerns that he resorts to the most ingenious devices—existential, linguistic, and secularistic—to becloud their existence. Because theological renegades ask the wrong question—How transform Christianity to enlist the secular man?—they come up with the perverse answer: Restructure the Gospel! rather than: Regenerate the sinner!

Much of the popular reading of our day, as well as some technical literature, mirrors man's spiritual evasion and equivocation, his moral ambiguity, his self-compromise in the face of ultimate concerns. The theological faddists provide a tidy formula capable of easy memorization and useful as a "shocker" by modern Athenians ever on the prowl for something new, always suspicious of a faith "once for all delivered to the saints," and therefore incapable of finding an intellectual resting-place. In hushed tones they impart the latest secret of the cosmos: "Christian faith is gone; Christian hope is gone; all that is left is Christian love—but that's enough."

To a generation dangling over the abyss of despair, any rope, however slim, is welcome. If agape can bear the burden of late twentieth-century doubt and anxiety, then agape is perhaps worth a try. If the supernatural and transcendent must go, if the historical is all that is left, especially the example of Jesus, perhaps that will patch up our raveling existence, even if this "agape" at times overtly justifies what the divine commandments and Jesus of Nazareth disapprove. It is not the inner logic of this proposal but the dire futility and emptiness of modern life that shapes a bare interest in this possibility—and, for that matter, in a hundred and one other contemporary cults. The linguistic theologians never tell us why human life ought to hold together; nor why Jesus alone holds it together; nor that this religious belief is objectively true; nor why it is logically superior to a contrary view. Nor can they.

Few college students are won to Christian faith by the modern proposals, which elevate the dated prejudices of the modern mind into status symbols and conform even the revelation of God and the Gospel of Christ to them. The man in the street and the layman in the pew shun such appeals because men desire truth no less than emotional satisfaction and cultural acceptance. None of the non-metaphysical theologies from Barth to Bultmann to Tillich to Robinson has nourished any great revival of lay interest in the Christian religion.

Back in the early 1950's Homrighausen noted that the entire "Word of God" movement in contemporary theology had failed to produce a single evangelist. How irrelevant to the Great Commission can theologians get? Where do modern men flock around Bultmann or Tillich or the linguistic theologians or the "death of God" theologians, crying out: "You have restored authentic Christianity to us!" The captive theological students in ecumenically minded seminaries are their main "converts"—Tillich made Tillichians at Harvard, Hamilton makes Hamiltonians at Colgate Rochester, Van Buren makes Van Burenites at Duke, Altizer makes Altizerites at Emory, and Loomer will be making Loomerites at Berkeley Baptist. But modern men hungry for spiritual reality will not be flocking there. They will fill up the Los Angeles Coliseum, or Madison Square Garden, and the other huge modern arenas to hear Billy Graham preach the New Testament evangel—and they give Graham a hearing in Europe and Africa no less than in North America and Latin America. Those who are always revising the Gospel to protect its power to persuade modern men seem curiously to leave the hard-core secularists as unpersuaded as ever.

The great modern tragedy is not the problem of the man in the street. It is the spectacle of the theologian who assures him that he can repudiate supernaturalism, and that he must do so, to become a Christian. This means not "the death of God" but the death of Protestant theology, however ecumenically respectable it may be.

Today skepticism has overtaken an ecclesiastically entrenched vanguard of pseudo-theologians disposed to restrict valid knowledge to the world of nature and to man as described by the sciences. Whatever criticism empirical scientism offers of the Christian religion and of the

Bible, these pseudo-theologians accept; they no longer know what it is to contemplate the higher criticism of the prevailing philosophy of science. But it is precisely the contemporary theological reluctance to probe the possibility of attaining knowledge of transcendent reality and the significance of cognitive reasoning in religious experience that is the crucial neglected theological issue of our century.

While theologians dismiss cognitive knowledge of God, they remain intellectually powerless to compete with the sensate-empirical outlook of the modern age—whether they appeal to faith, to experience, to intuition, or to dialectical or existential varieties of "revelation." Alasdair MacIntyre considers Tillich and Bultmann atheists, because these guiding theologians of Robinson's "Honest to God" reject a literal objectifiable theism ("God and The Theologians," in *Encounter,* September, 1963). Yet MacIntyre himself, bypassing the "death of God" stop on the expressway from theism to atheism, goes to the end of the line. Karl Barth was surely right in saying that the distance was not great from the domain of Tillich and Bultmann to that of Feuerbach, but he was profoundly wrong in thinking that the mansions of dialectical theology were securely located in the suburbs of supernatural theism.

If Christianity is to win intellectual respectability in the modern world, the reality of the transcendent God must indeed be proclaimed by the theologians—and proclaimed on the basis of man's rational competence to know the transempirical realm. Apart from recognition of the rational Creator of men made in his image and of the self-revealed Redeemer of a fallen humanity, who vouchsafes valid knowledge of the transempirical world, the modern Athenians are left to munch the husks of the religious vagabonds.

Editorial   July 16, 1965

63 *The Uncommitted*

JAMES WESLEY INGLES

In the deep wood, no road,
on the dark sea, too many stars,
through old and new ways faring,

without direction, mapless,
wanders the untrammeled mind.

Pale in the west, the sickled moon
after the bright sun's dying,
faint the perfume of the fading rose
and red as blood the dogwood leaf
when beauty touches the unsuspecting heart.

But what is beauty? What is good?
Who are the guilty? What is truth?
A wrinkled brow, a knowing shrug,
a sleepless night perhaps,
and then a little washing of the hands.

Twisted vine and upper room and olive grove
recall nothing to the mind;
Golgotha and the Emmaus road
bring neither tear nor burning,
and the white moveless stone Pietà
impresses only as a work of art.

Is it not wiser to withhold judgment,
to withdraw the hand, avert the eye,
to keep the head unbowed, the knee unbent,
to walk into the Shadow companionless,
still testing all things and committed to nothing?

                                                    May 8, 1964

64   *Bishop Robinson and His Paperback*

J. D. DOUGLAS

John Robinson, Bishop of Woolwich, is 44, a ban-the-bomb marcher,
member of the Labour party, defender of *Lady Chatterley's Lover,*
opponent of capital punishment, and campaigner for reform of severe
legislation against homosexuality ("a peculiarly odious piece of Eng-

lish hypocrisy"). On his consecration in 1959 he publicly vowed to be "ready with all faithful diligence, to banish and drive away all erroneous and strange doctrine contrary to God's Word."

A few months ago Robinson's paperback *Honest to God* hit the market (SCM Press, London; Westminster Press, Philadelphia). Currently at the top of the non-fiction best-seller list in England, sales to date total some 200,000. The effect it has produced is astounding. Despite a boost from the pulpit of Westminster Abbey from a preacher who turned out to be the publisher of the book, it has been denounced by the Archbishop of Canterbury as rejecting the concept of a personal God as expressed in the Bible. An Oxford don complained that the bishop was making it increasingly difficult to be an atheist; a humanist-agnostic acknowledged the bishop's "gratuitous contribution to our basic standpoint"; a left-wing columnist welcomed the idea of "a non-Christian bishop"; and London's *Daily Herald* hailed the "agonising and unusual spectacle—a bishop gasping for truth."

In a confused opening section Robinson scoffs at what he considers our outdated image of God as "up there" or "out there"—neither the liberal nor the symbolic view will do. He suggests the Freudians might be right: that "the God of traditional popular theology is a projection, and perhaps we are being called to live without that projection in any form. . . . Actually the Bible speaks in literal terms of a God whom we have already abandoned." Does it? Have we? What is not at all clear is what Robinson is putting in place of the view "we" are discarding.

In other sections of the book the argument becomes clearer, but the tone ceases to be speculative and becomes astonishingly dogmatic. Thus pages 118, 119: "The only intrinsic evil is lack of love. . . . This is the criterion for every form of behaviour, inside marriage or out of it, in sexual ethics or in any other field. For nothing else makes a thing right or wrong." Unless words are carefully defined, this is dangerous nonsense. "When we want to read of the deeds that are done for love," said George Bernard Shaw sixty years ago, "whither do we turn? To the murder column."

Of the Atonement, Robinson says: "The whole schema of a supernatural Being coming down from heaven to 'save' mankind from sin, in the way that a man might put his finger into a glass of water to rescue a struggling insect, is frankly incredible to man 'come of age'. . . . The 'full, perfect and sufficient sacrifice, oblation, and satisfaction for the sins of the whole world' supposed to have been 'made' on Calvary requires, I believe, for most men today more demythologizing even than the Resurrection" (pp. 78, 79). Apart from such destructive criticism, many will find offensive the impression given that these are the sort of conclusions necessarily arrived at if men are thoughtful about religion, and don't want to be branded as incorrigibly square. The impression is confirmed when we read page 70 on the Incarnation: "The belief that we are at this point and in this person in touch with God has increasingly been left to the religious minority that can still accept the old mythology as physically or metaphysically true." But on this subject the bishop goes further. "Jesus was not a man born and bred," he asserts, "he was God for a limited period taking part in a charade. He looked like a man, but underneath he was God dressed up—like Father Christmas." Well, he's got the point across, but many will never forgive him for the way he did it.

At other times Robinson shows an odd pseudo-pragmatic approach. In one section redolent of engaging candor he tells how the whole of the teaching on prayer he received in his theological college meant little: ". . . it was an impressive roundabout: but one was simply not on it—and, what was worse, had no particular urge to be." Because what his teachers said here rang no bell with him, that was the end of it—he found then, and confirmed later, that he was not "the praying type," that he had no "proficiency for it" (pp. 20, 92, 93).

In this book the names of Bonhoeffer and Tillich are freely bandied about, and both are extensively quoted. The latter scholar's name especially might serve to explain an incredible reference on page 21, where Robinson admits: "I cannot claim to have understood all I am trying to transmit." He might profess not to know what the message was when it left him, but when it gets to us it seems perilously like a major and determined attack upon Christian orthodoxy—though on occasion the Tillichian big guns are called into service to demolish a pitiable caricature of the faith.

Dr. Ramsey said that he was "specially grieved at the method chosen by the Bishop for presenting his ideas to the public." Dr. Ramsey is completely right: his words go straight to the heart of the situation. That Robinson realized the potential offense, as any intelligent man would, can be seen from his preface, which forecast that many would consider his book heretical.

After indulging in his little exercise in controversial divinity, Dr.

Robinson continues in office as a bishop in the Church of Christ. Perhaps on September 30, the fourth anniversary of his consecration, he might read again in the Book of Common Prayer words addressed to him on that occasion: "Be to the flock of Christ a shepherd, not a wolf; feed them, devour them not. Hold up the weak, heal the sick, bind up the broken, bring again the outcasts, seek the lost. Be so merciful, that ye be not too remiss; so minister discipline, that you forget not mercy: that when the chief Shepherd shall appear ye may receive the never-fading crown of glory; through Jesus Christ our Lord."

Current Religious Thought   June 21, 1963

65 The Temptation of Relativism

G. C. BERKOUWER

Everyone at some time in his life encounters the problem of relativism. It is said that our own time is characteristically relativistic, that we do not dare to speak of absolutes. This has its good side. We recall the absolutism of certain totalitarian states, which also reminds us that not everything is relativized in our century. We live in a time when some things are illegitimately absolutized. But still the relativizing of life is a profound matter, playing a role in the reflections and the viewpoints of the Christian faith.

Not everyone is sensitive enough to be greatly bothered by it, but some are almost overwhelmed when they first meet the suggestive and intoxicating idea that the Christian faith is a subjective conviction which is on the same plane with other no less earnest convictions. This is not merely a contemporary phenomenon. It elbowed its way into the environment of the Christian Church centuries ago. It was the syncretism of an early age; later it was the problem of "the absoluteness of Christianity" raised by the History of Religion school in the nineteenth century. In the latter instance, the problem arose through extensive research into other religions, which uncovered a depth and wealth of thought and conceptions of deity in pagan religions. The sharp line between Christianity and other religions was erased, even though there was still talk of the superiority of Christianity. The religions—including Christianity—were compared on the same basis. The conclusion was drawn that Christianity was not the one true religion, but an example of the many religious currents, a special form of the general essence of universal religion.

This so-called essence of religion had, through innumerable circumstances, taken various forms, including Christianity. It may have been acknowledged that Christianity was a very special form, but still only one of the many forms which arose out of the essentially religious structure of the human heart. A religious a priori was conceived, to be added to the theoretical, ethical, and aesthetic a prioris of the human mind. In the varying circumstances of life this religious a priori was actualized and specialized into this or that particular form of religion. There was no cleavage between Christianity and the other religions. Scholars pointed to the strong convictions that existed in every religion, to common forms of religious practices, such as a defined way of religious communal life, prayers, sacrifices, worship, notions of immortality, and so on. It was said that we could not conclude that a religion is unique and special because of the existence of a specially strong conviction, since strong convictions prevailed in many religions, notably in Islam. Thus, a general relativism began to prevail through the comparison of religions.

A clear example of this is seen in the so-called parliament of religions which was held in Chicago in 1893. There representatives of all religions joined together in the Lord's Prayer. All religions were joined; none was absolute. From this resulted a sharp criticism of any religion which pretended to possess a unique character. Such a pretension was considered impossible in the light of research into both the various religions and the human spirit. Religion had been discovered to be a disposition so close to the essence of the human spirit that we needed no longer to be surprised at the universality of religion.

It is evident that in this conclusion we encounter what may well be the most profound question that has faced Christian faith. It could hardly be otherwise than that many would be deeply impressed once the results of the study of comparative religions were popularized. People would say: Yes, there is a Bible, but there are also a Koran and many other holy books. There is a Redeemer, but other religions also concentrate their ideas of redemption around a specific redeemer. Does not all this come forth from a single law of the human spirit? And, hence, is the Christian faith, is the Bible, actually unique? Such questions collided head-on with the confession of the Church. The

Church was consequently criticized for trying to hold to her pretensions of absoluteness, a lost cause. The Church was not challenged to give up her religion, but to sacrifice her pretensions of the absoluteness of her religion.

The proclamation of the Church was directly involved. The message with which she had gone into the world was not an appeal to the special value of the thoughts of churchmen, but a trumpet sound, an invitation, a calling to the one way of salvation. Now, the witness of the Church in her missions to the heathen was up for question. This facet of the problem came quickly to the attention of the advocates of comparative religion. Troeltsch wrote, in 1906, that the common conception of missions had to undergo a radical change. It would, he claimed, be thereafter impossible to understand missions as a deed of sympathetic Christianity going into a dark world where salvation was unknown, to free the people from corruption and doom by conversion to the living God. Troeltsch supported the idea of missions, but suspected that much missionary effort stemmed from an overestimate of the worth of Western culture, a culture which other peoples could well claim to be unnecessary for them; they could find their own ways to salvation without the unwelcome assistance of the Christian message and culture.

One may ask, then, why a Christian church should be established in the East. Why not just as well a mosque in Paris?

The acceptance of the relativity of the Christian faith naturally produced a crisis in the missionary consciousness of the Church. Perhaps more accurately said, it brought a crippling of such consciousness. It may be possible to maintain missions on a cultural basis for a while, but in time the elan will die. This is the more evident as the cultural development of the non-Christian peoples proceeds, making it less and less possible to establish missions on the basis of one's own cultural aristocracy.

This process of relativizing does not involve only the theology of the philosophy of religion. It involves man, who sees no way to avoid the vacuum of relativity. He begins to make comparisons of his own. An attitude like that of Pharaoh's magicians begins to prevail in his heart. We recall how Jehovah said to Moses and Aaron: "When Pharaoh asks for a sign, take your staff and throw it on the ground before Pharaoh. It shall become a snake." But when the sign was given, Pharaoh was not convinced. He called his wise men and magicians, but "the magicians of Egypt, they also did in like manner with their enchantments. For they cast down every man his rod, and they became serpents." And Pharaoh's heart was hardened. He did not see in the signs a unique evidence of Israel's God. They were relativized by what Egypt's prophets could also do. The special character of a sign was removed from what Moses and Aaron did. The sign was not absolute, but relative. The same relativizing occurs later when Moses and Aaron threw a staff over the Nile and the Egyptians did the same. But finally the imitation of the Egyptians failed to work. Then Pharaoh's magicians said to Pharaoh: "This is the finger of God."

This throws light on the process of relativizing. The absoluteness of God's revelatory action for Israel in Egypt became irrefutably clear. Subsequently God led Israel out of the house of bondage by his mighty acts. Israel was under the impression of this; they were not long under the impression of the temporary parallel between Moses and Aaron and the magicians. But this is explained by the fact that the parallel was suddenly and demonstrably broken. Perhaps there are those who say that it would be convincing if, in the midst of the relativizing of Christianity, there were suddenly a special revelation that the Christian faith is after all something unique and absolute. But as long as this absoluteness is not clearly demonstrated, they will remain impressed with the certainties, convictions, intimations of immortality, and reverence within other religions, which make them parallel with Christianity. Thus they are tempted to go along with the current of relativity, a current which erases all exclamation marks and replaces them with question marks. This is hard; for it is frightful to live while questioning the ultimate.

The question marks are not taken away with a new voluntary decision to attribute absoluteness to Christianity. It would be a stout-hearted decision to regain a sure foundation in this world. But it does not work this way with the Christian faith; Christ will not thus be served. We do not find our way out by desperately writing exclamation marks over the question marks. The New Testament is clear that faith in the absoluteness of Christianity is not a decision of flesh and blood, not even when it is a stout-hearted decision. It also tells us that the apostles went forth into a syncretistic world possessed of many gods, without question marks after their witness to the one Redeemer. But their exclamation marks were pure gifts. They knew that they did not have them because they could prove precisely and convincingly for themselves the absoluteness of their faith. Neither were they the results of raw courage, but of human decision. Nor did they go with a kind of conviction that Jesus Christ was a superior Redeemer, but one among the many redeemers who were preached in the world. It did not work that way. It cannot work that way today.

It is, as it was for Paul, a struggle against flesh and blood, a struggle that only Jesus Christ can win for us through the Holy Spirit. There will be temptations to object to the idea that our faith in Christ does not arise from flesh and blood. It is not self-evident that we should seek our certainty in him alone, in the most exclusive way. Yet it is in that way alone that we can overcome the temptation to relativize our faith. It is profoundly remarkable that a man may know and maintain this as a treasure, that Jesus Christ is not preached by us as one way, but as *the* way, and that we can find in him everything needful. Yet this is the way that he walked among his own people. "I am the way, the truth, and the life." He said this after Thomas complained that he did not know the way. Thomas looked for a humanly possible way. But Jesus turned his eyes suddenly in another direction: *"I* am the way."

The disciples had enough difficulty along that Way, and they soon had no more reserves within themselves to draw from. They left it all to him. But when the Spirit of Christ was poured out, everything was changed. "Now must everything, everything change." And it was changed. There was a trumpet sounded over the world. And the hearing of the sound was saturated with blessing. From our human sentiments, we would rather first be convinced with rational certainty. We would rather first make certain that the sound of the trumpet is clear, and whether there may not also be other compelling trumpet sounds in the world. We would rather be certain of ourselves. But the amazing thing is that the farther we go along this way, the farther away the mystery of Christ fades from sight.

No one ever came to faith this way. The closer he may seem to have come in his search for proof, the farther away he actually walked. He may hear the message of Christ, but he wishes first to examine it. He hears that Christ first asks his question, but he demands that his own questions be answered first. But as he puts his questions to the fore, Christ's question is tabled. Christ's Word and Christ's question are not enough. He hesitates uncertainly, as did Philip, who heard Jesus and was impressed, but still reserved a feeling of unrest and uncertainty: "Show us the Father and it is enough." Christ answered: "Have I been so long with you and have you not known me? He who hath seen me hath seen the Father."

Only presumption would lead us to say that we understand fully what Christ meant. There are many thick volumes about it; the Church has stuttered when it has spoken about the Son and the Father. It has spoken of "Light of Light." And he who can comprehend it, let him comprehend it. But if we cannot comprehend it with our rational understanding, the absolute answer of Christ to Philip still stands. "He who hath seen me hath seen the Father," Jesus said. The answer sets everything in a wonderful light. John the Baptist, imprisoned, did not ask questions of the Pharisees and Sadducees. He sent his disciples to Jesus. And he received his answer: "Blessed is the man who is not offended in me." A new benediction! Who seeks more than this, seeks something less. It is on this way alone that the problem of the way on which men need never wander is solved.

Article   October 14, 1957

66   Civil Rights and Christian Concern

History will evaluate 1964 with its decision on the civil rights bill as one of the critical years in our national annals. The issue now before the country is more than one of integration versus segregation; it has to do with the integrity of our democracy.

As the Senate debate moves toward the day of decision, one senses a feeling of inevitability. This is a time of hard choices, not just for the senators who must cast their votes but also for the rank and file of their fellow Americans. We are all involved. The hour is long past—if it ever was at hand—when a man or woman might stand and watch the civil rights struggle as from a window overlooking the busy street.

What is happening this spring in the Senate is not an academic debate in which one listens to affirmative, negative, and rebuttal, and then awaits the judges' decision. No American, and least of all no Christian American, has the right to follow the civil rights debate unconcerned and unmoved. The vote on H.R. 7152 will indelibly affect the nation's future.

Patriotism demands individual concern in a matter so close to the public welfare. And patriotism is neither sub-Christian nor outmoded, even in this sophisticated age. For Christians it is plainly enjoined in Scripture. Moreover, ethics are united with patriotism; no Christian can stand passively by when the good of others is jeopardized. Obedience to the law of love for one's neighbor requires concern for the welfare of one's neighbor.

The kind of civil rights bill the nation will have depends in the first instance upon how the Senate votes. But it is equally true that how the Senate votes will reflect public opinion. In fact, the extra weight that will tip the balance one way or the other will come from the people. As James Reston, the well-known Washington correspondent, has said, "In the end, the temper of the country is likely to decide the issue."

What, then, are some guidelines for Christian concern regarding this great question? Four in particular may be listed: (1) The necessity for informed opinion. (2) The right of all Americans to equal rights of citizenship. (3) The obligation to respect those whose conscience leads them to convictions different from one's own. (4) The recognition that, essential as legislation is, moral problems are ultimately solved not by passing laws but by changing hearts.

First, informed opinion is demanded of every Christian who is in earnest about fulfilling his civic responsibilities. Valid opinion cannot be derived from ignorance nor developed out of a fog of second-hand ideas. With an issue so important as civil rights, it is not enough to let others do one's thinking or to reach conclusions based largely upon emotion.

If, as has already been stated, the climate of opinion will tip the balance in civil rights legislation, Christians to whom the moral aspects of the question must be paramount will have to take time and trouble to inform themselves about the issues at stake. This not only means reading what Senator X or Senator Y declares, what commentator A or pundit B writes, or what this newspaper or that news magazine says; it also means being familiar with the bill itself so as to know what its provisions are. Then, knowing what is involved, a Christian is obligated to come to his own conclusions thoughtfully and prayerfully. Only so does he earn, as it were, the right to add his weight to the growing amount of influence that is bound to affect the voting in the Senate.

Second, there is a major premise on which concerned opinion must rest. That premise is the constitutional right of all Americans to full citizenship. In particular, this means that no American should, because of his color, be deprived of his rights to vote, rest, eat, sleep, be educated, live, and work on the same basis as other citizens. Anything short of this is an intolerable deprivation of rights for one segment of the population, a deprivation that, by reason of its inherent injustice, violates basic morality.

Third, there is the obligation to respect the conscience of those who differ with their fellow Americans and fellow Christians regarding constitutional aspects of the legislation under consideration. The civil rights question is more than a controversy; it is a great conflict. In a conflict of such dimensions there are divergent convictions. Surely it is no compromise to recognize that however wrong one's neighbor may appear to be, he may be sincerely and honestly wrong.

Therefore, to dechristianize those who disagree with certain aspects of the civil rights bill is incompatible with Christian love and tolerance. Moreover, to equate any particular position regarding the bill with the Gospel of Jesus Christ may come perilously close to the Galatian heresy of proclaiming "another gospel." While justice for all, regardless of race, is an inescapable outcome of the Gospel, it is not itself the Gospel any more than any other fulfillment of the law of love is the Gospel. Let race prejudice and hatred be unmasked as the sins they surely are (and in the North as well as the South who is wholly free from them?); but let not a stand for civil justice or participation in demonstrations be confused with the Gospel through which alone men are redeemed by faith.

Fourth, there is the principle that law of itself, essential though it is, can be only a proximate, not the ultimate, solution of the deep problems of society. For the maintenance of the structure of society and the control of evil, laws are essential. Yet it may be that one of our national failings is the misconception that once a law is passed, a problem is forever settled. But laws must be obeyed, and ultimate obedience is a matter of the heart, not of compulsion, necessary though enforcement is. Sin is common to all, regardless of color. Therefore, Christian concern demands the ceaseless proclamation of the Gospel as the ground of ultimate reconciliation of the racial revolution.

There are also other matters of concern. While the Church should not engage in politics, as many evangelicals hold, it is nevertheless an inescapable obligation for Christians to take part in public affairs. Historically, amelioration of social problems has come through men and women whose hearts and consciences God has touched. The classic evangelical position is that the Gospel must be preached and that those whom Christ has redeemed will go out and serve as he leads them. If some Christians feel it their duty as individuals to stand side by side with their Negro brethren in the struggle, who is to say them nay? Are they not free to exercise their right of protest just as their more socially conservative brethren are free to respond in their way to the racial question? Yet granting this, it must also be said that restraint in demonstrations and respect for law are urgently needed. Extremism and threats of violence will only impede the processes of legislation.

But what of the civil rights bill? Constitutional aspects of the methods of enforcement specified in it require safeguards against possible misuse of the great powers conferred. Thus the position of some that the bill must be passed without the alteration of a word is unwise. At certain points it should and probably will be amended. But the need for legislation exists.

Christians may differ about the civil rights bill. Yet the path of Christian responsibility is plain. It leads inevitably to a position worked out before God. And that position ought to be made known. If individuals ask, "What can I do?" let them voice their convictions to their senators now and in these troubled days pray for the Senate and all in places of leadership.

Evangelicals, and indeed the Church as a whole, have lagged in racial relations. Especially has segregation within the churches been a stumbling block. Had the Church really practiced the love and brotherhood it preaches, the present crisis might have been averted.

These failures have indeed been lamentable. But once they are confessed, they must be put aside and attention centered upon the needs and obligations of the present. In this time of decision, evangelical spectatorism must give way to evangelical action that supports, as conscience leads, such legislation as assures all citizens the freedoms guaranteed them in the Constitution.

Editorial   May 8, 1964

67   *We Built a Temple*

LON WOODRUM

We built a temple, beautiful and tall;
we made it stronger than a Berlin-wall.

We built an altar brighter than a star,
where we could pray, forgetting hate and war;
where we could find a refuge from the heat
of human anger in the violent street.
We heard the gentle voice of one who told
of Him who talked of peace in days of old.
Calmed were our souls till it would almost seem
that Calvary was rather like a dream.
Here we, caught in a tranquilizing trance.
could meditate in holy arrogance.
We built a church out in the suburbs, far
from where the noisy, frantic people are.
We built a ghetto out of shining stone;
walled in from Man, we serve our God—alone.

March 4, 1966

68   *The March to Montgomery*

FRANK E. GAEBELEIN

The co-editor reports the historic civil rights march from Selma to Montgomery, Alabama.

Under the bright spring skies of Sunday morning, March 21, a crowd
of 8,000 stood before the twin-towered brick facade of Brown's
A.M.E. Chapel in Selma, Alabama. On the steps, an ecumenical service was in progress, the prelude to a historic fifty-mile march from
Selma to the state capitol at Montgomery.

"Those of us who are Negroes don't have much because of the
system," said Dr. Martin Luther King. "We don't have much education and some of us don't know how to make our nouns and verbs
agree. But thank God we have our bodies, our feet, and our souls. We
want to present our bodies and feet so the world will know the truth as
we see it. We'll march with great love for America, because we have a
great faith in democracy."

Shortly before one o'clock on the fifth day, the marchers, who had
come from the grounds of St. Jude's Church and Hospital in Montgomery, now numbering some 25,000, were massed before the white

capitol, from the classic dome of which the state and Confederate flags were flying, the U.S. flag being on a separate staff in a corner of the grounds. It was a symbolic picture—the orderly assembly of demonstrators headed by the 300 who for fifty miles had presented their bodies and feet for the cause of freedom, and the capitol, representing the power structure of segregation. In purpose and dramatic context, it was a decisive civil rights demonstration.

At the close of a 2 1/2-hour program, King spoke with moving eloquence. "We stand," he said, "with the conviction that segregation is on its deathbed in Alabama. . . . We're on the move now and no burning churches will deter us."

At four o'clock the assembly was over. A committee of twenty Alabama residents whose names had been approved by acclamation went to the capitol to present their petition but were told that the Governor's office was closed.

The Selma-to-Montgomery march was executed with the permission of a federal judge and under the protective escort of National Guardsmen mobilized by President Johnson. It began at 12:40 P.M. Sunday, on the same street where two weeks before a group of some 500 marchers were attacked by police, an event which aroused the conscience of millions. This time they crossed the bridge spanning the muddy Alabama without incident.

It was a varied multitude—young and old, white and black, educated and uneducated, a few beatnik types, and ministers in clerical garb. As they moved out of the city, most of the crowd turned back, the federal court order having limited the core participants to 300. All but about twenty in the actual line of march were Negroes from Alabama. Precedence was given those who had faced police violence.

So the march continued. Some in the line carried American and U.N. flags. The over-all spirit was cheerful; disaffection was not noticeable and the torrential rains on the third day elevated, rather than depressed, morale.

Among those in line was a one-legged young man on crutches, two nuns, a number of clergymen, and numerous women and children.

A Negro Methodist minister said that the march represented the American melting pot. He saw it as an expression of concern for constitutional rights. The ultimate solution, he declared, lies in the grace of God. He recognized the historic manifestation of grace at the Cross, yet felt it was being silently proclaimed at the march.

A young engineer from Philadelphia, a graduate of Columbia University, said bluntly that he had no faith and didn't care whether God or Christ ever existed, but that he left his wife and children to take part because of the issue of justice.

A young dropout from Queens College, New York, also professed no religious faith. "I'm here," he said, "because I don't like to see people stepped on."

A member of the militant Student Non-violent Coordinating Committee from Fort Collins, Colorado, declared that he wants to be "where there's action."

From Los Angeles came an actor-producer who said that his involvement built up until one morning he looked at his wife and children in his comfortable home and decided that he had to be in Alabama. "There comes a time," he said, "when benefit performances are not enough."

The Rev. Robert G. Long was there as a representative of his synod and of the Presbytery of Chicago. Richard Jackman, a leader in a New York labor union local, called himself a "Presbyterian socialist" and saw the marchers as an "elect group."

A number of theological conservatives participated in the march. Among them were several Christian Reformed ministers, including the Rev. Gordon D. Negen of the Manhattan Christian Reformed Church of Harlem; the Rev. Raymond Opperwall of Ridgewood, New Jersey; and the Rev. James A. Bonnema of South Windsor, Connecticut. These men viewed participation as an expression of their Calvinist heritage.

Another evangelical and Calvinist was James White, a Negro middler at Westminster Theological Seminary. Still another evangelical marcher was Bruce Crapuchette, a student at Fuller Theological Seminary, who came with a letter from Dr. David Hubbard, Fuller president.

From Seattle came the minister of music and the minister to students at the strongly evangelical University Presbyterian Church where Dr. Robert Munger is pastor. Both men said they gained "great respect for King's leadership."

Present also were Missouri Synod Lutherans and representatives of the Lutheran Church in America and the American Lutheran Church. Their placard read: "Lutherans care because Christ cares."

Among Pentecostal participants was Dr. J. Harry Faught, pastor of Danforth Gospel Temple in Toronto. Fought, executive secretary of the newly formed Evangelical Fellowship of Canada, said he was present to let people know that the evangelical conscience is sensitive to the issue of human dignity.

The extent of evangelical involvement is believed to have been without precedent in the current civil rights movement. Never before have conservative Protestants identified themselves so demonstratively with the Negro struggle for liberty.

The unifying factor in the midst of the theological and social diversity was clearly the constitutional issue—protest against abridgement of the right to vote and peaceable assembly to petition the government for redress of grievances.

The motivation and convictions of the marchers are one side of the event. The other side is the conviction and emotion felt by many people in the South. Just as the police brutality stirred world-wide emotion, so Judge Frank Johnson's court order and President Lyndon Johnson's speech before Congress greatly consolidated support of Alabama Governor George Wallace, whom large numbers of citizens consider a man of integrity and principle.

According to much Southern opinion, the march has set back the cause of racial relations and intensified bitterness. Alabama and the Deep South are seen as victims of gross injustice through biased reporting. There is also widespread public concern about reports of flagrant immorality among certain demonstrators.

Ministers in Alabama almost unanimously deplored the participation in the demonstrations of their fellow clergymen from outside the state. A leading Selma pastor, told by a visiting minister friend, "I felt relaxed and at peace after this demonstration," replied, "Yes, but I have to live with the tension here." Some contend that it takes at least as much moral courage for a pastor in the Deep South to maintain a moderate position as it does for his brother in the North to speak out.

Underneath the anxiety, there is genuine concern on the part of devoted Southern ministers and others for the constitutional questions.

The Alabama countryside through which the march passed is beginning to show the bright promise of spring. And the human condition is likewise capable of renewal. The march was a memorable witness to justice and human dignity. Through it, constitutional rights have been reaffirmed and Alabama and the nation have again been confronted, for all the world to see, with the inescapable responsibility for consistent application to Negroes of the liberties guaranteed by the

Constitution. Great problems remain, but a new page of history has been turned.

News   April 9, 1965

69 *Recasting the Ecumenical Posture*

When evangelicals evaluate ecumenical endeavors, the importance of "unity in truth" seems always to challenge a bare "unity in Christ." Evangelicals have constantly asserted that Christian unity without doctrinal unity is a sort of doubletalk. And this is true. Any new searching of Scripture in respect to the doctrine of the Church demands also a new searching of Scripture in respect to her Saviour and her Lord.

But evangelical failure to delineate Christian unity in a positive way should trouble our conscience and provoke evangelicals to exemplary leadership. If unity based on theological concession is undesirable, disunity alongside theological agreement is inexcusable. Evangelicals suffer from divisive internal competitions. To deplore the theological inclusivism that tries to overcome the fragmentation of Protestantism as a whole without earnestly seeking to overcome the proliferated witness of the evangelical segment is to remain spiritually vulnerable. It is time for evangelicals to find their ecumenical posture, and to set forth a doctrine of biblical unity which will preserve the vitality of the Gospel without compromising the witness of the Church.

Where would such an effort begin? In the first place, it would begin by a reaffirmation of the New Testament emphasis upon the essentially spiritual nature of the Church's unity. In the fourth chapter of Ephesians Paul's expression of Christian unity proceeds against the conspicuous background, not of identification with some earthly organization, but of spiritual union with Christ. The Church is identified by the permanent indwelling of the Holy Spirit. Paul's exposition of spiritual unity, therefore, is primarily concerned, not with organizational cohesion but with "the unity of the Spirit," that is, a unity authored by the Spirit of God. As Christians are individually united to Christ, so are they to be united in positive communion with God and to each other by the Spirit.

One of the unfortunate aspects of the competition among the National Council of Churches, the National Association of Evangelicals, and the American Council of Christian Churches is the extent to which organizational identification is made a test of personal devotion to Christ. It is shameful and sinful when Christians answer the question "Is he one of us?" by any other reference than to the body of regenerate believers of whom Christ is Saviour and Lord.

Secondly, the unity of which Paul speaks is not only a future prospect; it is a present reality. It is true that our Lord's most specific utterance on unity was spoken in the form of a prayer (John 17), but Pentecost stands between that prayer and the Christian Church. Paul does not say, "Let there be one body"; for the grammatical construction would then require, "Let there be one Lord . . . one God . . . one faith." No, there is one Lord. And under his lordship the true Church is one and has always been one. It is no coincidence that Christianity has been strongest when its leaders have preferred to be martyrs rather than to allow an encroachment on this lordship of Christ.

In spite of a real and essential unity, however, the immense practical problem of realizing the unity remains. The unity of believers is indeed God's gift, but believers can threaten or deny this unity in Christ. In some respects, all our contemporary ecumenical expressions are reactionary compromises against the modern ecclesiastical predicament that threatens this essential oneness.

This practical consideration throws light on the ecumenical problem itself. The ecumenical task is not one of simply relating presently existing denominations, because these denominations are themselves torn by theological divergencies. In point of fact, the existing proliferation into separate and competing movements, each of which virtually claims authentic identification as the true body of Christ, is as much if not more of a scandal as the denominational divisions. If Christians are to discover authentic, lasting unity in any practical sense, the ecumenical endeavor must begin with the ecumenical problem itself—in the egoistic and divisive appetites of the human heart.

What can be done to recast creatively the current ecumenical posture? The frankest way to show our eagerness to overcome the endless Western distinctions within the Christian Church is to concede the temporary, parochial, and quasi-reactionary character of the ACCC, the NAE, the NCC, the WCC, the WEF, the ICCC, and all the other existing ecumenical expressions. None of them adequately overcomes the embarrassment of the competitive structurings of the modern Christian witness. Why not then urge Protestants simply to use the one term *Christian:* the Fifth Avenue Christian Church, the Tenth

Christian Church, and so on. The New Testament reflects no single church polity. Why then should the twentieth-century Christian Church be embarrassed by plurality of polity? And if a parenthetical denominational suffix such as (Presbyterian) or (Anglican) is dispensable, let us not insist that a replacement like (NCC-related) or (NAE-related) or (ICCC-related) is indispensable.

Can we make headway in eliminating features of the present proliferation which all recognize to be undesirable, and yet remain true to the biblical revelation? We cannot speak for one another's constituencies. But we can each resolve to bring our own parochial or limited expressions of Christian unity continually under the scrutiny of the biblical norm and to prod believers on the local level to conscientious and creative effort to seek the Spirit's fullness in the fellowship of believers.

Whatever the cost in terms of denominational prestige, service opportunities, or organizational promotion, we can be ready to debate the issue of Christian unity in terms of first-century priorities rather than of the latest twentieth-century proposals. The important point is that we hear what the Spirit has actually said and is saying today, and that we do not let our modern prejudices or our favorite proposals obstruct the recovery of the biblical orientation of the Church in the world.

We are confronted today by an inescapable conviction that this generation of history demands a new posture from us all. The sincere hope is that the evangelical Christian witness might yet recover more of its unanimity, and by God's Spirit play an active role in shaping a new day.

Editorial   October 26, 1962

70 *Protestantism's Amazing Vitality*

KENNETH SCOTT LATOURETTE

We are repeatedly hearing the statement that we are living in the post-Christian, and especially the post-Protestant era. The data adduced to support this analysis are sobering. But to generalize from them is to be blind both to history and to the current global situation. Indeed, the opposite is true. If mankind is viewed as a whole, never has Christ been as great a force in the human scene and never has Protestantism played as large a part in the human drama.

The evidence for the sombre diagnosis is obvious. If we are to appraise the world situation in its full dimensions we must not dodge it. We must face it in all its stark reality. The march of atheistic communism across much of Europe and Asia and now with its footholds in the Western Hemisphere is a grim fact. Within the past 45 years, communism has brought approximately a third of the human race under its sway. Wherever it has control, the Church has been beleaguered and has lost in numbers. Less spectacular but in some respects more ominous is the growth of what we call "secularism"—the dismissal of religion and especially of Christianity as irrelevant and intellectually untenable. In Western Europe, the traditional heartland of what we have been accustomed to call Christendom, church attendance has sharply declined. That is true not only in the cities, where the forces of the evolutionary age in which we are immersed are centered, but also in many rural districts. It is common to both Protestantism and Roman Catholicism. In Latin America the process of de-Christianization of what in an earlier era was seemingly the most successful Roman Catholic mission field has continued. The overwhelming majority of the population regard themselves as Catholics, but only a decreasing minority can be regarded as "practicing" their religion. The two devastating world wars of the present century were fought with weapons and methods that were first devised in "Christendom." The first of the wars broke out in "Christendom." The second can be said to have begun with Japan's attack on China in 1931 and 1937, but it attained global dimensions with the explosion in Europe in 1939.

Most of the forces which have challenged Christianity had their inception among peoples regarded as Protestant. The deism which contributed to the skepticism of the eighteenth century and to the French Revolution was first formulated by men who conformed to the (Protestant) Church of England. Communism was given its classic formulation in predominantly Protestant England. That was by Marx and Engels. They had been reared as Protestants but believed that the stubborn facts of contemporary society and scientific knowledge made necessary the abandonment of the faith. Much of the scientific achievement which has undermined the faith of millions, including especially the formulation of the theory of evolution, has been by men of Protestant upbringing. Two among many were Charles Darwin, who had once intended to enter the ministry of the Church of England, and Herbert Spencer, who had his boyhood and early youth in a strongly evangelical atmosphere. The Industrial Revolution with its creation of machines and the factory system and a type of urban society which has made difficult the maintenance of church life, had its inception in Protestant Great Britain. The atomic bomb, with its threat to civilization and the survival of the human race, was first developed in what we once regarded as Protestant America.

These indisputable facts could be given in more detail and to them others could be added. Were they the entire picture, we Christians, and especially we Protestants, would have to acknowledge, regretfully, that we are in the post-Christian, and especially the post-Protestant era. Were they all, we would be forced to say that Christianity, notably Protestantism, had been giving rise to forces which are destroying it—that Christianity has been digging its own grave.

But those who focus their eyes on these facts ignore both important features of history and significant movements of our day which tell a very different story.

First of all, there has never been a Christian era. To be sure, the first five centuries after Christ witnessed the winning of the nominal allegiance to him of the large majority of the population of the Roman Empire. We have rightly called it an amazing achievement. But the Roman Empire embraced only a small fraction of the earth's surface. Most of mankind was outside its borders. It included only a minority of even civilized mankind. To the east of it were Persia, India, and China, together far more populous and certainly as highly civilized. In the first five "Christian" centuries the first two were touched only slightly and the third not at all by the Christian faith. Even the Roman Empire was only superficially Christian. The morals of the majority of its population had been affected very slightly. The rise of monasticism was a protest against the non-Christian lives of the millions who bore the Christian name—the earnest attempt of minorities to lead the full Christian life.

For several hundred years even this superficial Christianity seemed to be on the way to extinction. In the seventh and eighth centuries a new religion, Islam, espoused by the followers of Mohammed, became the dominant religion in about half of the erstwhile "Christendom." Not far removed from them in time, hordes of "barbarians"—the ancestors of most of those who will read these lines—swept down from the North in successive waves which lasted for about six centuries and threatened to obliterate the portions of "Christendom" which had not come under Moslem rule.

In time these barbarians were "converted." But for the majority, conversion entailed no thorough commitment to Christ. We are often told that the European Middle Ages witnessed the high-water mark of the Christian tide. But medieval Western and Southern Europe, nominally Christian, and containing the majority of those who bore the Christian name, embraced even a smaller proportion of civilized mankind than had the domains of the Caesars and only a very small section of the land surface of the globe. Moreover, although Christianity made a deeper impress upon the culture of medieval Western Europe than it had on that of the Roman Empire, Western Europeans were far from fully conforming to the standards of Christ. For example, recall the Crusades. The Papacy stimulated these successive wars of conquest which in the name of the Cross cost the lives of hundreds of thousands and left a legacy of hate which still embitters relations between the West and the Arab world and which deepened the gulf between the Orthodox East and the Roman Catholic West. By a strange irony, Pope Urban II, noted for his efforts to reform the Church, initiated the First Crusade, and Bernard of Clairvaux, esteemed as one of the outstanding saints of all time, preached the Second Crusade.

The Reformation, both Protestant and Catholic, raised the level of the lives of the Christians of the West and was followed by emigration and missions which planted the faith over a wider area than in any preceding era. But even then, in Asia, the most populous continent, Christians remained small enclaves and until the present century numbered only a few thousand in Africa south of the Sahara.

In the sense of mankind's conformity to the Christian faith, there has, then, never been a Christian era. As a second fact we must recognize that in no previous age has that goal been as nearly attained as it is in the present century. This is seen in at least six ways:

1.   Never has the Christian faith been as widely accepted as it is today. Indeed, no other religion has ever had as extensive a geographic spread as has Christianity in the twentieth century. It is true that the world contains more non-Christians than at any previous time, but that is because of the population explosion of the past two or three centuries. In the past 50 years the percentage of those who bear the Christian name has mounted in land after land—notably in India, Indonesia, and Africa south of the Sahara. In the United States

the proportion of the population who are church members has grown from about one-twentieth at the time of our independence from Great Britain to nearly two-thirds in 1961.

Significantly, in contradiction to the assertion that this is the post-Protestant era, in the past 150 years the spread of Christianity has been more by Protestantism than by any other branch of the faith. Much of the geographic expansion has been through Roman Catholics, but more has been through Protestants. A century and a half ago Protestantism was confined almost entirely to Northwestern Europe. Today it is the prevailing form of the faith in the United States, Canada, Australia, New Zealand, and South Africa, and it is increasing by leaps and bounds in Latin America, the Philippines, Africa south of the Sahara, India, and Indonesia. Much of the growth has been by migration from Northwestern Europe, but it has been chiefly by "home" and "foreign" missions.

2. Christianity is more deeply planted among more peoples than ever before. Until the last half century the churches among non-European peoples were mostly dominated by Westerners. The anti-colonial, anti-imperialist surge of the past four decades might have been expected to have weakened these churches; but because of the inner vitality of the faith in land after land indigenous leadership has been emerging. Among some peoples, the faith continues to spread with little or no help from the churches of Europe and America. We are seeing this, for example, among the Bataks in Indonesia, in the Southeast Asia Christian Conference, and in the Pentecostal movements in Brazil and Chile. The circumstance which we accept as axiomatic that the churches of peoples of European origin in the United States, Canada, Australia, New Zealand, and South Africa produce their own leaders, lay and clerical, and do not depend on Europe for them, is evidence of the manner in which the faith has become rooted in these lands.

Here, too, although the Roman Catholic Church has made striking advances, the gains have been more pronounced among Protestants. For example, the Roman Catholic Church in the United States still depends in part on Ireland's Catholic South for its clergy, and only a few clergy come from Europe to the Protestant churches of this country.

3. In no country—with the possible exception of North Korea (where we do not have data)—has Christianity been erased by communism. In Russia both the Orthodox and the Baptists persist and attract adherents from the younger generation. On the mainland of

China, although diminished in numbers, the churches go on and baptisms of adults as well as children are known to be taking place.

4. New movements are appearing in the churches—proof of continuing vitality. Often they enlist only a few and are what Toynbee has called "creative minorities." Some are much larger. In the Roman Catholic Church are the liturgical movement, the increase in Bible study, and Catholic Action, all of them engaging growing numbers of the laity. In Protestantism are the Evangelical Academies in Germany, Kerk in Wereld in The Netherlands, Iona in Scotland, "house churches" and "retreat centers" in England, and numberless movements of many kinds in the United States.

5. As never before Christians are approaching an answer to our Lord's high priestly prayer "that they all may be one." In a day when our contracting globe with the emergence of a world neighborhood— tragically quarrelsome—challenges them to a united witness, Christians are coming together. That is happening in a variety of ways— partly through the "Ecumenical Movement" and partly through other channels. Christians are still far from attaining to the unity implied in our Lord's command that his disciples love one another as he loved —and loves—them, but advances are being made. These, too, are primarily among Protestants and on Protestant initiative.

6. Christ is having a wider effect upon mankind than ever before. That, too, is chiefly through Protestantism. Among the many examples are the Red Cross and the United Nations, both clearly of Protestant parentage, and the influence upon Gandhi, and through him on all India, this through Gandhi's contacts with Protestants.

What is the meaning of this strange and striking contrast—on the one hand between the growth of movements antithetical to the faith and chiefly through a perversion of Protestantism, and, on the other hand, the amazing vitality and growth of the Christian forces, also largely through Protestantism?

Both are foreshadowed in the teaching of our Lord. On the one hand is his breath-taking Great Commission to make disciples of all nations, baptizing them, and teaching them to observe all that he has commanded. On the other hand his parable declares that both wheat and tares are to grow until the harvest. As Christians seek to obey the Great Commission they witness the progressive fulfillment of the prophecy in the parable. "The children of the kingdom" increase in numbers and in their fruitage in the life of mankind. "The children of the wicked one" also multiply.

Is God to be defeated? We are told that he sent not his Son into the world to condemn the world—the world which crucified his Son—but that through his Son the world might be saved. Clearly, as the Church has long known, we are living between the times. God's purpose is to sum up all things in Christ, whether in heaven or on earth—a staggering promise of cosmic significance. The "all things" must embrace this vast universe. It was through "the Word" that "all things" were made —through his Son God created the world—and the Son has been appointed "heir of all things." We are warned against seeking to establish a chronology for the attainment of God's goal or for a resolution of the contrast. But our faith is in God. We will not allow his Word to fail in the mission to which he has sent it. In his own good time and his own way, not ours, he will accomplish the purpose which he has in Christ.

Article   March 2, 1962

71   Russian Orthodox Church Voted into WCC Membership

CARL F. H. HENRY

The ecumenical movement reaches behind the Iron Curtain. The editor reports from New Delhi.

During the long week preceding the opening sessions of the World Council of Churches' third assembly, one topic dominated almost every discussion. But when Britain's Ernest Payne gaveled the Monday morning business session into action, only 31 minutes were required to dispose of what may go down in history as the most significant action of the assembly.

Anticipations of the delegates for fiery rhetoric went completely unrealized when the application for admission to the World Council by the Orthodox Church of Russia was presented. Speeches of approbation by other Orthodox groups were greeted by enthusiastic applause. Two speeches of abstaining votes (Hungarian Reformed Church in America and Russian Orthodox Greek Catholic Church in North America) brought only stony silence.

Ten minutes after the voting, an interim report stated that already far more than the necessary two-thirds majority had been received.

Final tabulation of the vote to admit the Russian church was announced as 142 for, 3 against, and 4 abstaining. Those voting against were not identified.

Delegates showed brisker opposition to the admission of Pentecostal churches in Chile than to the Russian Orthodox. Eight churches voted against Iglesia Pentecostal de Chile and against Misión Iglesia Pentecostal (Chile), with three abstaining in the former case and four in the latter.

Outside the fence surrounding the Vigynan Bhavan, two men paced back and forth with placards reading "AGENTS OF K—NOT SERVANTS OF GOD" and "RUSSIAN CLERGY—COMMUNIST AGENTS."

One Ernest Zingers from Latvia declared, "The Russian Orthodox Church is controlled by the Kremlin and not by Jesus Christ." He added, "The Soviet government is sending out spies and agents of their conspiracy under the cover of clergymen. No one is able to come out from Russia who is not going to follow the Communist line."

The Russian application significantly enough was followed chronologically—not preceded by—the applications for admission from churches in other "Iron Curtain" countries. Questioned as to why the Russian application was admittedly delayed for some time, Dr. Franklin Clark Fry stated that the Russians found trends within the World Council that they did not like—those trends being according to Fry an overemphasis on social activity and an underemphasis on things purely spiritual.

Fry commented wryly that these were the same objections raised by the ultra-conservative groups and that it was amazing how the extremes finally emerged so closely together.

The prospects for the Russian church in council activities are encouraging. Members are eligible for appointment to WCC commissions and to membership on the powerful Central Committee, the number to be determined in a numerical ratio to the membership of the church, which is said to be about 50 million.

Some future WCC meetings will undoubtedly be held in Russia, but the Russian church has with the capitalistic colleagues the responsibility of contributing financially to WCC coffers. A strange commentary on the overwhelmingly favorable vote was the fact that privately few delegates seemed in favor of it.

One top representative of a major American denomination was shocked to learn that each church was entitled to only one vote. He was totally unfamiliar with the man voting his church bloc in favor of the action and began trying to determine when or where his church had caucused to emerge with a favorable vote on the Russian admission. When the interim report assured the admission of the Russian church, Zingers leaned his placard against the fence and gave up his pacing—at least for this assembly.

At a press conference following the vote, the Russian delegation's leader, 32-year-old Archbishop Nikodim proved an agile dodger of questions. To repeated questions on the same theme he maintained that there is no interference in church affairs by the Soviet government, that priests are free to preach as they will and that the Gospel, not the government, determines church policy.

The limiting of questions mainly to representatives of wire services and secular newspapers virtually excluded the religious press from asking significant questions. Nobody asked Nikodim whether he agrees that a Christian cannot be a Communist in theory and practice. Questions were cut short after a half hour. Nikodim gave more candid answers privately than publicly.

News   December 8, 1961

72   *Ecumenical Matrimony*

My eleven-year-old daughter was listening to her mother and a friend talk about churches.

"I once belonged to the Episcopal Church," said the friend.

"Aren't you an Episcopalian?" my daughter asked.

"No, I'm a Congregationalist now," was the reply.

"And I used to be a Methodist before I married your daddy," said my wife.

"Hmmmm," muttered my daughter. "Cross-pollination!"— ROBERT O. REDDISH, JR., Medina, Ohio.

Preacher in the Red   October 14, 1957

73 *A New Mystic—Teilhard de Chardin*

PHILIP EDGCUMBE HUGHES

A new mystic has burst upon the contemporary consciousness in the person of Pierre Teilhard de Chardin, a French savant who died some half-dozen years ago but whose writings are only now being translated into English. Besides being a Jesuit priest, de Chardin was a paleontologist of distinction who spent many years in China. The last four years of his life were lived in New York. The translation of his book *The Phenomenon of Man,* which appeared in 1959, has already gained for him a remarkable posthumous reputation in the English-speaking world, despite the difficulty and novelty of much of its thought and language. In it he presented an evolutionistic perspective of man as developing into a new species, the category of which has been defined by the Incarnation.

It is evident that in setting before himself the task of reconciling the concepts of evolution and incarnation de Chardin has been faced with the necessity for breaking with the classical mystic concept of matter as an impediment to the soul and of bringing about some kind of reconciliation between the categories of "nature" and "grace" which for so long have been divorced in the theology of Roman Catholicism. This he has attempted to achieve through the development of a kind of "materialistic" mysticism which sees God everywhere—"in all that is most hidden, most solid, and most ultimate in the world." The meaning and method of this mysticism, which is central to the thought of de Chardin, are expounded in his book *Le Milieu Divin.* An English translation has appeared under the same (untranslated) title.

In the first place, de Chardin calls for the "divinization" of our activities. Viewing the universe as a single whole, the center and sun of which is Christ in whom all things consist, he conceives the power of the Incarnate Word not only as animating the higher reaches of existence but even as penetrating matter itself. "Nine out of ten practicing Christians feel that man's work is always at the level of a 'spiritual encumbrance' . . . that time spent at the office or the studio, in the fields or in the factory, is time taken away from prayer and adoration," with the consequence that they lead a "double or crippled life in practice." The Christian, however, should experience the "sur-animating" power of God in his daily activity which enables him to collaborate in building the Pleroma and thus to "bring to Christ a little fulfillment." Moreover, his work should be to him "the very path to sanctity" and "a manifold instrument of detachment," so that, through the divinization of his actions in Jesus Christ, it is not selfish ends but "God alone whom he pursues through the reality of created things."

The next stage on this spiritual journey is described as "the divinization of our passivities," that is, of the things which we endure or undergo. There are "passivities of growth," such as the life force within man, and there are "passivities of diminishment," such as misfortunes suffered outwardly and, in the inward sphere, "natural failings, physical defects, intellectual or moral weaknesses, as a result of which the field of our activities, of our enjoyment, of our vision, has been pitilessly limited since birth." There is, too, the inescapable deterioration of old age. Death, finally, is "the sum and consummation of all our diminishments." But we must welcome death by finding God in it, by embracing it as our "excentration," as our "reversion to God" and the step "that makes us lose all foothold within ourselves."

A consideration of de Chardin's doctrine of matter in relation to the mystic's ascent to the contemplation of God in his essence indicates, however, that it is not radically different from ancient Pythagoreanism, even though he avoids the crude dualism of the latter by placing matter within an evolutionary process that leads to an ultimate spiritual state. He is, indeed, able to speak of "holy matter," redeemed by the act of the Incarnation and informed with a spiritual power. Matter, for him, is not so much a weight as a slope, up which we may "climb towards the light, passing through, so as to attain God, a given series of created things which are not exactly obstacles but rather footholds"; and he maintains that "the soul can only rejoin God after having traversed a specific path through matter." De Chardin would have been quite at home with Socrates!

But it is not only the soul that is to achieve this spiritual fulfillment: the world itself, by means of progressive sublimation, is to attain its consummation in Christ Jesus, so that de Chardin is able to speak of "the general 'drift' of matter towards spirit," until "one day the whole divinizable substance of matter will have passed into the souls of men; all the chosen dynamisms will have been recovered: and then our world will be ready for the Parousia." His, however, is still the age-old objective of mysticism, namely, to escape from the world. Thus he writes: "The pagan loves the earth in order to enjoy it and confines himself within it; the Christian in order to make it purer and draw from it the strength to escape from it."

What de Chardin envisages is, in fact, nothing less than the transubstantiation of the universe, brought about by "the omnipresence of christification," the dynamism of the divine milieu. "The eucharistic transformation," he says, "goes beyond and completes the transubstantiation of the bread on the altar. Step by step it irresistibly invades the universe. . . . In a secondary and generalized sense, but in a true sense, the sacramental Species are formed by the totality of the world, and the duration of the creation is the time needed for consecration."

De Chardin's writing is beautiful and calmly passionate. But it is Gnostic rather than distinctively scriptural. His philosophy is incarnational in the sense of an evolution which gradually incorporates all into the Incarnation. His theology would seem to leave aside the Cross except as significant of a divine participation in the sufferings of his creation. It will be a great day when at last a Roman Catholic thinker breaks free from the tyranny of the *analogia entis*.

Current Religious Thought   March 27, 1961

74 *Oversimplifying the Remedy for the World's Woes*

The evils and sorrows that afflict the earth have called forth many suggested cures. A simple remedy offered frequently by evangelicals is the proclamation of Christ and him crucified. This has been termed by some an oversimplification of the answers to world problems. Such criticism has justification since the Scriptures clearly indicate that more is required than simply preaching the Atonement. Application of the Gospel to the various evils and problems of society must be made.

Paul informed the Corinthian Christians that he determined not to know anything among them, save Jesus Christ and him crucified. By this the Apostle indicated what was basic to his theology and message. However, in his letter to the Corinthians he makes careful application of the Gospel to individual, ecclesiastical, and social life. He warns the individual of strife and lust. He admonishes the church on Christian liberty, idolatry, worship and love, and discusses social questions of marriage and poverty.

The Gospel affects all the powers and capacities of the individual and extends to all relations and conditions of human life. The Gospel does not leave the convert kneeling at the altar; it follows him into every avenue of life. The Gospel speaks to the church on doctrine, worship and government. The Gospel has a message for the sciences, the arts, and every social institution. The Bible does not deal with the individual in isolation from society.

The evangelical has often hobbled the Gospel unbiblically. He has not shown that a Christian is a new moral creation destined to be the salt of the earth and the light of the world. He should humbly accept criticism for his neglect and should endeavor to rear a superstructure of social justice and righteousness upon the foundation Christ Jesus. He must work out his salvation in its various relationships with fear and trembling.

The evangelical, however, rightly discerns that nothing short of supernatural faith in Jesus provides an effectual remedy for the disease of sin. His basic message must always be Christ and him crucified. Only this message delivers from sin and, attended by the Holy Spirit, carries the necessary power to cleanse the world from evil and error.

Editorial   March 4, 1957

75 *Ecumenicity at Work in a Northern Setting*

FRANK FARRELL

How does organized ecumenicity work? The assistant editor observes an assembly of an amalgamated denomination.

The Canadians headed north. From the Strait of Georgia in the West to Newfoundland's Conception Bay in the East, came some 400 of them. They were commissioners of the United Church of Canada, their nation's largest Protestant communion—more than 1,000,000 adult communicants—and for the first time their General Council meeting brought them to the fast-growing northern city of Edmonton, Alberta. Site of the nineteenth meeting of their highest court was the red brick McDougall United Church overlooking the wooded banks of the North Saskatchewan River which winds through prairie country where nineteenth-century Methodist missionary George McDougall labored so well among Blackfeet, Crees, and Stonys as to be largely credited with the absence of Indian wars in the area.

After sending an "Address of Loyalty" to the Queen, in which the Council pledged "allegiance to the Throne and Your Person," the commissioners sought fulfillment of their appointed task "to enact such legislation and adopt such measures as may tend to promote true godliness, repress immorality, preserve the unity and well-being of the Church, and advance the Kingdom of Christ throughout the world."

Commission reports produced only a moderate amount of debate, carried on in accents somehow reminiscent of a distant skirl of bagpipes. These were among the major issues:

Alcohol. The United Church has a strong tradition favoring total abstinence, unsuccessful efforts having been made in the past to condition church membership upon abstention. But some have complained of loss of members to the Anglican Church over this issue. A lengthy report slightly softening the church's stand was adopted with few changes and surprisingly little opposition.

Birth Control. The Council approved a frank 66-page report by its Commission on Christian Marriage and Divorce, which declared the sexual act to be "for the perfecting of husband and wife, quite apart from its relation to procreation." Ministers are to help those contemplating marriage consider factors relating to their decisions as to number and spacing of children, as well as urge them to get medical advice "concerning means of conception control that are both medically approved and aesthetically acceptable to both of them and in accord with their Christian conscience." Traditionally strong for birth control, the Council withheld approval of abortion except when pregnancy seriously endangers the mother's health. Artificial insemination by husband was sanctioned, while artificial insemination by donor was rejected as leading to "grave genetic, emotional, social and legal problems."

International Affairs. The Council adopted substantially a report of its committee on the Church and International Affairs which asked the Canadian government to "reassess" its defense policy. The report advocated surrender of Canadian sovereignty "to the extent necessary to establish world order," but questioned the wisdom of surrendering "decision making to such organizations as NORAD" and providing sites for U.S. missiles. Declaring Canada to be "faced with the urgent task of revising" her defense policy and her international posture, the report spoke optimistically of the possibility of Canadian alignment with the world's neutralist nations and unilateral renunciation of nuclear warfare.

There is strong pacifist sentiment within the United Church. One highly placed churchman estimated that 25 per cent of her ministers would like to see Canada disarm unilaterally. Economic and moral reasons are set forth, among others. Trumpeted one commissioner: "I don't want to die in nuclear war."

A motion favoring withdrawal from present military alliances, including NATO, was defeated.

The council voted for Canadian pressure toward an "international agreement (subject to international inspection and control) halting all nuclear tests etc. for destructive purposes." It also reaffirmed its opinion of 1952, 1956, and 1958 that Canada "should give de facto recognition" to Red China and support its admission to the U.N. Principal E. J. Thompson of Edmonton's St. Stephen's College urged the United Church to hold conversations with the leaders of Red China and U.S.S.R.

Capital Punishment. Abolition of the death sentence was urged, to be replaced by a statutory life term with treatment and "the possibility of remission and parole." Prisons are to be looked on as hospitals. Parole is to be withheld as long as retention is required by the well-being of society and the prisoner.

The United Church of Canada was formed in 1925 through merger of the nation's Methodists, Congregationalists, and some 70 per cent of its Presbyterians. The resultant polity has been described as "pretty Presbyterian," though little hope is seen at present for union with the "continuing Presbyterians." But the United Church wishes to be known as a "uniting church" and has been carrying on conversations with the All-Canada Conference of the Church of Christ (Disciples) and the Canada Conference of the Evangelical United Brethren Church. However, greatest interest is in conversations with the Anglican Church of Canada, which have had their ups and downs for some 15 years, the issue of Episcopal ordination providing a formidable barrier to the desired "organic union." A study guide outlining relationships between the two communions is now to be sent United Church congregations, the Council decided. The climate of the current conversations is described as "cordial" but actual cooperation as "spotty."

"Continuing Presbyterians" tend to look upon the United Church as lacking a theology—hotly denied by some United churchmen, who point to the statement of faith contained in the original Basis of Union. It is said that modernism in the church is fading. On the other hand, one leader claimed there is "practically no fundamentalism per se in the United Church," identifying this with "literalism," though he claimed there is considerable "orthodoxy."

Retiring moderator Dr. Angus J. MacQueen pointed to United Church weaknesses which are reflected in need for renewed zeal for missions and church reunion, as well as a revitalized spiritual life. Following church union in 1925 there was a surplus of ministers, but now a severe shortage of ministerial candidates has reached emergency proportions, according to one educator, and not only among French Canadians. Church growth is lagging well behind the nation's population increase. Every conference showed a drop in new members by profession of faith. Four-fifths of all money raised remains within the congregational treasury—"a shocking proof of self-centeredness," charges Dr. MacQueen. Remarked one minister who had transferred from another church five years earlier: "This is a fascinating church to work in but it's a sleeping giant."

But signs of hope were seen in Council action to enlarge industrial chaplaincy work and enter a new mission field—South America. It also voted merger of the church's two women's groups, hoping for greater effectiveness in missions support particularly.

Friends of the United Church would be encouraged by the Board of Overseas Missions' call for faithful prayer, stressing the imperative of reliance upon the Holy Spirit. Heartening too are Dr. MacQueen's words: "Christianity is not just one more among the world's religions. It is unique. God came in all the fullness of his truth and grace in Jesus Christ for the whole world. This is the story we have to tell to the nations."

News   October 24, 1960

76 *Existentialism and Historic Christian Faith*

ROBERT P. ROTH

It is always a risk to divine the future, but perhaps it is not foolhardy to say that theological controversy in the next quarter century will be centered in the questions put by existentialism. It is true that denominational lines still persist and their respective theologies will continue to occupy the attention of scholars. It is also true that the ecumenical movement will continue to grow and discussions of faith, order, life, and work will press for a hearing. But the real stage of theological controversy must necessarily be where the great battle of our entire age is being fought. The locus of this critical struggle may be found where the creative minds of our day are shaping the sounds, the colors, the forms of the brave new world that is coming to birth.

The plays of Tennessee Williams, Arthur Miller, Jean-Paul Sartre, the poetry of W. H. Auden, T. S. Eliot, Dylan Thomas, the painting of Picasso, Braque, Mondriaan, Miró, Kandinski, the music of Bartók, Milhaud, Hindemith, the architecture of Saarinen, Rudolph, Le Corbusier—these are some of the forces that have been shaping the structure of the world in which we live. These in turn had been shaped by nineteenth-century iconoclastic thinkers like Sören Kierkegaard, Fëdor Dostoevski, and Franz Kafka. If we are to understand the times in which we live, we must come to know what these names mean and what has been said about them; otherwise we shall be shouting against the wind and our preaching will be what Dean Inge said it is: "Merely spouting water over a host of narrow-necked bottles."

Theology properly speaking is not an aspect of culture, but culture is the product of basic theological underpinnings. Nevertheless, there are certain theological movements which follow the pendulum swing of history, and in this sense we may say that the theology of Kierkegaard, Barth, Brunner, Bultmann, Tillich, and Niebuhr is largely the existentialist reaction to the liberalism of Schleiermacher, Ritschl, and Harnack.

Liberalism, grounded in the work of Lessing, is an idealist philosophy with a historical method for ascertaining truth. Lessing said two things: 1. Revelation is the education of the human race, and therefore truth is to be found by studying the historical relations of things; and 2. No historical event can be the basis of eternal happiness, and therefore one must find truth in a rational, idealist philosophical system. Thus it happened that, in the liberal line of theology that followed, historicism, fully appreciating the relativities of history, was coupled with a naïve faith in the inevitability of social progress as well as the optimism of individual moral perfectibility. Moralism found expression both in the search for a genuine experience of personal piety and in the social gospel.

The liberals busied themselves with the search for the real Jesus in an attempt to find what is essential to Christianity, so that they might attach themselves to this historical Lord and bask in his moral influence. Harnack concluded that the essence of Christianity is the Fatherhood of God, the brotherhood of man, and the kingdom of Christ as a community of love. Clearly the Bible was not understood as the gift of God in which he declares news of salvation through his Son. Rather the Bible was seen as an achievement of human history. But the quest of the historical Jesus ended in failure. By 1910 Schweitzer was ready to admit that the historical Jesus is forever lost and that all we can say about him is that he was a mistaken apocalyptic visionary.

Liberalism is dead today because it had within it the seeds of its own decay. When the quest of the real Jesus failed, we might have expected the liberals to abandon their historical methodology, but this did not occur and historicism still dominates the modern mood. The side of liberalism which did collapse, however, was its cavalier optimism, exposed as it was by the two wars and the great depression. But out of its shallow grave arose a new spirit for our age. This is the principality or power which we call existentialism. The term is vague and almost indefinable. As diverse views as those of Eastern Orthodox Nikolai Berdyaev, Roman Catholic Gabriel Marcel, Swiss Reformed Karl Barth, Lutheran Rudolf Bultmann, Atheist Jean-Paul Sartre, Jew Martin Buber, and non-Christian Martin Heidegger have all been jammed into the same theological closet.

The broadest definition of existentialism is that it is a realist reaction against the shallow optimism and easy rationalism of the nineteenth-century liberals. But this does not say enough. Actually the existentialist spirit, in spite of its sophistication, is naïvely realist and therefore historicist. In that it adheres to historical methodology, one would not be wrong to say that existentialism is still fundamentally liberal, howbeit a chastened form of liberalism. It follows the old nominalist tradition in saying that existence is prior to essence. Indeed all reality is in historical experience. Essences are only abstract names. There is no real existence beyond history, neither in an ideal or mystic sense above history nor in an eschatological sense in future at the end of history.

This being the pervading spirit of our age, it becomes necessary for us, says Bultmann, to interpret the Christian message in terms which are relevant. This he ventures to do in his realized eschatology which makes both forgiveness and judgment present realities. He applies all the resources of his abundant genius to manipulate the tools of form criticism to demythologize the New Testament so as to strip away irrelevant offense. All pre-scientific myths, he says, must be cut away, such as the Jewish myth of an apocalyptic cataclysm, the Gnostic myth of the pre-existent Lord, the futurist myths of heaven and hell, the historical myths of angels, demons, miracles, virgin birth, empty tomb, and resurrection. What is left is the Cross and the kerygma of justification by grace through faith.

A great amount of energy and erudition has been expended by the existentialists on the subject of sin. Even the term original sin is accepted, but it is redefined to mean the limitation of human existence. Man finds himself bound by the all-pervasiveness of death, guilt, and meaninglessness. Sin does not enter through a fall in a mythical garden of Eden. Sin posits itself. Man is thrust into an existence in which he suffers a desperate calamity. He is inextricably the product of his past, yet he must accept full responsibility for himself as he is and not shift blame to either heredity or environment. He needs freedom from the past for his future within history. This he can find in the decision for Christ which brings him a believing self-understanding, a release from the powers of this world for service of that Power which man cannot control. Redemption is not through the objective work of a personal Lord but through the human decision made possible by the event of God's grace in Christ. In this moment we stand before God and accept our acceptance, thus freeing us from the dead past for a living future in history.

How does existentialist theology affect some of the historic doctrines such as Christology, Resurrection, the Church, the Word?

1. According to Bultmann the historical Jesus is the Christ, but not in the traditional sense as the personal Lord whose body was raised from the tomb. Rather Jesus is the occasion for the encounter between the Cross and the sinner who makes the decision for the Ultimate. Apart from this encounter there is no more significance to Jesus than any other martyr in history. Really it is not the Jesus of history that concerns the existentialist theologians, but the revelation we meet in the moment of decision.

2. Resurrection is redefined to mean not a future life in an incorruptible body in a new heaven or eternal age, but a regenerate life here and now free from the frustration of death. Although death is inevitable, we do not fear it because we accept it. As Niebuhr says: "Because of original sin man's destiny is to seek after an impossible victory and adjust himself to an inevitable defeat." Redemption is not a future victory. It is a present adjustment.

3. The concept of the Church is quite radically changed by the existentialists because of their category of Inwardness or Subjectivity. This subjectivism is not the romantic subjectivity of the liberals which was centered in a feeling of dependence upon God. Such a feeling would make God a projection of the human heart. Existentialists would consider this the idolatry of using God as a disposable object, and God is never an object. Always he is Subject; always Thou, never I.

The divine Thou can never be manipulated. He can only be spoken to in answer to his call. The call comes to me inwardly, not objectively or mechanically or casually. God always treats me as subject too and never as an object. Hence the relation between man and God is neither a cognitive one which can be apprehended by means of a set of propositions nor an emotional one which can be grasped by a genuine feeling. The relationship is rather one of speaking and responding to God's Word, hence it is one of decision. But no man can make this decision for another. Each must do his own believing just as he must do his own dying. The result of this doctrine, which is a one-sided truth, is an extreme individualism with no proper place for the sacramental community of the Church. Indeed for most existentialists the Church, as a visible structure, only gets in the way of the decisive conversation between the I and the Thou. There seems to be no place for the Church as the body of Christ, as Paul teaches, the living, historically continuous organism with prophets, apostles, martyrs, and saints in personal communion with the risen Jesus as head and Lord.

4. The same observation applies to the relation between the living Word and Scripture. The existentialists find the written Word to be a troublesome obstacle in the way of their decisive moment. How can an I meet a Thou if he has the written Word in between? The existentialists take the same offense in the written Word that the Jews took in Jesus: "Is not this Jesus, the son of Joseph, whose father and mother we know?" So they look at the written Word and say: "Is not this document of human hands, whose historical antecedents we know?" As a result the living Word is separated from the written Word and we are left without a rule or norm of authority. This is a new subjectivism, voluntaristic rather than intellectual or emotive, but just as earthbound as either rationalism or pietism. Moreover, as we might expect, the sacraments are embarrassing to Bultmann and the existentialists because in their concern to worship the hidden God they find the sacraments too terribly visible. The existentialists separate what they call Christ from Jesus, from the Church, from Scripture, and from the sacraments.

Is there anything good that can come from existentialism? We must go back to Sören Kirkegaard for an answer. It is salutary that we should avoid alliance with rational systems whether of Aquinas or Hegel. Quoting Shakespeare, Kierkegaard said it is better to be well hanged than ill wed. But we may extend this to include the liaison with existentialism too. In our well-meaning concern to make the Gospel relevant, we must be careful not to identify the Gospel with any of the periods of the historical pendulum.

Kierkegaard was a much needed theological gadfly. It was good for him to awaken us from our dogmatic slumbers and ask us what it means to be a Christian. The resulting new emphasis upon inwardness and the hidden God is also helpful so long as we keep it free of subjective voluntarism, and so long as we recognize that the hidden God is only the God of wrath whom the Jews and the Muslims also have. Nor does the hiddenness of God preclude his general revelation in nature, history, and conscience. We are Christians and our God is the revealed God, our Lord Jesus Christ, the babe in the manger and the man on the Cross. The realistic correction of liberalism's optimism and moralism has certainly proved acceptable. It is good for the Church to be reminded that she is still in this world and she may indeed get in the way between man and God. The Church like the Christian man is *simul justus et peccator*. One of the most alarming but nevertheless true judgments is that the world often articulates the kerygma more effectively than the Church, as in the case of Sartre's play, *The Respectful Prostitute*. This is the world's way of telling the parable of the Pharisee and the publican. It is time the Church learns to speak her message in the clear idiom of our day lest by default we give the message to the world and allow it to be perverted by the silky deception of Satan.

Article   March 27, 1961

77 In and Out of the Windows

EDMUND P. CLOWNEY

Every preacher knows that illustrations in sermons are windows to let in the light. Some sermons are like railroad coaches, with windows regularly spaced throughout their length; others are ranch style, featuring one picture window. Homiletical architecture, taking its cue from contemporary building, is using more and more glass. Indeed, to change the figure, as every illustrator must, many sermons have so many windows and so little structure that they resemble not so much a greenhouse as a fish net, classically defined as a large number of holes tied together with string.

A window does not only function to admit light. Recall the experience of my namesake at Troas! (Let me here deny categorically that Eutychus fell asleep on the window sill because Paul's sermon lacked illustrations.) Many a bemused hearer has been lost from a sermon via illustrationis, that is, out the window. Consider the folly of the young preacher who on a June morning is the victim of his repressed desires and pictures an approach shot to the ninth green to illustrate his second point. The greater his finesse with his homiletical iron, the more squarely he will loft 15 per cent of his hearers over to the wrong fairway for the rest of the service.

Illustrative windows have also been known to admit dust, bugs, and noise. Red herrings have been dragged through some; others are service ports from which thousands of canned anecdotes slide down an endless belt.

One preacher's corrective is to compare illustrating to harness racing. That illustrative critter must be lean and fresh, it must move fast on the inside track, and most of all, it must be harnessed. Unless it carries the point down the homestretch, keep that horseflesh off the track.

Still better, board up those windows and distill a limpid prose like that of this letter, which is free of all illustrative additives.

Eutychus   May 27, 1957

78   *The Winds of the Spirit*

There have been times in the life of the Church, as there were in the life of our Lord, when things began to happen because of a new and sudden movement of the Spirit of God. After thirty years had passed Jesus suddenly began his public ministry, healing the sick and preaching the Gospel of the kingdom. When the Spirit of God came upon him, he was abruptly thrust into the wilderness and on to the road that led to Calvary. And the abrupt "before" and "after" contrast that we see—the only one we see—in the lives of Jesus' disciples occurred because of the coming of the Spirit at Pentecost, a coming which happened "suddenly" (Acts 2:2).

Similarly, there have been times of sudden outbursts of expansion and vitality, of reform and renewal in the history of the Church because the winds of the Spirit blew through the garden of God. The Reformation, the Counter-Reformation, the upsurge of Revival in England and America and of Pietism in the arid rationalism of Germany, were emergents whose causation lay not in historical antecedents but in new and special stirrings of the Spirit. In such seasons of refreshing the Church recaptured the warmth and passion of her springtime and moved forward eagerly into her promised harvests. Indeed, for such times as these the Church has ever prayed: "Come, Holy Spirit."

We seem to be living today in such a season of spiritual excitement. There are new and fresh energies of God bestirring the Church to new obedience to her calling and new awareness of fresh opportunities.

In all her long history there has not been a mission concern comparable to the modern concern to bring Christ to the nations. Not since Reformation times has there been anything comparable to the expansive Luther-Calvin research of recent decades. Never before has there been such interest in the nature of the Church and in the eschatological nature of the Gospel. It has been a long, long time since we have experienced so great an interest in systematic and biblical theology, New Testament studies, the role of the layman, liturgical appreciation; such lively concern about Christianity's confrontation with non-Christian religions; such extensive probing of the Gospel and the problem of communication—to mention no more. Not until modern times did the Church become aware that as the holy, catholic Church, she is indeed a world church. Even those churches most critical of the ecumenical movement are practicing ecumenics within the limits of their provincial concerns.

To see in all this seething activity a movement of the Spirit is not to accept everything that occurs as Spirit-induced and acceptable to God. Not all the story of the Reformation is happy reading; yet who would deny it was a time of the Spirit? Even under the leading of the Spirit we are not to expect the infallible word, the perfect deed, the pure miracle. The Spirit works through people and churches who are always old wineskins and earthen vessels. Even the story of the Pentecost Church of the New Testament page is a spotted story. Much recorded there was not the fruit of the Spirit.

Moreover, we must not be surprised that those seasons when the Spirit moves are times of disturbance within the Church. Old familiar ways are strained, time-honored boundaries crossed, limits pushed back, accepted patterns of thought and practice broken, walls of human device crumbled, respected churchly machinery toppled, and long-established ecclesiastical structures disestablished or by-passed.

It is striking that much of the exciting action of our time has occurred among people and in places where some of us would least have expected it. Theological energy has come more from the liberal than the conservative side of the Church. The extensive Luther-Calvin research has not been carried on by the denominations that give their particular loyalties to these men. Ecumenical theology has not come from those specifically concerned about traditional denominational theologies and their distinctives. The earliest ecumenical impulse came not from the churches but from the mission fields, and the "younger churches" are more pained over the divisions of the older churches than are the older churches themselves. Today's mass evangelism began and continues outside rather than inside the churches. The fastest growth occurs within the segments of the Church that are highly flexible and little organized, not within the established and staid denominations. On all fronts the Spirit is breaking the old wineskins.

It is precisely the Holy Spirit's high disregard for our organized Christianity that intensifies the ecumenical question of the "nature of unity we seek." The Church's unity is spiritual; this, however, does not mean disembodied. The Spirit resides in the Church. The unity he establishes is spiritual, yet not merely mystical or ethereal. It is for the Church to pray: "Come, Holy Spirit," and to search amidst all the bustle of activity for the visible unity the Spirit demands.

Editorial   January 4, 1963

79 *The Reporter and the Klansman*

DAVID E. KUCHARSKY

In New York there is an incident with a strange twist relating to the Ku Klux Klan.

Pursuing a tip, lanky 37-year-old reporter John McCandlish Phillips of the *New York Times* sought a local Klan leader who was a Jew but hid his nationality and preached anti-Semitism. The confrontation between Phillips and Klansman Daniel Burros, 28, was that of a devout evangelical layman who keeps a Bible on his desk and a short, stocky follower of the Odinist religion, a Nordic supremacy sect, who was once an official of the American Nazi party. Their acquaintance lasted only forty-eight hours.

The two met in a Queens barber shop the morning of Friday, October 29. Phillips recalls that Burros was "civil, almost pleasant" until confronted with the facts of his Jewish parentage and upbringing. The Klansman retained his composure but told Phillips: "I'll have to retaliate. . . . I'll be ruined." He vowed to murder Phillips if the story was published.

The following day, Burros telephoned Phillips and said he would "shoot up" the editorial offices of the *Times* if his Jewish identity were revealed by the newspaper. If it meant that he would "catch some lead" in the process, Burros said he would go in a "blaze of glory."

How did Phillips feel about the threats? "I was scared, certainly," he says. "I had a sense of the power of evil, and I was somewhat panicky inside, although I managed to retain my outward composure."

Phillips wrote a story meticulously tracing the Jewish background of Burros and how he came to be involved with the Nazis as a teenager. The story was published on the front page of the *Times*'s Sunday edition.

Burros read the story, not in New York but in Reading, Pennsylvania, where he had an appointment with fellow Klansmen. According to their account, he came into their small apartment on Sunday morning with a copy of the *Times* and, in a state of extreme agitation, shot himself twice. Police found him dead, and an official suicide verdict was issued.

Although realizing that his story apparently prompted the suicide, Phillips has consolation in the fact that he was able to express personal concern for Burros' spiritual welfare. After questioning the Klansman at length, Phillips quoted Scripture to him, declaring God's love for him and the offer of salvation that Christ makes to all who believe. Phillips, who is a *Christianity Today* correspondent, also gave him a copy of *The Cross and the Switchblade,* a popular documentation of the Christian conversion of numerous young hoodlums. The conversation thereafter alternated between the newsman's witness and the Klansman's threats.

News   November 19, 1965

80 *The Aesthetic Problem: Some Evangelical Answers*

FRANK E. GAEBELEIN

In recent years, evangelicalism has been coming of age intellectually. With the strengthening of academic standards in many of its schools, colleges, and seminaries, its tendency toward anti-intellectualism has declined. More evangelical education institutions have been accredited by the great regional associations since 1950 than in the preceding half century. An increasing number of scholarly books are being written. And one of the major developments in religious publishing during the past decade has been the willingness of leading secular publishers to bring out the work of evangelical thinkers.

But a parallel tendency toward what may be called "anti-aestheticism" remains. In Dorothy Sayers' introduction to *The Man Born to Be King,* an essay every Christian student of the arts should know, she speaks of "the snobbery of the banal." It is a telling phrase, and it applies to not a few evangelicals. They are the kind of people who look down upon good music as highbrow, who confuse worship with entertainment, who deplore serious drama as worldly yet are contentedly devoted to third-rate television shows, whose tastes in reading run to the piously sentimental, and who cannot distinguish a kind of religious calendar art from honest art. For them better aesthetic standards are "egghead" and spiritually suspect.

The arts pose uncomfortable problems for many evangelicals. There are those who question the relevance of the arts to Christian life and witness in these days of world upheaval. "Why," they ask, "spend time in this tragic age talking about such things as aesthetics?" The answer is that art belongs to human life. Pervasive and influential, it is an essential element of man's environment. And when art is unworthy, man's spirit is debased. "The powerful impact of modern culture upon modern man . . . discloses," as Professor W. Paul Jones of Princeton says in an important essay, ". . . the overwhelming degree to which contemporary man is being formed by an 'art' not really worthy of the name" ("Art as the Creator of Lived Meaning," *The Journal of Bible and Religion,* July, 1963).

Art, though aesthetically autonomous, has deep spiritual and moral implications. Like the capacity for worship, the aesthetic sense is one of the characteristics that set man apart from the animals. Evangelicals turn away from art as a side issue or frill at the peril of their own impoverishment and at the cost of ineffectiveness in their witness. For art, which is the expression of truth through beauty, cannot be brushed aside as a luxury. We who know God through his Son who is altogether lovely must be concerned that the art we look at, listen to, read, and use in the worship of the living God has integrity.

Our God is the God of truth. According to the Gospel of John, "He that doeth truth cometh to the light." This great principle is just as valid aesthetically as in doctrine and in practical living. Art that distorts the truth is no more pleasing to God than any other kind of untruth. Surely it is not too much to say that the God of all truth looks for integrity in artistic expression as well as in theology.

Some evangelicals may not like art. Because of their cultural illiteracy, they may be ill at ease in the presence of worthy artistic expression. In their discomfort they may want to say to the aesthetic side of life, "Go away, I'm not interested. I don't want to be bothered by you." But it will not go away. Through millions of radios and television sets, through the printed page, through advertising, through the architecture and furnishings of public buildings, churches, and homes—in a thousand and one ways art is here, though often in unworthy forms, and no one can run away from it.

Moreover, Christians have an aesthetic problem not merely because of the ubiquity of the arts but because in one way or another much in the contemporary use of literature and the arts is debased and opposed to the truth and to the values to which Christians are obligated. Evangelicals had better be concerned about the aesthetic problem, if for no other reason than that a tide of cheap and perverse artistic expression is constantly eroding the shoreline of noble standards and godly living.

The situation is complicated by the multiplication of leisure hours in this automated age. How many now use their extra hours wisely? Gresham's law may well have an aesthetic counterpart in that bad art like bad money drives out the good.

As background for some answers to the problem, consider a very brief survey of the aesthetic situation among many evangelicals today with particular reference to music, the visual arts, and literature.

Music is an area in which "the snobbery of the banal" stands in strange contrast to the doctrinal discrimination of many conservative Christians. Not only does the mediocre drive out the good; there is also a certain intolerance of the excellent that refuses to see that great music can be a far more true expression of a biblical theology than piously sentimental music. Or it may be that certain kinds of music finding ready acceptance in some churches reflect a theology that, despite its high claim to orthodoxy, yet leaves much to be desired.

Religious music, however, is not the only music we hear. Much of non-religious music—serious and not just popular in character—betrays the spiritual rootlessness and moral anarchy of the times, as in the strident and heartless works of some of the atonalists or the irrationalities of some avant-garde composers. Thus there is all the more reason for inculcating in God's people higher standards for this great art that speaks so directly to the emotions and to the spirit.

Look next at the visual arts. Here, as in music, there are great riches. Granted that much in modern painting is related to the spiritual alienation of the day (although not all abstractionism is unworthy), how slight is the acquaintance of many evangelicals with the masters, past and present. How many know the works of American masters like Stuart, Inness, Ryder, Winslow Homer, Cassatt, Marin, or Andrew Wyeth? And what of the priceless treasures of great Christian art through the ages? There is vastly more in religious painting than the ever-present head of Christ that seems almost to have become a Protestant icon.

As for literature, where are the first-rate Christian novels and poems? Evangelicals have made notable progress in scholarly writing, but their achievement in more imaginative forms of literature is mediocre. Christian editors know the paucity of verse by evangelical writers that even begins to qualify as poetry. And in the field of fiction, distinguished novels and short stories written by evangelicals today are almost non-existent.

Perhaps one thing that holds evangelicals back is a certain cultural parochialism and fear of the world. The moral state of much contemporary literature is indeed appalling. Here the aesthetic problem is a spiritual one that cannot be divorced from the Christian conscience. But there are many books that evangelicals can and must read, including not only the great treasures of English, American, European, and other literature but also representative current writing.

At a Christian teachers' institute several years ago, I urged breadth of reading and ventured to give a brief list of some of the great works indispensable to a liberal education. In the discussion that followed, a young man asked, "What has Plato to say to a Christian?" The answer is that Plato and every other great writer and artist of the past or present has much to give a Christian not only because it is essential to know the main currents of human thought but also because genius comes only from God. The doctrine of common grace asserts that God distributes his gifts among all kinds of men—unbelievers as well as believers. But the gifts are God's and the glory is his. Amid the moral corruption of our day, some great and worthy books are being written. Christians need to know them.

In his *Confessions,* St. Augustine speaks of "the spacious palaces of memory." It is a wonderful phrase, suggesting Christian responsibility for the furnishing of the mind. But for the fulfillment of this responsibility, there is needed something more enduring than television, the ephemeral popular religious literature of our times, or best-selling Christian records.

Like much else, culture begins at home. Taste is formed by what we live with. The question might well be asked of evangelicals: "What does your home tell of your spiritual and intellectual and aesthetic interests?" Said Rudyard Kipling: "Men and women may sometimes, after great effort, achieve a creditable lie; but a house cannot say anything save the truth of those who have lived in it." What do the books on the shelves, the magazines on the living room table, the pictures on the walls, the music on the piano, the record collection say of us? What should we read, what should we hear, what should we look at? The Bible has its clear criteria, summed up in the great Pauline phrase, "bringing into captivity every thought to the obedience of Christ." In Scripture the truth is paramount. Therefore everything that is shoddy and false, even though piously so, is abhorrent to the God of truth.

But this brief survey, which might well be extended to other arts such as drama and architecture, while necessary as diagnosis, points clearly to the need for action. Let us consider, therefore, three proposals toward evangelical answers to the aesthetic problem: (1) The formulation of a Christian theory of aesthetics based first of all upon the insights of the Bible rather than upon extrabiblical sources; (2) the cultivation of good taste and the development of the critical faculty; (3) revision of educational programs to give a more adequate place to the arts.

Consider first the study by evangelicals of the theory of aesthetics. One of the hopeful signs of the last twenty years has been the development of a Christian and biblical philosophy of education. If evangelical education is experiencing renewal, the reason is that evangelical educators have been seriously occupied in considering the theological and philosophical basis of Christian education and in defining its goals.

But so far very little study has been devoted to aesthetics. Indeed, it is difficult to bring to mind a single published book by a conservative evangelical that deals competently with the theology and philosophy of aesthetics. Only comparatively recently have any Protestants given serious thought to this field. Professor W. Paul Jones, in the article previously referred to, says, "Despite a history of virtual indifference to art, Protestant thinkers within the past several decades have begun to explore in earnest the relation of religion to aesthetic matters." Evangelicals should be joining in this effort. It faces them with an exciting opportunity to explore new paths in applying biblical truths to their cultural milieu.

The bulk of the work being done in the field of Christian aesthetics represents Roman and Anglo-Catholic thought. Its roots go deep into sacramental theology, Thomism, Greek philosophy, and such great writers as Dante. But in large part it is extrabiblical. There is a radical difference between the thought-forms of the Bible and those of Western philosophy and humanistic culture. And while the Bible says little directly about the arts or aesthetics, its basic insights must provide not only the foundation for an authentic Christian aesthetic but also the corrective for artistic theory derived from other sources, however excellent these may be.

Moreover, what some liberal Protestant thinkers have been doing in the field of aesthetics also needs revision, as Professor Jones clearly points out. For Paul Tillich and others like him, he says, art is important because it is chiefly the indicator or "barometer of the 'faith' or 'ultimate concern' of a generation or culture," but the difficulty is that such a view of the function of art somehow fails to discriminate between first-rate, second-rate, third-rate art, the latter of which often reflects the present culture more truly than does the first. And furthermore art belongs to the only creature made in the image of God, the only creature to whom is given in a limited but real extent the gift of creativity, even though the gift is marred in fallen human nature. Thus considered, it is much more than the faithful mirror of culture. It is far more importantly a way-shower, leading on under God to fuller visions of his truth.

If there is, as we have seen, tension between many evangelicals and the aesthetic aspect of life, the reason lies in a contented ignorance of much that is aesthetically worthy and a satisfaction with the mediocre because it is familiar. Yet theological roots in the eternal biblical verities which never change do not necessarily imply enslavement to aesthetic traditionalism.

An essential element of true aesthetic practice is the adventure of new ideas and their development in new forms. The great artists of the past had in their day an element of newness and spontaneity, and the greater the art the more abiding the newness. In a time when the ugly and the formless have become a cult reflecting the confusion of the pagan world, the creative Christian spirit in art should be pointing the way forward and upward, but always with reference to the everlasting and ever-present truth of him who is "the same yesterday and today and forever."

A second proposal is that evangelicals must, if they are really to wrestle with the aesthetic problem, take seriously their obligation to develop critical discrimination in the arts. Good models are absolutely essential for sound aesthetic judgment. Good taste is not expensive; it is just discriminating. And it can be developed. Its formation begins very early.

It matters everything what kind of pictures are looked at by children, what kind of music is heard, what kind of television programs are viewed. Art exists in its own right, not just as a vehicle for moralism. Yet it cannot but affect those who are exposed to it. For young people to live day by day with shoddy literature and vulgar entertainment may tear down what they have heard in church and learned in Sunday school. Evangelical churches have picnics and hikes, athletic games and parties for young people—wholesome means of fellowship indeed. Why not also Christian fellowship in group attendance at a symphony concert, or a violin or piano recital? And it is surely not beyond reason for Christians to visit art galleries together. "The way to appreciate beauty," said Professor William Lyon Phelps of Yale, "is to keep looking at it, to appreciate music is to keep listening to it, to appreciate poetry is to keep reading it."

At the end of the first chapter of Romans, after his appalling catalogue of sins within the human heart and life, Paul states the ultimate condemnation of unregenerate man in these words: "They not only do these things but take pleasure in them that do them." As people look together at what is unworthy and debased aesthetically, they are together debased. But the converse is true. The shared experience of great music or drama, living with good pictures (even in reproductions)—these are group experiences in nobility and, let it be added, in reality. Not all music is joyous, nor does all drama have a happy ending. Yet, as Aristotle shows in his *Poetics,* tragedy purges the emotions through pity and fear. And at the pinnacle of involvement through experience in the company of others is the reverent worship of the living God, not for the sake of what we get out of it, but because God is God and because worship must be given him.

The time is overdue for evangelicals to outgrow their careless unconcern for aesthetic values and to develop critical standards that will enable them to distinguish good from bad in the art that surrounds them.

The third proposal, obvious but nonetheless important, concerns the more adequate place that the arts ought to have in Christian education. In too many evangelical schools and colleges the arts are little more than poor relatives of the curriculum. Yet in actuality they are not marginal, peripheral subjects; they are close to the heart of Christian life and witness. At present evangelical education is strongest aesthetically in music, although even here it yet has far to go. When it comes to the visual arts like painting and architecture and to the performing arts, including drama, much of evangelical education is like a fallow field that needs both planting and cultivating. Christian schools and colleges must practice the unity of truth they preach by giving the arts a greater place in the curriculum.

The compelling motive for Christian action in the field of aesthetics lies in the nature of God. Christians are obligated to excellence because God himself is supremely excellent. In the Hall of Fame at New York University, these words are inscribed in the place given Jonathan Edwards, the greatest of American philosophers: "God is the head of the universal system of existence from whom all is perfectly derived and on whom all is most absolutely dependent, whose Being and Beauty is the sum and comprehension of all existence and excellence." It is because of who and what God is, it is because of the beauty and truth manifest in his Son, it is because of the perfection of his redeeming work, that evangelicals can never be content with the mediocre in aesthetics. Here, as in all else, the call is to the unremitting pursuit of excellence to the glory of the God of all truth.

Article   February 26, 1965

81　*Michelangelo's Statue of David*

M. WHITCOMB HESS

From the recalcitrant marble his sure hand
Shaped this live image: See young David stand
Armed for the final conflict, poised to fling
That fateful pebble from the shepherd's sling
Hung over his strong shoulder: See his brow
Prayer-lifted facing old Goliath now—
The foe of ages to be overthrown. . . .
Here is the trust of Israel set in stone.

October 8, 1965

82　*It's Been a Long, Long Time*

RODERICK JELLEMA

A review of *Amazing Grace,* by Robert Drake (Chilton Books, 1965).

Anyone looking for a really good piece of fiction among the thousands
of titles streaming from the presses gets to feel like a boy at a muddy
rapids looking for a trout among rushing schools of spawning bull-
heads. It is too much for the eyes. If the thing he is looking for is surprisingly there, he is almost certain to miss it. Unlike the boy, however, the reader can come back, prompted by the reports of other
readers, and still find what he sought.

In 1965 such a book appeared: Robert Drake's *Amazing Grace.*
Those of us who missed it ought to go back. It is still available. And
it is the best piece of fiction to come out of evangelical vision, not
just in 1965, but in a long, long time.

Talking about "religious literature" is dangerous; it is like talking
about "political literature" or "therapeutic literature." That noun "literature" bristles with anger at the encroachment of any adjective that
would modify it. To modify, after all, is to alter, to limit. A modified
literature is less than literature as surely as the social gospel is less

than the Gospel or as a salvationist church is less than the Church.

Drake's book is not "religious literature" in that popular and limiting sense. Still, it is religiously oriented, religious in spirit and in its concerns. And it is literature. It is not contrived to be in the service of something else. It is written naturally and unself-consciously out of a sensibility that is essentially Christian. In our secular society, with religion pushed off into a separate compartment, such poise is rare.

As a young professor of English (Tennessee) and a committed Christian, Drake knows the problem of harmonizing the literary and the religious for a world which holds them apart. He is careful not to violate either for the sake of the other.

Amazing Grace does not capture its harmony with formula or calculation. The book's most impressive device is its honest simplicity. With unabashed warmth and nostalgia, Drake re-creates the scenes and thoughts of a boy growing up in a close Methodist county in western Tennessee. The structure is casual. The eighteen sections (tales and sketches—not quite short stories and not quite novel-chapters) can be read independently. But they do at the same time fuse into a cumulative and subtle unity that increases the simple force of the book.

Within this simple format, Drake focuses on the boy's concern with the meanings of things from within his simple, evangelical outlook. Woodville, Tennessee, loses its fundamentalist oddity because Drake can transform it into something downright normal. Unity is achieved by the dramatic repetition, at different stages of the boy's growth, of words from plain old Methodist hymns. It is achieved more subtly by the tones of the boy's voice as he tries to live with the words. He sounds a little like Holden Caulfield because he is a boy-narrator in the same tradition. But his voice is his own. And his situation is unique: he is not in quest of a community or a father, but is sensitively alive to the fact that he has a community and a father—that he has, in fact, in some growing sense, two of each of them.

Everything in the book works by quiet tones, innocent viewpoint, understatement, deceptive simplicity. There are no moments of high-pitched despair or exultation, no outbursts of eloquence, no grand encounters. Drake's tender sketches and muted tones create their own kind of power.

Amazing Grace is too good to talk about in the abstract. It is finally the boy who must promote the book. Here he is, for example, writing about the steel engravings that illustrate a fierce and loveless Bible story book:

Whoever made the pictures seemed to be real fond of showing angels coming down to straighten people out and make them mind, like the one that was leading Adam and Eve out of the Garden of Eden. . . . You could tell how he felt about it all by the way he looked. . . . He just looked like he was gwine where he gwine, as my nurse Louella used to say.

And as for the author of the same book:

Somehow I felt like she wouldn't ever have suffered anybody to come unto her, unless it had been her duty, and then she would have looked just like that angel with Adam and Eve.

Such tones are an excellent vehicle for Drake's theme: the spiritual growth of a boy through and beyond his quandary about "those hymns where you had to low-rate yourself and say you were a worm" to a ripened spiritual awareness of the grace of God, "always ready to reach out for you and bring you finally to Himself, not for any reason, but simply because it was His good pleasure."

This is a rare little book: genuinely human, warm and simple, almost brilliant, unself-consciously Christian.

April 15, 1966

83 *And Bless You, Too*

It was my first big church wedding. At the rehearsal the evening before, I had noted that the couple appeared to be more than usually nervous, so I had tried to ease their tenseness. "You do not have to worry about a thing. All you need to do tomorrow is follow exactly everything that I do."

Now the ceremony was nearly over. The couple were kneeling in front of me for the benediction. As I bowed my head and began to pray, I sensed that something was going wrong. I opened my eyes a bit—and I was stunned. True to my instructions the couple were following my lead. Like swords crossed as an honor walkway, they and I had our arms raised and almost touching, as I stood there pronouncing the benediction in the traditional arm-raised style.—REV. HENRY T. MONEY, minister, Hooker Memorial Christian Church, Greenville, North Carolina.

Preacher in the Red   July 3, 1964

84 *Engineering Peace in Prague*

J. D. DOUGLAS

The British editorial director reports from Prague on an unusual meeting.

Despite the counter-attraction of a parade featuring 100,000 Young Pioneers, many Prague citizens chose one Sunday last month to go to that same Bethlehem Chapel where Bohemian reformer Jan Hus preached five and a half centuries ago. There they joined visitors from more than sixty lands in a service to inaugurate the Second All-Christian Peace Assembly. Officiating were Dr. J. L. Hromadka, dean of the Comenius Theological Faculty; Metropolitan Nikodim of Leningrad; and the veteran German pastor Martin Niemöller. Rays of sunlight streamed through the tall Gothic windows as ancient Slavonic chants, delivered in the rich bass voices of Orthodox bishops and archpriests, alternated with Protestant hymns sung in different tongues. The gay turbans of Mohammedan mullahs and the saffron robe and shaven head of a solitary Buddhist monk from Nepal stood out even in that congregation of varied and colorful ecclesiastical attire.

Later, at its first meeting in Prague's Municipal House, the assembly heard the keynote address from its president, Dr. Hromadka, who the previous week in Geneva had led a delegation to discuss with World Council of Churches leaders the relation between the two bodies, and matters of common concern. In four languages above the platform were blazoned words from Malachi 2:5 that formed the assembly theme: "My Covenant Is Life and Peace." In discussing the Church's responsibility in the world, the ex-Princeton Theological Seminary professor attributed the turmoil in Southeast Asia to "the fifteen-year-old unsettled problem of People's China, her unity, and her participation in international bodies, notably in the United Nations."

Dr. Hromadka had received a personal letter of greetings from the Archbishop of Canterbury. Both Premier Khrushchev and President Novotny of Czechoslovakia responded warmly when the assembly sent greetings to various leaders, including Prime Minister Douglas-Home, who also replied, and President Johnson, who did not.

The first list issued of those attending made no distinction of category but lumped together delegates, observers, guests, and journalists, according to country, as "participants." Having provoked some indignant complaints, this was eventually superseded by four separate lists. These showed some 265 delegates from Communist Europe and the U.S.S.R., 270 from other European countries (71 of them from the United Kingdom), and a further 176 from thirty non-European countries (including 65 from the United States). There were also 73 observers, 74 guests, and 52 journalists (*Christianity Today* was the only U.S. or U.K. journal listed).

Western delegates included a large proportion of young people of both sexes (the average age of the British contingent was about thirty), but those from Communist countries, possibly excepting East Germany, were of a much older generation and were mostly ecclesiastics. It was impossible to ascertain which churches were represented officially, for some delegates had come on their own initiative. Those who were not delegates were put in an invidious position when told that, contrary to prior correspondence, they were the guests of the local committee but could contribute the equivalent of their hotel bills to the Christian Peace Conference.

Right from the start the dice were loaded against the non-German-speaking press, for simultaneous translation equipment was not made available to journalists. Strenuous protests were met with vague allusions to "technical difficulties" involved in extending for a further six feet wiring that already covered several hundred feet. This left many dependent on the official translation of major speeches and such documents as were made available in other languages, and on the inadequate English, if somewhat better French, of an amateur interpreter.

Paradoxically, further frustration was averted because the assembly did not permit free discussion in the plenary sessions, except for the closing stages. Challenged by *Christianity Today*'s correspondent on the absence of such discussion, an official at first stressed its impracticability in a 700-strong gathering, but under attack quickly abandoned this position for different ground: "The Eastern Europeans do not conduct meetings according to Western democratic procedures."

One-fifth of the assembly was German, and it was soon evident that visitors from the two states and from West Berlin had come to Prague with predetermined views on the vexed question of their divided fatherland. "This, naturally," commented the following day's news release rather naïvely, "endows the Christian Peace Assembly with an unexpectedly political flavour."

During the closing stages, delegates were asked to approve a "Mes-

sage to Churches and Christians" drawn up by a small working com-
mittee with scarcely a scrap of decent English among the lot of them.
(The British member of the committee denied authorship of the
English version but helped construct a readable amendment.) Sparks
flew over the political implications of a sentence that read: "Too often
Christian preaching is not yet free from overtones of the Cold War,
of anti-Communist crusades, and of slogans of political propaganda."
Many Western delegates objected strongly and suggested that if "anti-
Communist" went in, then "anti-Western" should go in, too. "The
integrity of this whole conference is at stake on the vote we take on
this particular proposal," said one speaker, drawing loud applause.

A proposed alternative substituted for the offensive phrase "hatred
against the political systems of other countries," but speakers from the
Eastern bloc did not like this. "We hear preaching from San Francisco
which is political and not Christian," shouted Archbishop Kiprian of
Moscow; "when I preached in a Western city people came to me and
told me I was preaching from the Gospel; in their churches they heard
only political preaching. . . . Anti-communism in their preaching
is a reality, anti-Westernism in ours is a fantasy."

The Rev. Harold Row of the United States, a minister of the Church
of the Brethren, scoffed at the notion of the East's total innocence and
the West's total culpability. A vote taken on the amendment made
things worse, for though the Eastern bloc had evidently carried the
day, the counting of hands was done in the most slapdash fashion, and
the announced result of 388 to 110 was wildly inaccurate. When this
was pointed out with admirable restraint by the British delegate, it
elicited some bad-tempered remarks from Secretary-General J. N.
Ondra, who took it as a personal insult that his staff's arithmetic
should be questioned. A sticky scene was avoided by the intervention
of Archbishop Nikodim, who confounded the gathering by suggesting
that perhaps "anti-Communist crusades" should be dropped from the
proposed wording after all. The bearded Russian was rewarded by a
most un-British kiss on both cheeks from Paul Oestreicher, religious
broadcasting director of the BBC.

The assembly issued also an "Appeal to the Governments, Parlia-
ments, and Authoritative Personalities of the World." This condemned
apartheid, urged that the U.N. prohibition on weapons to South
Africa be respected, and supported the appeal for an economic blockade against that country, "where the ruling classes affront humanity,
and thus bring about a serious threat to peace." The appeal called

also for a peace treaty involving East and West Germany, and peaceful settlement of the Chinese-Indian, American-Cuban, and Southeast Asian disputes. It deplored colonialism in such places as Angola and Mozambique, and suggested that economies in armament expenditure could represent a decisive contribution to the elimination of hunger. Communists spoiling for a fight would assuredly not find provocation in these findings.

It was apparent that people came to the conference with vastly different motives. Many were genuinely and exclusively concerned with peace, some of them for non-Christian reasons. One of the dangers of an assembly like this, however, is that it provides a rallying point for malcontents of various sorts.

One sensed behind the movement a group of men, dedicated and united on essentials, who did the real work and fostered the recurring implication just behind the surface that while Communist preaching against democracy was a wholly laudable pursuit, Western preaching against communism was a misuse of Christianity.

News   July 31, 1964

85 *Evangelicals and the Prophetic Message*

HAROLD B. KUHN

The nature and degree of the Church's involvement in the social order has never been a simple problem. The stepped-up rapidity of social change in this decade has served to give the question an increasingly urgent character. There are times in which, in the urgency of the situation, segments of the Church act without a great deal of self-consciousness, and certainly without taking adequate time for self-examination or self-criticism.

Those who believe in the basic integrity of the Judaeo-Christian tradition must recognize that unless the Church is to disown the tradition of the Hebrew prophets, she must incorporate into her total ministry something of the prophetic—something of the socially responsible—in regard to the world about her. Admittedly the relation between the Old Testament prophet and the Chosen Nation is not wholly the same as that between the Church and the world in general. If it were, then the concept of "Chosen People" would be meaningless.

Basic to the prophetic message is the element of responsibility. This inheres in the very nature of an ethical religion. But a perennial problem faces the Christian Church: To what extent must she stand outside the world as the fellowship of those who "are not of the world," and to what extent must she allow herself to be immersed in the world's life to serve as "salt of the earth"?

In answer to this question, some are appealing to history in general, and to the life of our Lord in particular, to see whether some direct guidelines may be found there. Some interpret the fourth century of the Christian era as being one in which the decadent powers of imperial Rome threw up their hands and left the Church to bear primary responsibility for the social order. Others of different orientation have liked to view our Lord as a political (and perhaps proletarian) rebel, whose major role was to challenge the existing socio-political order; his followers maintained this stance, these people say, until the movement was captured and domesticated by Constantine, whose minions transformed it into "a theological system of esoteric redemption" and thus destroyed the dynamic of its Founder.

G. K. Chesterton, in his book *The Everlasting Man,* develops the former view. He concludes that the Church proved inadequate in the face of her new responsibility and that as a defense she retreated into herself and became content with what is called the "monastic protest" against the world. The latter view has, of course, been characteristic of the left wing of the "historical Jesus" movement.

The dialectic implied by the expression "in the world but not of the world" haunts all the major segments of the Christian Church. Massive forces for social change, some of which seek social justice for the disinherited of the earth, present a challenge that no Christian can ignore. And it may be fateful for the Christian Church that she tends to permit herself to be polarized around one of two hardened centers, thus causing each position to seem exclusive of the other.

To put the matter baldly, there are those who, while professing full loyalty to the teachings of their Lord, assume a stance that not only smacks of social irresponsibility but also at times allies itself with the forces having a vested interest in maintaining social injustice. The sensitive evangelical cannot close his eyes to the fact that while all elements of the Christian Church have been timid when they ought to have been courageous—and we select the question of race and color as a test sample here—yet the area of our land in which men of color continue to be most conspicuously disadvantaged is also an area which is traditionally "Bible-believing" and in which a general adherence to evangelical Christianity is the order. This is, to say the least, embarrassing and humbling!

It must likewise be acknowledged that those who theoretically ignore or repudiate great sections of the historic creeds of the Church do nevertheless manifest a moral sensitivity and a willingness to "stand up and be counted" for social righteousness, even at great personal cost. Evangelicals simply cannot shrug this fact aside. It may be true, of course, that such crises as that of voter registration in the Deep South do afford a visibility feature that makes social action appealing. But this cannot be legitimately used by those of theological orthodoxy to excuse any lack of social sensitivity on their own part.

This writer is aware that some evangelicals will shrug off the involvement of those of more liberal persuasion by an appeal to some such theory as that of Harold D. Laswell, expressed in his *Power and Personality*. Laswell develops what may be called a "power view of politics" that tries to explain social and political involvement as resulting from an immature and frustrated personality rather than genuine ethical and social ideals. This simply will not do! It does not and cannot explain, for example, the dynamics of such persons as Dr. Martin Luther King.

Certainly we welcome any movement that seeks to assert the view, classically expressed by Aristotle, that ethics and politics are inseparable. The severance of these two elements, making ethics to be purely functional and instrumental, is the feature that makes communism so brutal and so insidious. Christianity rightly understood stands squarely athwart the path of Marxism at this point.

The burning question for evangelicals is, How can the prophetic message (and at the core of this lies the insistence that the heart of God is concerned for justice among his creatures) be made effective at the level of the individual Christian in the life of the world? It avails nothing to throw verbal stones at the Russian Orthodox Church for her inability to be prophetic. It is tragically possible for evangelical Protestantism in America, not faced by any governmental restraint, to retreat into a purely "priestly" form of ministry. To fall into this trap, she need only limit her emphasis to a narrowly confined advocacy of purely personal pietism. She can succumb to the pressures of her environment and feel exceedingly righteous in doing this, especially if she does so while avoiding the doctrinal errors of other segments of the Church.

Has the Church any directive from her Lord at this point? Both evangelicals and liberals might well "try this one on for size": "These ought ye to have done, and not to leave the other undone." And until those of evangelical persuasion correct the imbalance between private and public piety, they act in poor grace as they excuse their contemporary monastic withdrawal, their pious resignation from the human race, by an appeal to the defective theological basis of those whose social consciences seem more sensitive than their own.

Current Religious Thought   May 7, 1965

86   *Picking Flowers on Golgotha*

Despite "this terrible twentieth century," many people remain confident that the twenty-first century belongs not to Communist tyrants but to the free world.

Yet nobody with a sense of history sees any real hope of that outcome apart from radical spiritual renewal. A former United States Army chief of chaplains, Ivan L. Bennett, points out that our country was "founded and developed within the framework of faith and hope in God. Today no nation possesses such resources of power, such reserves of plenty, such technical skills, and such reservoirs of compassion. Yet our day of destiny has come. Either we shall walk with God, or we shall sink into the dismal darkness that envelops nations forgetful of God."

Any generation preoccupied with creature comforts and isolated from spiritual concerns is in the process of committing spiritual suicide. People who try to live without God cannot long live with one another, or with themselves. It takes moral earnestness and spiritual power to keep a civilization alive. To pay one's debts, to mind one's own business, to support the fight against cancer, and to keep the dog off the neighbor's lawn—important as this suburban code may be—is no sure preservative of a way of life. Dr. Joseph R. Sizoo has somewhere detailed the tragic cost of our popular credo, "Get what you can; get it honestly, but get it." It produces a society, he comments, in which people can eat caviar while a neighbor starves, or play solitaire on Persian rugs while slum children stumble in the streets because of malnutrition. Dr. Sizoo says of such a citizenry, "They can pick flowers on Golgotha while the Son of God dies and leave him hanging in the rain."

As descriptive of the contemporary American mood, Congressman Walter H. Judd singles out the discomfiting term "confusion." This confusion he locates primarily in the sphere of values. Is there or is there not a moral order in the universe? Americans answer ambiguously. The masses of our people, Judd contends, fail to see that the great conflict of our times is over the nature of God and the nature of man. They do not sense the heavy weight of moral duty placed on us by the question of values. "We haven't understood the nature of this conflict, nor the character of the adversary," he states, "because we have grown fuzzy about ourselves."

Secularism and materialism stifle the life-breath of our own society. Its moral decline is terrifying, its spiritual illiteracy alarming. Fifty million Americans no longer attend church or synagogue, and the younger generation places an incredibly cheap price tag on human life. Dr. Edward L. R. Elson, minister of the National Presbyterian Church of Washington, D.C., observes that millions of persons are inadequately fed and most people travel on foot in the modern world, yet the two chief concerns of many Americans are "How can I reduce?" and "Where can I park my automobile?"

No spiritual merit accrues from simply denouncing an enemy who blasphemes the divine source of human life, debases the dignity of man, and desecrates our noblest beliefs, while we ourselves neglect the fountains of spiritual vitality.

Traditionally, the American spirit found its deepest delights not in material things but in spiritual privilege. The Pilgrims left home and kindred, comfort and security, to cross an uncharted sea and to build a new society in the rugged wilderness for one supreme reason: to worship God in good conscience. The Pilgrim Fathers signed the Mayflower Compact which began, "In the Name of God. . . ." In 1776 the Founding Fathers were influenced by the Christian view of man in their charter of liberty, defining government as an instrument for the preservation of man's divinely given rights. Washington praying at Valley Forge, Lincoln pleading at Gettysburg, Marines fighting their way on Iwo Jima, soldiers establishing the Normandy beachhead, and American airmen repelling North Vietnamese aggressors today testify eloquently that life's most precious values do not consist in enslavement to material things.

Modern Americans no longer need to span unknown seas nor to

pioneer in an untried continent. But they do need to meditate anew on their nation's heritage and destiny.

The more we spin through outer space while stockpiling missiles at home, the more apparent it should be that love is no optional twentieth-century commodity, that righteousness is an eternal imperative, that faith is not outmoded, and that God's rule in human affairs is more requisite than ever. Those citizens who no longer honor the Lord's Day, who neglect the house of God, who utter no prayers and bow to no Scripture, had better reckon among their privileges their inheritance of the blessings of a way of life shaped by a society that honors the spiritual disciplines of life.

A nation not built on good men and good will must falter and fail. The will of the majority is no adequate substitute for the will of God.

E. Stanley Jones has said: "There is one unshakeable kingdom, only one. The kingdom of self is shakeable; the kingdom of health is shakeable; the kingdom of property is shakeable; the kingdom of nationalism is shakeable; every kingdom in this world is shakeable at least by death. But there is one unshakeable kingdom . . ." (*And Our Defense Is Sure: Sermons and Addresses from the Pentagon Protestant Pulpit,* ed. by Harmon D. More, *et al.*).

More awesome than the cold and hot war with Communist aggressors in which the nations are engaged today is the ultimate conflict for the soul and spirit of man. A member of the British Parliament, Sir Cyril Black, has put the decisive issue well: "It is a war of ideas, a war of ideologies, a war that can only be won in the hearts and minds of men and women. It concerns such fundamental questions as what we believe about man, his destiny, his way of life. Is man a creation of God and immortal . . . a human personality created by God . . . , or is he merely a pawn in the game of great tyrants and cruel dictators . . . ?" (*Ibid.*) A land in which the spirits of free men no longer compete for the highest ideals has one sure destiny: to march off the map. The only unshakeable terrain is Christ's.

For about $150—thirty pieces of silver—Judas betrayed Jesus of Nazareth. The lust for money still compounds that tragedy. "Shall we confess," asks Chaplain Frederick Brown Harris of the United States Senate, "that the ruling passion of half our citizenry is to build more barns and bigger barns (or more and bigger corporations), that the raging passion of the other half is to get more and more wages for less and less work—and that wealth and security have become the goals of our personal living and of our national existence?"

Recent American history is not all shadows; there are signs of strength. A people who once routinely drove Quakers from colonial New England later elected Herbert Hoover to serve in the White House. The clearer American ideals become, the more citizens proudly repeat the words "with liberty and justice for all" only as that Pledge to the Flag raises no embarrassment before the test of race, birth, color, sex, and religion. Injustice is seen more clearly as part and parcel of an ideology that renounces human dignity, that rules out God—in a word, injustice belongs to a society of the kind that the founding Americans disowned and despised, and that we reject in Communist tyranny.

But the vision of social justice is not self-sustaining. Its noblest ideals, its deepest insights, were nurtured by revealed religion. And in the long run redemptive religion alone has moral and spiritual resources to sustain and fulfill this vision.

In *Modern Man in Search of a Soul,* Carl Jung relates that among his patients over thirty-five he found not one "whose problem in the last resort was not that of finding a religious outlook on life." It is a tragic fact that multitudes of Americans today grope for spiritual reality. Even graduates of many church-related colleges complain that they were denied what they had a right to expect—a reasoned outlook on life centering in the realities of revealed religion. And members even of some evangelical churches complain that they are not really nourished in the deep central truths of the Christian religion.

The apostles of Christ who faced the first-century world nowhere claimed omniscience; about some things they knew much less than we do. Least of all were they armed with a political ideology for revamping the Roman Empire.

But one thing they knew beyond all doubt. They knew that God's promised Redeemer had come; they knew that he was crucified for sinners, and that he lives triumphant over death as Lord of all. They owned him as Saviour and put themselves beneath his Lordship. And they were true to their mission: to invite lost sinners to redemptive forgiveness and grace, and to proclaim the whole counsel of God. Theirs was a mission of love and righteousness in a world that had lost its way.

It is time to recapture the high and holy faith that exalts a people—faith in the Creator-Redeemer who forgives men's sins and who lifts them to newness of life. It is time Bibles were opened again. It is time to return to family worship and private devotions. It is time for church attendance. It is time to face the implications of "our most holy faith" for all of life. It is time for "the things of God" to find ready place upon our lips and in our hearts. ⌐

Editorial   May 21, 1965

87 *"What If . . ."*

JOHN LAWING

They've finally gone too far!

88 *Missing—One Knife*

L. NELSON BELL

The operating room was gleaming with the multiplied perfections of modern equipment. Not only was everything spotless, but the cool, conditioned air was constantly subjected to the purifying light rays which deduced even normal bacteria to a minimum.

Two surgeons, along with residents under training, were standing motionless in their pale green sterilized gowns and caps, their faces partially covered by germ-inhibiting masks.

Both the chief surgeon and his first assistant were men whose years of arduous training and experience had earned for them certification in their surgical specialty. They were members of a number of learned societies. The elder of the two had only recently been honored by his associates by being made chief-of-staff of the hospital, and just prior to that he had been the president of the society of distinguished surgeons.

The patient, draped with sterile sheets and towels, was breathing deeply as the anesthetic began to take effect.

Then the anesthetist looked up and nodded his head. The patient was ready.

On the Mayo stands and the tables adjacent to the operating table there was a shining array of instruments, each designed for a specific purpose—clamps, clips, retractors, spreaders, scissors, sutures of various kinds—everything needed to facilitate the operation.

The surgeon finished draping the patient, already thoroughly prepared by scrubbing and the application of antiseptic solutions. Then, looking around he took up first one instrument, and laid it down, and took up another, and laid it down.

No incision was made! He did not use the knife.

Fingering the various instruments, the surgeon went from one to the other, looking at one, making futile passes with another. It was a strange pantomime. Under perfect surroundings, with a patient who desperately needed surgery, the entire procedure consisted of meaningless motions. Naturally, some in the room were disturbed, others were confused, and some were exasperated.

After an hour, the patient was rolled from the operating to the recovery room. There he was cared for until he fully reacted from the anesthetic. Then he was taken to his room where relatives waited anxiously to see him. Friends sent in flowers and messages, evidences of their love and concern.

Before long it was obvious that the patient was no better. The same old symptoms recurred. There was still pain and weakness. Why was the patient no better?

Hospital authorities were asked to investigate. The surgical staff met and discussed the case and also a number of similar ones which had occurred in the same hospital. Every step in the patient's history was gone over again and again in an honest attempt to uncover the cause of repeated failures to cure these patients.

One night during a general staff meeting, the mystery was again under discussion. The internes and residents were encouraged to share in the procedures. One young man, not considered as bright or promising as some of the others, ventured to speak up:

"Mr. Chief-of-Staff," he said, "I have scrubbed in on a number of these unsuccessful operations and there is one thing I have repeatedly noticed: the surgeon does not use the knife. There is no incision, no bleeding, no going down to the source of the illness, nothing is removed; when the patient leaves the operating room, he is in exactly the same condition as when he went in."

"But," the chief surgeon said, "the knife is old; it is full of imperfections; I do not trust the quality of its steel; in fact I feel that it is more an ornament than an instrument—something suitable to keep on the table, but not necessary or effective in the complicated surgical conditions confronting us today."

The interne was subdued, but as we left the room we thought we heard him mutter under his breath: "Those poor patients! They are still sick; they leave the hospital just like they came in. Surely something is wrong. Why don't they use the knife?"

The Sunday morning service was about to begin. The sanctuary was filled with quiet, well-dressed, well-fed people. They were comfortable, thanks to air conditioning and cushioned pews.

In all of the city there was not a finer pipe organ, and the man at the console was a master in his profession. The choir was well paid and highly trained. The whole atmosphere was one of quietness, reverence, and expectancy.

The minister and his associate took their places and the order of service proceeded with the quiet dignity and efficiency of a thoroughly prepared program. At precisely the scheduled moment the minister stood up to preach. In his robes he was the epitome of scholarship and grace, and when he spoke it was obvious that he was a man of eloquence and conviction.

Prior to the beginning of the sermon, a passage of Scripture had been read; but the main appeal was to philosophical reasoning and a confrontation of today's problems along the line of one's personal responsibility and duty to engage in social engineering. Many authorities were quoted; there were frequent references to great leaders of our day; fragmentary quotations from some of our finest literature revealed the wide reading of the preacher, and many in the congregation were impressed.

At the conclusion of the service there was some subdued chatting among members of the congregation; the ministers greeted them as they went their several ways—some for a time of rest, others to spend the rest of the day in amusements or recreation.

With most of them there was an unappeased sense of spiritual hunger. One could see that the stone of human opinion was hard to digest. Like a serpent, sophisticated denial of divine revelation gnawed at the place where men desired peace and assurance.

Many realized that there was something wrong. Church officers discussed the problem. In the denomination intensive efforts were set on foot for evangelism, missions, and stewardship.

One day a member of the congregation remarked to a friend: "I wish we heard more about what God has to say. Sunday after Sunday, I hear what men have said or are saying. Occasionally the Bible is quoted and then there is light, conviction, and a sense of God's nearness."

"Yes," said the other, "the one thing that will change the situation completely is using the Bible in all of its wonder and power. After all, it is the Sword of the Spirit, the only weapon for an attack on the stronghold of Satan."

Word got around. The Sword was unsheathed. Sinners were saved, Christians were revived, and the church once more became God's house.

A Layman and His Faith   October 10, 1960

89 *Steadfast Taper*

LUCI DECK SHAW

"His candle shined upon my head . . ." (Job 29:3)

His candle shines upon my head.
He trims the wick and guards the flame,
And though the darkness creeps in close
The steadfast taper shines the same.

The flower of flame sways in the air.
Wing-fingers snatch and try to snuff
The stalk His careful hands protect.
The light shines through; it is enough.

His candle shines on me in love.
(Protective circle in the gloom.)
And through the dreadful night I know
That He is with me in the room.

Throughout the weary waiting-time
The liquid flame shines thin and pure.
When tiredness dims my faith, I look
And see His light, and I am sure.

October 29, 1956

90 *Your Theology Is Too Small*

HAROLD O. J. BROWN

A leading Russian Orthodox scholar has often said of one of the most celebrated and most difficult to understand of modern theologians: "Either what he is saying is true, but in that case it is trivial, or else it is false." Ambiguity is not found only on the modern stage; it is also well represented in much "modern" theology. In such theology, as on the stage, the ambiguity is sometimes deliberate, sometimes unconscious. In theology, it is partially technique, a way of securing attention for theological opinions in an intellectual market where, as in bookstores after Christmas, we find "all theology 50 per cent off." But it is at the same time also a symptom of a complex of problems in the modern intellectual climate. Both as a technique and as a symptom, it is self-aggravating. Every successful use means that the next time a heavier dose will be required.

In several currently popular schools of theology, such as the "new theology" of J. A. T. Robinson, the "religionless Christianity" of Dietrich Bonhoeffer, or the "death-of-God theology" of Altizer *et al.,* this ambiguity is not incidental but central. Modern theology depends on it both for its penetrating impact and for its wide appeal. Yet ambiguity is also deadly, and is in itself enough to ensure that none of these schools or fashions will ever be able to produce a "new Reformation" or renew the modern mind. As Georges Florovsky so aptly pointed out in lectures delivered at Harvard University last year, this ambiguity is itself ambivalent: is it what the new theologies mean that is in doubt, or whether they mean anything?

"Religionless Christianity," "death of God," and similar theologies have a fascination that the scholastic monologues of typical academic theology cannot match. Yet one cannot help feeling that it is not the fascination of the *mysterium tremendum,* of the mystery and majesty of the vision of God, but rather the perilous attraction of the brink of the abyss, or of the glittering eyes of the snake. Men touch, and claim to handle and even to dismantle, the highest things in time and eternity. This is fascinating and frightening, or both at once; but if indeed they succeed in this undertaking, then those things were neither high nor eternal, and the new theologians are not dragon-slayers but canary-fanciers. New theologies depend for their viability on being sufficiently ambiguous to pass for both piety and blasphemy. To cry, "God is dead!" as Thomas J. J. Altizer does, catches attention precisely because it is fraught with blasphemy and yet somehow claims to be said on behalf of God. Both the blasphemy and Altizer would be insignificant if God were not really there.

Altizer of course recognizes that if he were fully convincing, his outbursts would no longer be marketable; and this is why he makes the fundamentally illogical statement, "God is dead," instead of the more rational but quite colorless one, "There is no God." Altizer, however, is somewhat extreme and thus atypical among modern theologians, for there seems to be no satisfactory way to put a good, orthodox, conventional face on what he is saying. He lacks an adequate depth to his ambiguity, and in time his ideas will probably be expelled from the growing corpus of new theology. Others, such as Britain's Bishop Robinson and America's Harvey E. Cox, always speak and write with loopholes, so that a well-intentioned or muddleheaded reader can always think of them as eccentric but essentially Christian, and call them "not so far off the track, if they mean what I think they do."

This oscillation between shrill blasphemy and platitudinous conventionality is extremely frustrating to the orthodox theologian who tries to examine them fairly—witness the painstaking efforts of Professor Eric Mascall of London to be fair to Robinson and Paul Van Buren in *The Secularization of Christianity* (Darton, Longman and Todd, 1965). Like Ingmar Bergman films, the new theologies use and abuse powerful symbols and rouse ancient memories, playing on all the heights and depths of human experience and imagination, and thus are compelling and fascinating. The similarity goes further: Ingmar Bergman uses Christian symbols to say essentially nothing, and thus really says that Christian symbols mean nothing. A movie director is under no obligation to produce sound doctrine, but a theologian is— or used to be.

This ambiguity is evidently deliberate, at least to some extent. It is too protracted, and at times too farfetched, to permit one to accept Bishop Robinson's disclaimer that it is just "thinking out loud." Critics like Walter Kaufmann and Alasdair MacIntyre, both atheists, accuse the new theologians of dishonestly cloaking atheist ideas in Christian expressions, and acidly suggest that they do this because there are many professorships of theology but few of atheism. Such criticism may be unfair, but it cannot be refuted in a climate or frustrating imprecisions and apparently premeditated ambiguity. At the very least we are entitled to complain with Samuel Sandmel of "The Evasions of Modern Theology" (*The American Scholar,* Summer, 1961). In short, modern theology often does not read like real theology at all. The authors often seem to have assumed the kind of pose a *Scientific American* staff writer might assume if he were to try to write an account of rocket research today as though it had been written as science-fiction prophecy in 1875. Either he would reveal that he was not really the man he impersonated by obviously knowing too much, or he would have to falsify some things so as not to give himself away. Somehow it would be sure to ring false. So, too, there is something not quite right about these new theologies; it is as if their proponents are keeping something back—or putting something on.

Canon J. B. Phillips' little book *Your God Is Too Small* deals with problems that beset the man who has an inadequate idea of who God is and of what he can do. Phillips was writing for laymen, but he could have directed his title judgment at modern theologians. Much of the malady of modern theology is a problem of scale, or of proportion, or of position—like looking through the wrong end of the telescope. Forty-odd years ago, in *The Principle of Authority,* P. T. Forsyth warned that much nonsense was coming about because men were looking at the God-man relationship from the wrong perspective, e.g., starting with a consideration of man's rights. (Or, as a Bultmannite or Robinsonian might say, "Modern man simply cannot conceive. . . .") His warning has gone unheeded, and so today J. B. Phillips' expression would serve as a good title for a literary history of mid-twentieth-century Protestant theology.

Phillips has pointed out that often inability to believe in God is the result of a completely false idea of God—one that does not accord at all with the view of the Bible or of historic Christian thought. In an age when the presentation of Christian doctrine has been replaced to a great extent by platitudes from both the pulpit and the political podium, when churchmen can take comfort in such nebulosities as songs about "Someone in the Great Somewhere," it is not surprising that laymen often lack even an intimation of the majestic conception of God found in traditional Christian teaching and have not the faintest inkling of how well the great Fathers, Doctors, and Reformers stand the test of time and overshadow their contemporary detractors.

Denis de Rougemont remarked, in his piquant book *The Devil's Share,* that the penalty for not knowing the history of Christian theology is to have to make the same mistakes all over again. This is indeed happening in theology on the lay level, where we can observe a recrudescence of all the second- and third-century heresies amid wondering shouts of "How new! How brilliant! How relevant!" But why do the professional theologians, who should know better, come in for De Rougemont's penalty? It is not always easy to conclude, as Georges Florovsky does, that they too are simply ignorant of the grand dimensions of Christian thought—not that they have never been exposed to them, but that they have exhibited toward them that invincible ignorance with which the church of Rome was wont, in more controversial days, to charge Protestants. With examples at hand of how each of the "new" theologians mentioned above has distorted, sometimes consciously, a facet of Christian teaching as a necessary step to his own restatement of it, ignorance would be the most charitable explanation one could suggest, although ignorance too is culpable in a man's specialty in which he claims authority to teach.

Paul Van Buren is the most courageous of these radicals; he does not seek to veil his questionable and misleading statements of Christian doctrine by quoting them from others, as Harvey Cox does, or by merely saying that Christianity "almost teaches" them (whatever that may mean), as John Robinson does. Even so, the misstatements of half these men, particularly in works intended for popular consumption, are often so crass as to point us back to the question of basic honesty raised by Kaufmann and MacIntyre.

Thus, in ridiculing the creed of the Council of Chalcedon in *Honest to God,* Robinson distorts it in a way that will not be recognized by the average reader unfamiliar with the text and history of that fifth-century document, but that can only produce embarrassment and suspicion in the reader who knows something about the magnificent vision of God held by the fourth- and fifth-century Fathers.

A great deal of modern theology suffers chronically from such a shriveled view of God (e.g., the volumes of idiotic but perfectly serious discussion on whether modern science permits God to produce a virgin birth) that it hardly deserves to be called theology but would be better suited by some such term as anthroposophistry. Such a designation could even be applied to the monumental work of the late Paul Tillich (and probably would have received a tolerant and approving smile from that universally educated giant), and it is certainly appropriate for his lesser and more banal imitators. The charge that it implies is warranted and, if proved, would deprive much of what is called "new theology" of the right to be recognized as a voice in any Christian dialogue. Since few Christians have the courage to point this out, the observation has come from atheists, or from a Jew like Samuel Sandmel, who seems to feel somewhat cheated at discovering that the "Christian" theologians are not firm enough for him to challenge them.

Leaving other allegations aside, it seems abundantly clear that a whole generation of "theologians" not only have no vision of God themselves but also are unaware of the vision others in the history of the New Testament people have had. Their theologies lack substance, and they try to make up for it by providing a constant series of sensations. In this, at least until they have exhausted the range of possible stimuli, they are successful.

A sidelight on the smallness of "new" theology may come from another angle. Why is so much of it so shallow, even though, following Tillich, it is fascinated by the idea of depth? A comparison with Greek drama provides a clue. Aeschylus and Sophocles were concerned with the dread underworld divinities, the powers of the earth, blood, and death; and their Olympian deities by contrast shine in a luminous glory. Euripides, only a few years their junior, trivialized the forces of evil, and his Olympians are feeble wraiths—or, as the Christian classical scholar Nebel puts it, "his heavens are an empty facade, with only blackness behind the empty windows." Even the severest orthodox critic of Paul Tillich must recognize the grandeur, intensity, and depth of his thought. Tillich throughout his life was always sensitive to the personal, mysterious, and superhuman nature of the power of evil, and this gave to his vision at least an Aeschylean, if not a Christian, sweep. Cox, by contrast, considers the very idea of the demonic the opposite of New Testament faith (*The Secular City*, Macmillan, 1965, p. 154), and Robinson would emasculate all evil to "the benign indifference of the universe," interpreted by love (*Honest to God*, SCM Press, 1963, p. 129 *et passim*). Is it an accident, then, that these men do not share, like Tillich, in the breadth of an Augustine or the intensity of an Aeschylus, but only reproduce, in the modes of the twentieth century and in the mythical conventions of a bloodless, post-Christian, academic Protestantism, the tired trivialities of a Euripides, too pale even to reproach the gods for forsaking man?

Despite the validity of the observation that this whole school of theology is simply too small, it will remain fascinating, for it has the fascination of any attempt by the small to handle—or manhandle—what is great. There is in all of us enough of the desire of Faust—or Jean-Paul Sartre—to be God that we will continue to be intrigued, though perhaps with a trace of horror, by such attempts. And, as long as these attempts are made by man furnished with all the accomplishments of the human intellect, and with at least a fragmentary record of wrestling with God, they will continue to show flashes of insight and of the sharply valid criticisms of more complacent traditionalists. Perhaps we can indeed hope that the fate of these new theologies will finally be that of Mephistopheles in Goethe's *Faust*, who wanted to be "a part of that power, which always wills evil, and always causes good."

In trying to decide what to do with the schools of thought and the books produced by the new theologians, one is led to the suggestion made by some wag on resolving urban traffic jams. Wait, he said, until all the highways are fully congested, and no automobile can move, and then plaster over all the cars with a second layer of highway and begin again. Attractive though it is to one who has painstakingly shared the analysis of Mascall or the frustration of Sandmel, such a suggestion is more easily applied to cars than to men. Yet beyond a certain point, it really is necessary to plaster over some of these movements, by recognizing that they are indeed no longer theology at all and simply ignoring them, living, to paraphrase Bonhoeffer, as if there were no theology. Above all we should recognize that this smallness of theology is a hunger phenomenon, and that the hunger results from the scarcity of the Word of God and from the lack of the vision of God. To feed these men themselves may not be possible, because they have largely rejected fact and chosen fancy and fantasy in theology. But we must not be led by them into neglecting the people they are not feeding the truth.

The loss of the vision of God, the pitiable smallness of what passes for theology today, must be counteracted by those of us who hold the Word of God, who are the legitimate heirs of the prophets, apostles, and martyrs. We must counteract this inadequacy in the vision of God with a theology not merely accurate in detail but also adequate in scope, soundly based biblically, and recapturing some of the magnificence of historic Christian thought. If these poor men had caught but a glimpse of the splendor of the Christian vision of God, they might never have lost the substance of its faith. To the analysis of J. B. Phillips, so painfully applicable to "new" theology, "Your God is too small," there is added, inevitably, the solemn sentence, "Where there is no vision, the people perish" (Prov. 29:18).

Article April 15, 1966

Notes on Contributors

L. NELSON BELL is executive editor of *Christianity Today*.

G. C. BERKOUWER is Professor of Dogmatics and the History of Dogma at the Free University of Amsterdam.

ANDREW W. BLACKWOOD was Professor Emeritus of Homiletics at Princeton Theological Seminary.

GEOFFREY W. BROMILEY is Professor of Church History at Fuller Theological Seminary.

HAROLD O. J. BROWN, a former resident tutor at Harvard College, is on the staff of the International Fellowship of Evangelical Students.

F. F. BRUCE is Rylands Professor of Biblical Criticism and Exegesis at the University of Manchester, England.

GEORGE BURNHAM was first news editor of *Christianity Today*.

EMILE CAILLIET is Stuart Professor Emeritus of Christian Philosophy at Princeton Theological Seminary.

EDWARD JOHN CARNELL is Professor of Ethics and Philosophy of Religion at Fuller Theological Seminary.

GORDON H. CLARK is Professor of Philosophy at Butler University.

LESLIE SAVAGE CLARK, who lived in California, published several books of poetry.

JIMMIE R. COX is an editorial writer for the Fort Worth (Texas) *Star-Telegram* and a news correspondent for *Christianity Today*.

RAYMOND L. COX is pastor of the Foursquare Church in Hillboro, Oregon.

RACHEL CROWN teaches English while studying for her doctoral degree at the University of Kansas.

JAMES DAANE, formerly assistant editor of *Christianity Today,* is Professor of Practical Theology and Director of the Pastoral Doctorate Program at Fuller Theological Seminary.

J. D. DOUGLAS is editor of *The Christian* (London) and British Editorial Director for *Christianity Today*.

ELMER W. ENGSTROM is president of the Radio Corporation of America.

FRANK E. FARRELL is Adult Editor at Gospel Light Publications, Glendale, California.

SUE FIFE is a poet and writer who resides at Lithonia, Georgia.

HELEN FRAZEE-BOWER of Campbellsville, Kentucky, was a writer of religious poetry.

FRANK E. GAEBELEIN is Headmaster Emeritus of The Stony Brook School; he was co-editor of *Christianity Today* (1963–66).

CYRUS H. GORDON is Professor of Near Eastern Studies and Chairman of the Department of Mediterranean Studies at Brandeis University.

BILLY GRAHAM is an internationally known evangelist.

DOROTHY L. HAMPTON is active in the work of the Metropolitan Association for Retarded Children of Denver.

EVERETT F. HARRISON is Professor of New Testament at Fuller Theological Seminary.

CARL F. H. HENRY is editor of *Christianity Today*.

M. WHITCOMB HESS is a poet and essayist, residing at Athens, Ohio.

PHILIP EDGCUMBE HUGHES, editor of the *Churchman* (England), is currently Guest Professor of New Testament Exegesis at Columbia Theological Seminary.

JAMES WESLEY INGLES is Professor of English and Chairman of the Department at Eastern Baptist College.

RODERICK JELLEMA is Assistant Professor of English at the University of Maryland.

PETER R. JOSHUA, a retired United Presbyterian minister and evangelist, resides at Port Hueneme, California.

DAVID E. KUCHARSKY is news editor of *Christianity Today*.

HAROLD B. KUHN is Professor of the Philosophy of Religion and Chairman of the Division of Doctrine and the Philosophy of Religion at Asbury Theological Seminary.

KENNETH SCOTT LATOURETTE is Sterling Professor Emeritus of Missions and Oriental History at Yale University.

JOHN V. LAWING is art-production director at *Christianity Today*.

ADDISON H. LEITCH, formerly president of Pittsburgh-Xenia Theological Seminary, is Distinguished Professor of Philosophy and Religion at Tarkio College, Tarkio, Missouri.

CALVIN D. LINTON is Dean of Columbian College of George Washington University.

ELVA MCALLASTER is Professor of English at Greenville College.

CHARLES H. MALIK, former president of the United Nations General Assembly, is a native of Lebanon and a Greek Orthodox layman and is presently on the faculty of the American University of Beirut.

HENRY T. MONEY is minister at the Hooker Memorial Christian Church, Greenville, North Carolina

HAROLD JOHN OCKENGA is minister of Park Street Church, Boston, Massachusetts, and Chairman of the Board of *Christianity Today*.

EVANGELINE PATERSON of St. Andrew's, Scotland, has published religious poetry.

J. HOWARD PEW is president of the Board of Trustees of the United Presbyterian Foundation and an elder in the Ardmore Presbyterian Church, Ardmore, Pennsylvania.

BERNARD RAMM is Professor of Systematic Theology and Christian Apologetics at California Baptist Theological Seminary.

ROBERT O. REDDISH, JR., editor and publisher of the monthly magazine *Sine Qua Non,* is an Episcopal minister on leave from the diocese of Ohio.

PAUL S. REES is vice president of World Vision, Inc., Monrovia, California.

ROBERT P. ROTH is Professor of Systematic Theology at Northwestern Lutheran Theological Seminary.

LUCI DECK SHAW, of Western Springs, Illinois, is the author of a number of published poems.

SAMUEL M. SHOEMAKER was rector of Calvary Episcopal Church in Pittsburgh and a contributing editor to *Christianity Today.*

RUTHE T. SPINNANGER was born in Norway and is a teacher and writer of poems and essays.

KENNETH STRACHAN was General Director of Latin America Mission.

J. WILLIAMS was a minister in Cinderford, Gloucester, England.

SHERWOOD ELIOT WIRT is editor of *Decision* magazine.

LON WOODRUM is conference evangelist in the Evangelical United Brethren Church.